D0860967

Dread

for all
refusing
futureless futures

Dread

Facing Futureless Futures

———————

David Theo Goldberg

polity

First published in 2021 by Polity Press

Polity Press
65 Bridge Street
Cambridge CB2 1UR, UK

Polity Press
101 Station Landing
Suite 300
Medford, MA 02155, USA

ISBN-13: 978-1-5095-4444-8
ISBN-13: 978-1-5095-4445-5 (pb)

A catalogue record for this book is available from the British Library.

Library of Congress Cataloging-in-Publication Data

Names: Goldberg, David Theo, author.
Title: Dread : facing futureless futures / David Theo Goldberg.
Description: Cambridge, UK ; Medford, MA : Polity Press, 2021. | Includes
   bibliographical references and index. | Summary: "A brilliant diagnosis
   of the ubiquitous mood of our times"-- Provided by publisher.
Identifiers: LCCN 2020052818 (print) | LCCN 2020052819 (ebook) | ISBN
   9781509544448 (hardback) | ISBN 9781509544455 (paperback) | ISBN
   9781509544462 (epub) | ISBN 9781509548699 (pdf)
Subjects: LCSH: Risk--Sociological aspects. | Anxiety--Social aspects. |
   Civilization, Modern--Psychological aspects. | Future,
   The--Psychological aspects.
Classification: LCC HM1101 .G65 2021 (print) | LCC HM1101 (ebook) | DDC
   302/.12--dc23
LC record available at https://lccn.loc.gov/2020052818
LC ebook record available at https://lccn.loc.gov/2020052819

Typeset in 11/13 Sabon by
Servis Filmsetting Ltd, Stockport, Cheshire
Printed and bound in Great Britain by TJ Books Ltd, Padstow, Cornwall

For further information on Polity, visit our website: politybooks.com

Contents

Preface and Acknowledgments

As 2016 unfolded, a recognition gathered pace that the world was less settled than it had seemed. Syria had torn itself apart in a seemingly endless civil war, and fleeing refugees were overloading Lebanon and flowing into Europe. ISIS had maximized its power and territorial spread as the year opened, expanding beyond Iraq, controlling much of Northern Syria, and mobilizing in other Middle Eastern and North African countries while recruiting more broadly in Europe. A series of coordinated attacks in Paris in November 2015 had killed 130. Six months later, a supporter gunned down nearly fifty people in an Orlando nightclub catering to a largely gay clientele. Rather than liberating Afghanistan and Iraq, the sustained "securing" had extended the devastation and unsettlement. The June 2016 outcome of the Brexit referendum and Trump's support, locally and globally, propelling him to election in November confounded the complacent. Sexual harassment and racist violence were openly proliferating. The planet surpassed the carbon threshold, global temperatures soared, the ice cap was melting at a record pace, storm systems became more devastating, and species were being wiped out.

By early 2017, many were waking each morning to wonder what disaster faced them, what sinister arrangements, what enclosures and exclusions, would be enacted by authoritarian leaders worldwide with smiling approval from their thrilled supporters. I couldn't quite put my finger on the uncanny upset pouring from most everyone with whom I interacted, in person and virtually. That summer, the sensibility manifested more clearly for me. Dread had gripped life.

Over the ensuing year, the feeling grew. Others readily concurred. But it was also becoming apparent that the rising authoritarianism across a growing number of societies was symptomatic, as it invariably is, of a deeper set of structural forces, while exacerbating them. This book is an attempt to make sense as much of the range and proliferation of underlying prompts as of the sensibility itself. A great deal has, of course, been written about the impacts on our lives of the technological revolution, of climate change, and of racial conflagration. Over the past year, the COVID-19 pandemic quickly became the pressing subject of our time, perhaps understandably eclipsing most everything else. The experience produced not just an explosion of scientific literature but also a slew of writing on the experience, the racial and class differentiations, and compelling critical contributions on the turn to the empirical, detection, the immunological, and the right to breathe.

The pandemic, however, also prompted predictable critical accounts by notable public philosophers intent on fitting breaking events into their preconceived theories. Slavoj Žižek (2020), for one, focused, perhaps predictably, on the contorted political panics to which the pandemic inevitably gave rise, the improbably renewed prompting of socialism's possibility as the driving viral fallout. Bernard-Henri Lévy (2020) dismissed everyone else's stupidity in accepting thoughtlessly the curtailments of their freedoms. Mostly more nuanced, Giorgio Agamben (2020a, 2020b) stressed how readily governments – he was especially concerned with the Italian state response in the early days – elevated a "techno-medical despotism," looking to the disciplinary technologies of delimiting liberties, the devaluation of human sociality underpinning these moves, and the fascistic reduction to "bare life."

A tendency among some analysts to forgo a more subtle, relational, and intersectional account of social positioning prompted an occasional declaration that all members of a racial group, for example, would be subjected to the same deathly experience in an emergency room no matter what their class standing and professional networks. Dread takes hold of the unexpecting. The pandemic nevertheless neither materialized nor has operated in a social vacuum. It is implicated in and has magnified a compound of social factors, at once enabling or advancing novel modes of control while fracturing social forces in less containable fashion. This calls for a more interactively nuanced analysis of the social field than any reductively self-replicating and self-reinforcing account warrants (cf. Hartman 2020; and Cottom 2019 for a more subtle reading of the social field of health).

Dread, as I conceive it, has emerged as the driving social sensibility in our times. There has been a quiet uptick in the term's popular usage, perhaps unsurprisingly. Yet there has been little theoretical analysis since Kierkegaard's novel focus on the concept, Heidegger on "angst," Sartre on "anguish," and, more passingly, Freud's later analyses of anxiety. Neel Ahuja (2016) speaks of "dread life" less as an analytic than as a shorthand for fear at the interface of race and species, architectures of power and security.

Dread, I will argue by contrast, is driven now by the socially specific interaction of currently impactful conditions. As the expressive manifestation of complex social fields, then, dread is a general index of contemporary specificities. The book is intended less as a comprehensive account than as a means of prompting a critical vocabulary and analytics for understanding what dread is, why it manifests as it does now, what its modes of articulation and expression are, what its implications are for the politics of our time. My starting point is the American context because dread has manifested so clearly in its shadow. The account, nevertheless, is intended to apply more generally, if variously, across wider contexts, as many examples drawn on will suggest.

The argument opens with two introductory chapters conceptualizing dread. Two chapters follow on the operative logics underlying contemporary dread, including digital automation and the driving technologies of contemporary capitalism, notably consumptive, political, and cultural tracking. A chapter each is then devoted to the looming devastations of the interlacing viral disasters of disease and climate change, as dread's materializations. I close with two concluding chapters, one reflecting on civil war as contesting conceptions of how to be in the world; the other on the politics in which dread manifests, contrasting between the material infrastructure of racism and infrastructures of care. Instead of a specific chapter devoted to race and its repressions, I thread racial articulation throughout as it is repeatedly, renewably, and interactively constitutive of the conditions of the social, and dread-making especially.

*

No work is authored alone. This book has benefited from layers of interactions and conversations with colleagues, friends, authors long engaged with and newly discovered. A number of people were kind – or concerned – enough to review a full draft of the manuscript. Ackbar Abbas provided me with characteristically insightful and probing feedback. Anjali Prabhu offered suggestive revisions too. Extensive conversations with Anirban Gupta-Nigam throughout the writing process drew my attention to ideas and literature I otherwise too self-satisfiedly would have skated past. Achille Mbembe in Johannesburg kept pushing me further, as did Lisa Leung in Hong Kong. Jenna Ng nudged my thinking along over these years on algorithmic logic and being. My lifelong friend filmmaker and incomparable surf movie director Michael Oblowitz made me uncomfortable with the taken-for-granted (in this case, regarding dread), as he always does. Gaby Schwab arranged a conversation on the coronavirus chapter with members of the University of California Humanities Research Institute (UCHRI) residential research group she was convening on "Artificial Humanity." The group prompted me to clarify and sharpen ideas key to that chapter's analysis. A passing question about dread's etymology from Sarah Farmer between our morning laps at the pool led to a little revision.

Early on in my thinking, the *Los Angeles Review of Books* published an outline version of my argument, causing me to extend my analysis. A shout-out to Brad Evans for opening that door and fueling me with invites throughout the book's elaboration. A public discussion on civil war with Brad, Adom Getachew, Libby Anker, and Achille Mbembe prompted some tweaks to Chapter 7. The driving dynamic ideas central to this book were the subject of keynote presentations to the Postcolonial Studies Association in Manchester, a conference at Radbout University in Nijmegen, and a CEMFOR conference at the University of Uppsala. The ensuing discussions all extended my thinking significantly. Cheers respectively to Helen Cousins and David Firth, to Anya Topolski and Josias Tembo, and to Mattias Gardell and his colleagues Daniel Strand and Mehek Muftee for the engagements. My colleagues in the Asia Theory Network devoted meetings in Taipei, Seoul, and Tokyo to various ideas germane to the book. I am grateful to all the members of the group for their rich generation of insights and ideas, and to Li Hung-Chiung for his tireless and self-effacing organizational energy. Extensive exchanges with Sarah Nuttall, Yogita Goyal, Alex Taek-Gwang Lee, and Woosung Kang especially opened my eyes to different ways of seeing points in the book.

The folks at Polity, as always, have been a pleasure to work with. Jonathan Skerrett gently steered me towards clarity and creativity. Karina Jákupsdóttir reminded me of tasks and deadlines with the lightest of touch. Justin Dyer, an incomparable copy-editor, finds deft ways of making one sound so much better without changing one's meaning; filling in missing or mis-stated detail without making one feel foolish. Cheers also to a number of anonymous reviewers who raised questions large and small in the spirit of producing a book both clearer and (hopefully) more compelling.

As always, the incomparable staff at UCHRI saw me and my colleagues through all the challenges of our time. Their tireless work and commitment, and their spirit of collective collaborative engagement, have always provided the possibility of thinking differently together and supporting sustained critical work. Wujun Ke, in particular, tirelessly compiled the concepts and names filling out the Index. The book would not have seen completion without their ceaseless engagement.

I have spent the past two-plus decades in constant conversation with Philomena Essed, between homes and continents, pleasures and social pains. The periods of pandemic and political turmoil throughout 2020 pressed us into more intense and sustained daily conversation, shaping my thinking on matters of the book and much else. Interlaced with humor and delight, her caring concern pushed me to be more caring too.

My son Gabriel's world has been upended by worklessness, family illness, and ecological challenge. He has made his way through it all with spirit and creativity. This book is written with his and his generation's futures in view.

Irvine, California,
January 2021

1

A World of Dread

The social screws have been turned, the social fabric has been torn apart.

In 2018, an academic colleague was returning to the United States from a work trip in Europe. Landing in Minneapolis, she passed through the Global Entry lane machine-expediting entry for US citizens into the country. Declaring no illicit materials, she was exiting through the baggage pick-up area when accosted by a Customs and Border Patrol agent. Rifling through her shoulder bag, the officer discovered an apple, illegal to import into the country. My colleague had carried the fruit onto the plane, intending to eat it in flight. The haze of long hours in the air dulled her into forgetting about it. Refusing any explanation, the officer accused her of lying on her entry form indicating she carried into the country no fruit or firearms. Reports of similar treatment were beginning to proliferate as increasingly intrusive Trumpian border management was ramping up. My colleague was spot-fined $500, and stripped of her Global Entry privileges for the foreseeable future. In Italy and Spain under pandemic lockdown, police fined people up to €1,000 for straying a couple of public meters beyond the prescribed limits. A steep cost for violating confinements or for forbidden fruit at the bottom of a bag.

Seth Harp, a Texan journalist, re-entered the United States at Austin airport in May 2019 following an exhausting investigative trip to Mexico City. He was "randomly selected" – in non-bureaucratic speech, picked out – for additional screening, his first in a lifetime of crossing the southern border. Harp was interrogated by a series of three Customs and Border Patrol officers about the story he was investigating – on weapons purchases by a drug cartel in Mexico – and then on his various war reporting contacts in Iraq and Syria. His computer and smart phone were taken from him without requesting permission, removed from his presence for hours. There followed a warrantless search of his digital footprint. It included social media postings, digital photograph albums, his browsing record, interactions with family and friends, including encrypted communications with informants in various parts of the world. It is quite likely his computer and smart phone contents were downloaded and stored by the government, though the officers denied doing so.

US law currently requires a warrant only if one is under arrest (now under legal challenge). Given that he had not yet legally been admitted into American territory, Harp was denied access to a lawyer. He was threatened with denial of entry if he didn't cooperate, despite being a US citizen by birth. Whether any state to which he would be sent – likely Mexico – would accept him is an open question. This suggests that Trumpian America was committed not just to deporting the undocumented living in the country but also to rendering its own citizens completely stateless, literally with no country in which to land, if critical of the administration.

The officers denied having recorded Harp's interrogation. A Homeland Security response to a later complaint filed by him, however, admitted that the "port director" had reviewed "the tape," presumably of his interactions with the officers. Harp was released more than five hours later, the interrogation having turned up no illicit activity. Secondary screenings of American citizens returning from international trips were conducted more than 33,000 times in 2018. That's nearly 100 per day across the country's principal ports of entry (Harp 2019).

These are not new experiences, especially for members of targeted populations, racially and religiously defined. Muslims especially, and those with Arabic-sounding names, more often than not find themselves the objects of additional interrogation when seeking to enter nation states across the global north. Colleagues fitting this characterization have repeatedly told me they avoid transferring transnational flights in Paris as they will invariably face immigration interrogation. Shahram Khosravi (2011) has written movingly about the harrowing conditions to which a stateless refugee is subjected in seeking a safe place to land and live.

Migrants are confronted by increasing hostility no matter where they pass through or land. But in the past few years, the pervasive sense across the global north that any and all are under suspicion, surveillance, and but a step away from erasures of rights has ramped up significantly. In the United States, Latinos promised or in some cases granted citizenship for service in the US military have been stripped of citizenship and deported after completion of their service and having risked their lives in war zones. Even naturalized citizens with decades of US residency have been threatened with revocation of their citizenship for minor legal violations, especially if originally from countries considered *non grata* (Wright 2018). Similarly, Brexit has reified the insularity of British self-identification, placing in question the right of access and residency status of those perceived as not belonging. China's insistence on its power to extradite Hong Kong citizens to the mainland for trials concerning political violations likewise blurs legal distinctions that were once more or less clear.

The abrupt arrival of a global pandemic ramified all of this. If the fluidity of global movements was already coming under some stress, COVID-19 brought the world to all but a screeching halt. In February 2020, almost three months after the first case was recorded in Wuhan, China, a party of thirteen Californians boarded a plane for France. All healthy and fit men in their thirties and forties, they competed in a team sporting event. Upon completion, they flew to the Italian Alps for a day of helicopter skiing. Upon arrival, one of the party was feeling under the weather but soldiered through the day they had all excitedly anticipated. By day's end, he was hospitalized, had tested positive for the coronavirus, and was in a critical condition. His team members returned to the United States via JFK in New York. At immigration, they were asked whether they had visited China, and were waved through when indicating they had not. By then, the Trump administration had restricted non-US residents' travel directly from China. Within a week of return to California, nearly all the team members had come down with the virus, half of whom landed in local hospitals.

A virus seeming to take hold first in provincial China had consumed much of Italy and its neighbors, spiking the global spread pretty much in all directions. Limited travel restrictions for a subset of those coming from a single source failed completely to comprehend or care about the dynamics of global circulation and viral spread. The world was about to clam up.

*

It has been a struggle to put a collective finger on the feeling, the broad social sensibility, to which rampant experiences like these are currently giving rise. The gnawing sensibility that seems to have been eating at us collectively of late is represented by this range of border-crossing experiences grown customary. The micro-experiences are joined by larger threats to the disruption of life meant to signal a warning to all engaged in critical political action. These events assume broader and deeper significance once connected to the culture wars festering into what even national legislators across political divides in a wide variety of national contexts are characterizing as "civil war."

The escalating conflicts are the expression of contested conceptions of how to live and be in the world today, and the everyday border, policing, and rhetorical violence conducted in the name of the nation and its supposed protection. Heightened anxiety in the face of these seemingly discrete events is made more concrete by the surge across the globe in dictatorial authority and authoritarian assertion, both petty and pervasive. This, as I will argue, is not so much a civil war in the conventional sense as a war against civil society itself.

There are, accordingly, numerous other factors, including structural shifts, that have unsettled social sensibilities of late. Remunerated work has become increasingly individualized, more self-producing and self-sustaining. Over the past thirty years, unevenly across different societies, people have been rendered more individually responsible for costs of health insurance, retirement savings, even public education, as the viral lockdowns globally have made overwhelmingly evident. A greater range of work functions are being automated, threatened with robotification. Even the contrasts between work, home, and recreation have been blurred.

Work now is not so much the anchor of dignity, something many aspired to and worked to realize as central to non-alienated life. Rather, recreation itself has become something to work at. Work, too, has become more widely a work-out: staff hiring contracts for desk jobs often inquire whether one can squat, lift, climb, and stretch. Intrusive employer surveillance of work computers and productivity has become more widespread, further blurring the line between material working conditions and private communications, records, and lives. Ubiquitous artificial intelligence has transformed the very culture of work.

human / tech

The lines dividing human from technological being accordingly are quickly blurring. We no longer just wear technology; it is increasingly inserted into us, a feature rather than an appendage. This technology generates reams of data about our physical and mental makeup, our momentary location, habits, patterns of consumption, and indeed individual desires. While designed to inform individual wellbeing, the data produced require constant vigilance regarding their potential to abuse privacy or be exercised against one's best interests.

The flood of information deluging our lives has exacerbated the concerns. The next news cycle begins before the last one has ended. Every lead item is tagged as "breaking news." The election of reality TV personalities, sitcom characters, and comedians to leadership positions across the world, including major political economies, has grounded both fascination and anxiety. More or less local concerns make waves globally, just as the rumble of globally significant events may shake the ground instantaneously beneath one's feet at home. Daily reports of child abuse at US border facilities concentrating infant and adolescent kids into unsanitary disappearance camps have been punctuated with chilling images of the dead bodies of those refused safe passage or appropriate asylum procedures floating face down in a Texas border stream or across the central Mediterranean. Large structural arrangements such as Brexit or repeated foreign interference in local elections reshuffles the economic and political deck. Mass shootings and mass bombings mar everyday life with alarming frequency.

The stories about forbidden fruit, names, and travels

with which I started have proved enormously unsettling. We wake each day to questions about serial events and structures made event-like: what's the next episode, what horror is facing us now? In fact, they turn out at a deeper level to be the same question.

*   Robotiaized War

Social sophistication has failed in part to keep pace with technological prowess. War machines increasingly came to drive the economy of twentieth-century modernity. The world went between global wars from machine weaponry and automobility to long-distance bombers and aircraft carriers, nuclear destructiveness threatening sustaining environments and existence alike. A new generation of military machines has now emerged. As before, their impacts pervade everyday life: automatic weapons, drones, GPS, driverless vehicles, handheld facial recognition devices, stealth technology, and so on. The once seemingly clear lines between military and civilian cultures have blurred.

Today, war – like work – is becoming increasingly roboticized. Drones are the first step. AI-driven warfare involves the managing of, strategizing about, and increasingly execution of war. Machinic warfare is fast developing to the point of autonomy, of algorithmic self-definition. Like automobiles and financial transactions, war machines are in the process of operating themselves, making auto-generated decisions on the basis of data inputs and reiteratively calculating formulae. Technological instrumentalization wedded to producing only instantaneous satisfaction has pushed aside more nuanced affective responses. The latter are increasingly nowhere to be found.

Omer Fast's remarkable video *5000 Feet is the Best* (2011) offers telling insight into these tensions. US military drone operators based in Las Vegas target for killing at a distance mostly anonymous people on the ground in Iraq and Afghanistan. Operator emotions are formulaically squeezed out. Five thousand feet, it turns out, is best for target determination, the height from which a brand of cigarette or make of shoes is most readily determined. But then buried emotions return to haunt. "The nightmares began," confesses the drone operator central to the video. A sinking feeling inched up on him as he stealthily crept up from on high, from worlds away, on his unsuspecting target-turned-enemy. The growing grip, taking hold vise-like, refuses to leave the stricken "technologist" any peace.

The movie *Eye in the Sky* (2015), directed by Gavin Hood, grappled with the psychological and moral dilemmas gripping the executioners of military violence from a bird's-eye view. Video wargames may train their players in technicalities such as response time and accuracy. They fail dismally to prepare them for the draining psychic demands of actual war violence. Anonymity, counter-intuitively, breeds unconscious remorse. There is emerging neurological evidence that first-person shooter games and prolific use of GPS in place of physical maps contract users' hippocampus, permanently diminishing brain function over time. The irony is that increased auto-repetitiveness may dangerously diminish functionality over the long haul (Edwards 2010; O'Connor 2018).

The algorithmic furnishes the logic running this new generation of technology. It is quickly becoming the mode not just of production but of sociality. Its operating logic deepens the increasing inscrutability of the logics of economic production and social relation. By extension, this imperceptibly curtains off the loss of control as both sensed condition and factual outcome. Hence the contemporary concerns about transparency, self-determination, and sovereignty.

The triangulation of unpiloted technological targeting, acceleration (e.g. in nuclear capacity), and relative loss of control in this proliferation intensifies the incipient unease taking hold worldwide. The benefits of contemporary warring machines consume our everyday functionality now, further blurring the distinctions. Much of common technological prowess has roots in military R&D, from automobiles to computing technologies, energy efficiencies to clothing. There are now likely more privately owned assault weapons in the United States than there are in the American military. We can speak today with some accuracy of "warpeace" proliferating to the point of indiscernible low-intensity wars or microaggressions, law enforcement, warlike border policing, even recreation. Games of war and war games are not so readily distinguishable. Slow violence, and not only of the ecological kind (though that too), pervades everyday life.

Life proceeds now not simply in a time of constant states of war, but in the shadow of more or less undiminished and continual anxiety at their prospect, spread, or intensification. This includes anxiety about their outbreak, conduct, violence, effects, and costs. About war as such, conventionally comprehended, but more generalizably about *a* war (the indiscernibility of the indefinite article indicative of the proliferated insecurity) on everything: on poverty, on drugs, on crime, on the environment/nature/the climate, on neighbors, on immigrants, migrants, and refugees, on terror fought with terrorizing ferocity. Before global economic activity was decimated overnight by declaration of a war on "the Virus," it was dominated by trade wars. Public places throughout the world had become targets of mass violence, from places of religious worship to places of consumption such as malls, fairs, markets, clubs, bars, and sites of learning such as schools and universities. We have come to live, then, in proliferating dread, even of dread itself.

*

Even before the pandemic lockdown, more than half of high school students in the United States were reporting stress and anxiety, much of it racially and gender driven. This was a dramatic increase from just 7 percent in the years prior to the presidency of Donald Trump, and the social aggression his unruliness licensed. The viral lockdown has increased trauma for children, from Spain to Lebanon, much as youth across war-torn landscapes have experienced. The agitation is intensified, even exaggerated, by the proliferating threat of gun violence, as much from within the expected safety of the home and school as from without. It is ramped up, in turn, by the incessant violent social media engagements making up everyday life, and in the case of youth much of their waking moments. COVID-19 has exacerbated rather than alleviated political intensity, across a wide swath of societies.

Societies find themselves slipping into civil war when within or between them they are wrought by irreconcilably contesting conceptions of life. For the state's inhabitants, living is largely made unbearable. Those at least nominally controlling the state apparatus insist on obedience and deference to its way of being, on pain of erasure or disappearance for refusal or resistance. Fights over the impacts on everyday life of climate conditions, from Brazil's Amazonia to the Maldives, from the coal-based economy of Australia to Zimbabwe's recovery-defying droughts, reveal the intensifying political fallout. Civil wars more broadly conceived become struggles over competing ways of being in the world. They are struggles over their underlying conceptions, ways of living, and over control of the state and its apparatuses to materialize and advance these commitments.

Colonial existence, as postcolonial theorist Achille Mbembe (2016) has noted, riffing off anticolonial philosopher Frantz Fanon, is a permanent state of agitation, a state of constant alarm. This is a constitutive condition of coloniality, not just a by-product or occasional affective state in colonial societies. The sovereignty of colonized states was always in question. Globalization has updated and heightened this alarm by blurring anew boundaries between states, drawing into question the absoluteness of even metropolitan state sovereignty. As state sovereignty has frayed at the edges, if not eroded altogether, social conflict has gripped state culture, within and between states. The escalating tensions within and across the European Union, between the EU and Brexitannia, and within states offer a range of driving examples. State force is readily invoked, insisted upon even, where sovereignty is deemed under duress, for example in the wake of waves of ongoing migration crises. Where politics is indistinguishable from civil war, dread has become its leakage.

Ionesco once famously quipped that "God is dead, Marx is dead, and I don't feel too well myself." If religious experience once purported to be about spiritual enchantment, the implication of Ionesco's pithy insight is that today the politics of religion seems driven by disenchanted resentment, more often taking on an apocalyptic articulation. Post-apocalyptic survival looms as large in this cultural imaginary and its commercial materialization as post-life ascendancy, from survival training and entertainment programs to exobiological investigations and cryogenics. The pandemic expression of this, perhaps, is that in the interest of survival we have all become virologists.

In a world with no more transcendental gods and the unleashing of generalized uncertainty, race can be characterized as the secularization of the religious (Goldberg 2015: 8–10). As religion had previously led in doing, race offers an artifice, a narrative, of common and distinct group origins, a projection of kinship and belonging, a set of protocols for social life

Race replacing religion [handwritten margin note]

and interaction, genealogical inheritance and generational reproduction. Social warrings, whether cultural or weaponized, are invariably about insisting on the maintenance of these boundaries to the exclusion of the projected non-belonging and non-committal. They cut off renewal, closing down the possibility of regeneration and reconstruction.

*

Feeding and feeding off these developments is the exploding culture of fabrication and a politics predicated upon the ballooning sociality of make-believe. Fabrication emerges out of these contemporary social and technological developments, while in turn interactively exacerbating them. The culture of fabrication and aggrandizing self-fabulation is enabled by technologies that readily sponsor making things, manufacturing them virtually. The virtually made are represented as readily existent, as the real. 3D printing is an obvious example. Maker culture has quickly licensed the emergence of make-believe culture.

The resulting product is double-sided. On the one hand, there has readily emerged the circulation of alternative realities, of alternative truths. These are made-up accounts of events, conditions, states of affairs. They may include strands of the actual and existing but twisted into fabricated accounts not or not fully reflecting the real. Our equation of the fabricated with the real has translated quickly into tolerance of the fabricated. The recent emergence of "deepfakes" exemplifies this trend. But it has a deeper history, as exemplified by the slew of fake memoirs, of misrepresented or fabricated credentials, of accounts of events that did not take place or at which the storyteller falsely claimed to be present. On the flip side are constant dismissals, sometimes weaponized, of the real as fake: fake reality, fake news, the produced by design as mere happenstance.

Make-believe operates in two registers. First, there is the operation of making things up, of fabricating them, of giving a fully or partially fictionalized account. Michel Foucault (1980–1/2017: 34fn) characterizes "biopoetics" as "personal fabrication of one's own life," presumptively for self-advancement. Second, there is the compulsive in the operations of make-believe, compelling others by force of will, control of technologies of mediation, or sheer threat to believe (in) the account.

This unsettling of the given, the real, the true and false, the believable and incorrigible has further tightened the knot in the social stomach. It frays the seams of sociality, leaving nothing but quicksand, all the way down.

*

Political depression is too common to capture this gnawing sensibility seeping across all aspects of social life, like a pit bull with jaws clamped around one's leg, tightly locked, not letting go. One gets politically depressed in the face of losing an election or vote, say. But that tends to pass more readily when one re-commits to the political process or struggle to ensure a better outcome next time. There has been some of that currently, to be sure, but this lingering sense seems deeper. It is not a momentary presence of a political candidate, burning issue, or world-historical caricature with whose commitments one basically disagrees. Political depression may cut more sharply in one cycle or another, depending what side of the issues one occupies. Nor is it simply the inconvenience of an unfortunate more or less random experience. There is something else at work now, responding to larger, more tectonic, shifts. Dread and its mutations act as a symptom, pointing to something not yet quite discernible or understandable, an uneasy sense of the anticipatory.

Indistinction has become generalized. It has become

much more difficult to distinguish between war and peace; illness and wellness; everyday practice and corruption; desire and demand (or command); interest or preference and internet feed; truth and fabrication; even a beautiful and a "killer" sunset. As borne out by the experiences of those with whose stories I began, authority is often giving way to petty authoritarianisms. The latter morphs in a discretionary moment and policies into more despotic intrusions, often legally defying or bending. Consider the terrible conditions imposed upon women, men, and children migrants in the hundreds of invisible refugee camps across Europe, or on Nauru and Manus islands off Australia, or in the disappearance camps at the southern border of the United States. There is a reach for absoluteness as all evidence points to the contingent and conditional. The next ecological disaster or pathogenic virus occurs with greater frequency and ferocity. As, too, do the not so random searches and attacks on streets, in schools, at work. No matter how much security technologies are proliferated, or guns purchased in supposed self-defense, we start each day feeling less safe, more socially insecure.

In the wake of all of this, dread has become the driving affect best characterizing the palpable anxieties of our time. Where meaning can be identified, there is little room for dread. Dread operates in the space of indiscernibility. Outrageous racist expressions are known to be wrong, but the transgressing exhilaration of their assertion delays or buries otherwise certain dread. Similarly, everyone in China knows the Cultural Revolution was awful. But they at least can claim to comprehend it, hence the nostalgia for it at a time of proliferating uncertainty. These otherwise outrageous transgressions offset or displace the generalized uncertainty now.

Prolonged dread, then, is the mark of this moment, of its seeming inscrutability, its illegibility, where the improbable has become likely. Repeated raging hurricanes, the quaking earth, indeed pandemics, are rationalized as acts of nature. But like famines, floods, and fires, the destruction they manifest is invariably anthropocenic. They merge politics and culture with nature, ideology standing in the way of science, politics refusing to own up to the facts. They are prompted and enabled by human shortsightedness, inaction, overaction and overreaction, or immediate instrumentalizing intervention parading as "nature."

There is little recognition, if not often outright denial, of the long-term conditions giving rise to these repeated upheavals. Random screening and interrogation have become prolific, though not quite indiscriminate. Race still determines likelihood, as borne out by secondary screening data at ports of entry and less formal "stop and frisk" or updated "sus law" policing practices on city streets, as well as viral infection and mortality rates. The quick uptake of racist expression as an instrument of political blame and advancement is as revealing about the disturbing latencies of the populations moved by such expression across global polities as it is about the leaders committed to such racist instrumentalization. Dread drips from the pervasive sense that incomprehensible and indecipherable extinction or disappearance could strike in a blinding second.

Incomprehension follows assuredly from this mixing of genres, from their indistinguishability. The distinctions have blurred. They are no longer those we came to assume as a matter of course. We are deeply conceptually confused or, more pointedly – to borrow a purple phrase – "phenomenologically fucked" (Abramovich 2009). We seem not quite able increasingly to discern the true from the false, the actual from make-believe, war from peace, friends from foes, gender from biological identity, gain from loss, safety from insecurity. Is Britain European, Hong Kong Chinese, Israel Middle

Eastern rather than European, as South Africa, once European, is now African, or Mexico North American? Our conceptual self-understanding and social arrangements have failed to keep up with the accelerations in the shifts, economically, politically, technologically, culturally.

The world is awash with uncertainty, both phenomenal and conceptual. Dread now is literally at the door, in the home. It is as if dread pandemonically has seeped into every crevice of our ambiguous and ambivalent being today. We are living in its grip. Colonial agitation has become replaced by post-political (I am tempted to say post-historical) anxiety. It is not that political dread has no precedent in taking hold of a world, the world at large. Perhaps this sense engulfed the enslaved on plantations in the nineteenth century, or in the hulls of slave ships. The enslaved, I think, will have been gripped more readily by the complex of fear and resentment, exhaustion and modes of quietly persisting resistance. Dread likely gripped many across Central Europe especially between 1933 and the outbreak of World War II. It no doubt suffused the lived condition of the colonized in dealing with the colonizing, and to some degree the postcolonized coming to negotiate the constant reminders in inhabiting the metropole of the colonial legacies structuring their everyday experience (jastej 2019). The dread of the moment, the experience, after the fact the memory, individually and collectively. Dripping from the voices of Nina Simone and Billie Holiday, from Edvard Munch's 1893 painting *The Scream (of Nature)* and Joan Miró's 1938 lithograph *Summer*, from the writings of Richard Wright and Primo Levi. Perhaps, too, it coursed through bodies diving under desks during nuclear drills.

For all of that depth, dread historically did not seem to assume quite the pervasive global reach of hopelessness now haunting life's prospect. The abiding anxiety-inducing uncertainties seeping across worlds today, I have been suggesting, are prompted by both structural shifts and the attendant political and cultural representations circulating in their wake. These include the impacts of new technologies on our work, social structures, cultures, and everyday lives. They give rise to social ruptures and warring tensions. The resulting impacts are enabled and exacerbated also by social foreclosures. These restrictions, mobilized and enacted as violent refusals, take specific aim at the quickening demographic shifts and their accompanying cultural unsettlements spilling out across social worlds.

The stories with which I started reveal an incipient shift in emphasis: from the politics of movement and migration and their technologies of surveillance (my colleague's forbidden fruit and Seth Harp's interrogation) to a politics of health and their technologies of tracking (the Californians returning from Italy). What else is at work to promote this shift, and what are the implications? The following chapters trace these transformations, the mutations in dread historically, the novel social regulations to which dread's articulations now give rise, dread's operating system and logics, and the concerns and resistances pushing back against them.

*

What, then, to make of dread? How is it related to fear, and how does it differ? What complex of social conditions has prompted its hold on the world today, its range and varying intensity of expressions? How do the developing and changing material conditions shift its very meanings, experiences, and significance from one period to another, and what do these conceptions reveal about the conditions underlying them? What are the foreclosures and refusals to which all this directs pressing attention?

In the following chapter, I address the conceptual

nature and workings of this emergent dread, the politics it conjures and promotes. The social conditions
underpinning the proliferation of dread include the hold
the digital revolution and its logics of operation have
exercised on everyone, and the social shifts fueled by it.
This Technological Turn has fueled a series of developments in political economy. These include the gathering
disappearances and changes in work, as well as invasive
intrusions and the population that tracking has licensed
for purposes of consumption and political surveillance.

Techno Turn

While these technological developments and impacts
have been central forces in the gathering sense of unease,
they are neither singularly determining nor alone. The
gathering ecological threats to collective ways of being
and the pandemic challenges to our taken-for-granted
social lives have boosted the anxiety. These boosts, in
turn, are inflated in interaction with the technological
developments and the politics of social constraints ripping in sometimes deadly fashion through increasingly
heterogeneous societies today. New technological developments emerge as well out of these socio-ecological
developments. To twist the Soviet avant garde's insistence that technological developments take the form of
social relations, I proceed throughout on the understanding that for every historical formation new technologies
both shape and are shaped by the social relations in
which they are invested. We know more about the conditions facing us as a result of the data technologically
gathered and analyzed. But this, too, can heighten the
anxiety in the absence of means to tackle the emergent
challenges. The chapters of this book address in turn the
tangle of new digital technologies, the political economy
these technologies drive, the viral pandemic, and the
social impacts of climate change.

Principle:

What, then, does dread reveal about the worlds we
relationally inhabit otherwise hidden from view? In
closing, I consider whether the interactive power of

these conditions is producing a social logic in which the war on everything is inevitably prompting a proliferating civil war, an internalizing of war within and among ourselves. And in reflecting on this, I consider whether it will be possible to outline a politics of refusal and resistance, helping to shape and direct a creative politics countering the social life of dread.

2

Sensing Dread

In mid-2018, Jem Bendell (2018) famously sought to publish his article on "inevitable near-term social collapse" following from "climate chaos." The paper was rejected by a notable journal for failing to address (non-existent) literature in the field concerning climatic impact on "eco-systems, economies, and societies." Bendell's paper was subsequently published by a research institute with which he was associated at the University of Cumbria, UK.

The findings and insights were so strikingly alarming that the publication went viral. As of March 2019, it had been downloaded more than 110,000 times (Fawbert 2019). Bendell concludes that by 2030 at current trends we collectively face "disruptive and uncontrollable levels of climate change, bringing starvation, destruction, migration, disease and war." He adds, "Our norms of behavior – what we call our 'civilization' – may also degrade."

Bendell's paper has contributed to producing an identified psychological condition called "eco-anxiety," causing some to seek therapy and join support groups (Ambrose 2020; Tsjeng 2019). Eco-anxiety is taking hold of increasing numbers of people as worries over environmental threats are ramping up. Environmental stress is rising so rapidly it has received a formal definition from the American Psychological Association as a "chronic" concern about "environmental doom." The current global pandemic only broadens the concerns, bringing the time horizon of end-times more sharply into view. Lars von Trier's film *Melancholia* (2011), about passively watching impending, inevitable apocalypse, signals one sort of response to the cultural dread beginning to envelop our planet as a consequence.

*

For Kierkegaard (1844/1944), dread as a psychic or affective condition is produced in the face of Nothing. Dread oozes into one as not-being, non-occurrence, absence become more palpable. Kierkegaardian dread arises from the absence, the impossibility, of forgiveness. Redemption from sin is unavailable should God fail to exist. The ancient history of dreadlocks – dating at least to Egypt and perhaps also India – suggests a longer entanglement of dread and deity. This expressed itself as concern over godly abandonment. But it also manifested – as with the Rastafari movement, from its earliest spawning in critical rejection of industrialism's discipline and regulation – as the dread of not living up to God's commandments or perceived expectations. Dread here suggests being ill at ease, unsettled, in the face of desanctification and disenchantment.

An affect is an intense and shifting emotion no longer understood because it has become socially disconnected from its predictable set of prompts, or one not yet comprehended because responding to a condition still unrecognized. (I owe this insight to a helpful conversation with Ackbar Abbas.) Affect accordingly stands in stark contrast to the simplism of sentimentality because unnamable and unnavigable. Dread, then, is less like fear and more analogous to melancholia. One knows what one fears, just as one knows whom one mourns. Like melancholia, by contrast, dread has no exactly defined object. But where for melancholia the object is lost, unrecovered and seemingly unrecoverable, in the case of dread one remains unsure of what exactly its object is, how to define or find it at all.

Dread follows from lack: of definitive object and cause, of predictability, of legibility and discernibility, from denial or complete absence of principle. Women fear rape, but generally dread toxic masculinity. One may think one knows what one doesn't know. But these "known unknowns" are often obtuse or opaque, as the pandemic experience has brought home, and so to some degree really unknown (unknowns). Dread follows not only from lack of information or predictability; it grabs subjects, as the eco-anxiety proliferating in response to Bendell's environmental provocation bears out. It manifests especially where doubt proliferates about what information or evidence would count. How do we actually know a catastrophic storm is the effect of climate change? What world-historical transformations will pandemic impacts bring about?

The drone operator in Omer Fast's *5000 Feet is the Best*, mentioned in Chapter 1, may be capable, hawk-like, of discerning the make of the target's car, and its tires. He thinks he is sure of the driver's identity, a marked man. He would admit that neither he nor his commanders ever quite know whether there are any other passengers. They presume that if there are, they are fellow political travelers. The missile strikes, secure in its targeting. A family is wiped out, children and parents politically uninvolved. There precisely, in the face of utter unknowability and its implications, the emptiness is filled with dread.

Dread responds to obscurity, to lack of transparency. It registers a sense that something pressing or important is being withheld, kept secret from one, done behind one's back. Or that, in other cases, what is better to have left untouched, dormant, secret, is now unsettlingly being brought to attention, made visible. To make the familiar strange, in one set of cases; in another, to make visible the strange, the estranged, the alien and alienating. These are the two dominant senses Freud (1919/1955) gives to his notion of *unheimlich*, the uncanny. (I am drawing on Freud's conceptual insights here, not on his broader theory that the uncanny follows from *psychic repression* of the familiar, especially "repressed infantile morbidities" or "primitive beliefs" [1919: 249; cf. Fisher 2017].) In the first sense, the uncanny is that which renders secret, and obscures. Here, dread is chained to the condition of unknowability. In the second, there is leakage, a secretion. The dread-filling feeling is more a horror at the way catastrophe or disaster comes out of nowhere.

Dread thus operates messily. It unsettles, haunts, disenchants, shocks. Dread can also "unsense," de-sense or cut off, foreclosing or voiding established meaning. It can desensitize, make foreign, defamiliarize, thereby alienating and reducing care about its ill-defined domain of concern. Like the pandemic, ecological disaster can be named. But their extension and impact are so far-reaching, touching every facet of our lives, that their underlying, less visible triggers are more readily obscured or repressed. The irrepressible dread nevertheless tends to freeze most in place. But can it also serve for some to sound an alarm, that something is amiss, and so a ringing call to action?

Dread emerges out of an unpatchable tear in being, existential or social. It seems always drawn to what will increase its own velocity, deepen its hold, magnify its unsettlement. Dread is enigmatic: one can't quite put one's finger on it. One cannot even define or identify the sense that is dread itself. It is not exactly sadness, approaching rather something like unfathomable torment. Dread is depthless, bottomless, lacking insight. It is an agony with no single definable object giving rise to it. It expresses a general anxiety the prompt of which is indefinable, a nagging sense that has no singularly compelling explanation.

As intensified and permeating anxiety, dread offers a warning of sorts, an alarm that impending threat is at hand though not quite definable. Freud, in his later theory, suggests that anxiety signals pervasive worry about helplessness and the lack of adequate support in the face of threat. As eco-anxiety reveals, dread freezes out all other feeling. It is world-surrounding, world-infusing (cf. Blanchot 1986). Dread seeps, in a manner of speaking, into one's bones, into one's very moral fiber. It leaks into one's being in the world as a silent virus. Once sufficiently settled in, dread will reveal itself in taking over life as such. It can paralyze one in place, immobilizing one in the face of the worry.

*

The unpredictable proliferation of dread's prompts and multiplicity of its articulations prime the pump of its political field. Hortense Spillers (2017) has commented that "actual power" produces "fear." "Symbolic power," she argues, by contrast, does not necessarily do so, as one "can take it or leave it." Sticks and stones, but not names, Spillers seems to be insisting. Expressions of symbolic power, I suggest, are more likely to unleash dread. This has only magnified in the wake of social media, where throwaway comments or "hot mic" moments become "shit storms."

Dread is phobogenic, in the Fanonian sense. It is phobia-inducing, constraining if not clouding both clear-mindedness and productive or at least effective action. It tends to prevent identification of the causes of expression or action, or to mis-identify them, and by extension curtails response to the conditions or actions that are dread-inducing. Paul Gilroy (2005: 101) characterizes the resentments directed at immigrants to former imperial countries like Britain as the product of their being "unwitting" reminders "of the imperial and colonial past." The nagging dissatisfaction and anxiety lacking any materially well-defined identifiable prompt or cause is displaced onto targets of opportunity. Dread of being faced with the faceless, ghostly return of the repressed, on one side; and with the incessant worry of being subjected to racist invective or worse, seemingly coming out of nowhere, on the other.

As COVID-19 began to take hold across Europe and the United States, there was a surge in racist verbal and physical attacks on those taken to be Asian for introducing the virus. Some Eastern European countries saw a surge also in attacks on Roma. An EU Parliament member from Bulgaria, for example, identified "Romani ghettoes" as "the real nests of contagion" (Matache and Bhabha 2020). In the wake of white supremacist mass shootings in the United States, apologists for Republicans and the National Rifle Association put the outbursts down to "mentally sick" individuals rather than to the toxic mix of rampant racisms and lax gun possession legislation. The most vulnerable, least accepted, the perennially non-belonging, become the objects of mounting violence. Last arrived, the most powerless, are the first to be despised. Vulgarity and violence, bigotry and brutality against the vulnerable become the bitcoin, the stealth cryptocurrency, of the politics of dread. Assault weapons are now the arms of choice. The self-promoting invest in both in moments of political crisis and challenge to their authority.

In September 2018 in an American city, a young black Uber driver picked up three white barely twenty-somethings, two men and a woman. As he climbed into the back seat, one of the men tipsily exclaimed, "white privilege, white privilege." The fragility of the claim's presumption requires repeated insistence, as if only for self-assurance in the face of its relentless questioning.

The driver, remaining outwardly calm, quietly asserted his authority. The insulting man demanded music; the driver refused. Both male passengers kept touching and moving contents in the car. The driver, his voice even and firm, his disposition respectful throughout, requested they return the contents to their rightful place. The woman tried talking her two friends out of their racial belligerence, at least for the length of the ride. A few minutes along the way, the driver pulled over, ordering the passengers out. As the more belligerent man exited, he erupted: "You're one fucking bitch-assed n*****." The driver, anger mounting but in full self-control, non-violently dressed down the man. (He is clearly better than most of us.) As he returned to his car, the driver turned first to him: "Be thankful that I'm a calm, collected dude"; and then to the woman (who ordered the ride): "Rebecca, that kind of mentality, if you are not like that you should stay away from people like that." He drove off, retaining his considerable dignity throughout.

This makes evident the racial dimension frequently shadowing elaboration of dread. Black cab drivers, having just experienced or read about an unsettling racist attack, cannot be blamed for dread creeping over them when picking up future white rides. Would the next bigoted passenger be disrespectful, or carry a concealed weapon? Knowing Rebecca's name abstracts violence into "civil" exchange, the one-to-one evaporating in otherwise squeezed-out sociality. Race becomes a driving vehicle for dread.

In recent years, supporters of Israel, especially in Britain, Europe, the United States, and South Africa, have leveled charges of anti-Semitism at those criticizing Israel for its treatment of Palestinians. A number of prominent global intellectuals, mostly people who are not white, have had prizes and prominent speaking invitations withdrawn as a result of this coordinated effort and mischaracterization of their views. The charges have unleashed a barrage of racist and violent attacks against those targeted. The media discussion around these questions in Germany has revealed ongoing anxiety about the country's own racisms, the dread at possibly being called out for ongoing anti-Semitisms while largely evading much introspection about its broader culture of racisms.

Intellectual representations around bounded identity groupings tend to ontologize what are actually historically produced formations. Experience of the Holocaust as incomparably evil, a genocide like no other, almost invariably is accompanied by the insistence that it is irreducibly constitutive of Jewishness as such. Similarly, Afro-pessimism understands "anti-Blackness" and black enslavement as constitutive of "Blackness" and "the Human" in the European-derivative mindset (Wilderson 2020; cf. Cunningham 2020). Comparative studies of each group tend to shape hierarchical claims of evil, with each respectively experiencing gradations of suffering. Persistent dread of the world as currently ordered is seen to attach to the group so understood.

If comparativist formulations of these sorts ontologize historical experiences, relational accounts seek to understand how dreadful experiences are both historically prompted and relationally realized and sustained. When Europeans "see" a black man, Mbembe (2017: 32) remarks, they historically see "Nothing." The point is generalizable to whiteness at large, to those self-identifying, asserting themselves as white. It's not that Europeans or whites literally see nothing. The fact that it is specifically a black person they see *as* nothing implies they must see the black man as black in order to see him as Nothing. They are not seeing nothing but seeing the black person – women are subjected to this too – as a non-entity, without value. They must see in order not to see, to disavow, discount, disvalue, deny. This, Mbembe concludes, is the delirium or mania of race.

bell hooks (1997) claps back at the racism. A black person sees whiteness, the white man qua white, as the embodiment of terror and violence. There is plenty of historical evidence to bear this out. After all, up through the 1950s, those taken to be not white were characterized as "non-Europeans," whether on South African park benches or less formally by whites in Europe. But there is also plenty of contemporary evidence to make clear that it is far from a thing of the past. The likes of Frances's *Génération Identitaire* (see Chapter 7) identify "non-Europeans" as all those not white, those they take by implication not to be European, to have no place in Europe. This is now taking on renewed and expanded form. Europeans have long targeted a range of racially conceived monsters: Blacks, Jews, Muslims, Roma. In other states, the monsters may vary: for Hindu nationalists, they are Muslims; for Turks, Armenians and Kurds; for Israelis, Palestinians; for Myanmar Buddhists, Rohingya; for Chinese Communists, Uyghurs; and so on.

*

If delirium produces manic expressions, invariably violent, dread tends to fixate, to fix in place, to render the dreading subject immobile in the face of the dreaded condition. Where the manic becomes a generalized social condition, one never knows exactly when delirium will take over, with violence lashing out. Dread takes hold as anticipation of violence, foreshadows its eruption, much as an eerie moment of silence precedes an earthquake. When delirium dances with dread – a *danse macabre* – it invariably ends disastrously. Heightened violence, ultimately death, is the likely outcome, precisely because little else will satiate its drive.

Where racially disprivileged subjects suffer dread – and whiteworld pretty much has always prompted this suffering – they do so as a lived condition of their constraints. The dread takes on the specificity of fear as the prompt hardens into palpably identifiable objects of concern. The always possible police stop and frisk, the official knock on the door, a burning cross on the lawn, the cleaving asunder of families. The racist remark out of nowhere is followed almost inevitably by the denial of its racist intentionality, accompanied by the silent presumption of racially privileged innocence and dis-privileging guilt. The codes, structural impediments, and institutional barriers are taken for granted, as, too, are a sense of belonging and the entailed occlusions. The fears of those constituted as not white are set in relief against a canvas of accumulated experiences.

Dread, in short, envelops. It inhabits the world it comes to constitute, to define. That world, the "dreadsphere," is interactively dreadful and dreaded. So much so that the dread itself becomes preoccupying, all-enveloping, claustrophobic. Many of those suffer-ing eco-dread, after all, require therapy, as indicated above. We have shifted, perhaps, from the condition of planetary fear (what Virilio [2012] calls "cosmic fear") in the wake of Hiroshima to planetary dread today. Fear and dread are like vectors of Being crisscrossing sometimes through, sometimes past each other, DNA strands of affective life. Planetary dread is unleashed and licensed by a foreboding in the face of globally dis-tributed forces ranging from weaponized destruction to viral technological displacement, cross-generational and constitutively gendered sexual molestation and viola-tion, soaring precarity for many with outlandish wealth for the few, and the eruptive effects of viral and environ-mental collapse. Will I be touched by it? When? How? In short, a rampant politics of alienation, elimination, erasure. The incessant dread of disaster, as the impact of Bendell's environmental predictions makes evident, fueled by the twenty-four-hour news cycle and incipi-ent viral circulations, erases any distinction between expectation and the unexpected. It produces what a patient of Freud (1919/1955: 240) characterized as an "omnipotence of thoughts," that chattering in the mind that won't let up.

The production and feeding of dread trade on two entangled modes by which people are demeaned. One is the standard practice of demeaning: of saying nasty, disparaging things about another, diminishing the target's dignity, debasing, degrading, or discounting their value. The demeaned are positioned by the demeaning as less valued, non-belonging, unworthy of social standing. The disparagement may take one of many articulations: gender, race, class, disability, and so on. When the demeaning is even implicitly racial, not least a dog-whistle, it is racist; when gender driven, it is sexist. It may – mostly will – interactively be both. Perhaps surprising is how these demeaning expressions have so readily resurfaced at a time when they are increasingly under critical attack.

There is another mode of de(-)meaning which has become a general strand of contemporary culture. Terms are denuded of their established meanings. With racist expression, there is a constant casting of doubt on terms' meanings. In repeatedly demeaning four Congresswomen of color in July 2019, Donald Trump characterized them in tweets as "Racist . . . and not very smart." The ignorant racism he is projecting is theirs, not his. The charge of racism, no matter the contextual applicability, is wielded as a shield against his own. The complete denuding of meaning from the concept seeks to render the charge of his own racism meaningless, without force. If everything is, nothing is, and his cannot be.

It has likewise become commonplace when called out on racist or sexist expression for public figures to declare that "I [or they] said nothing about race/color/gender." The conventional meanings of terms or codes, acquired over a long history of racist expression, are erased, then filled with a different, more "neutral" or contrarian meaning, or none at all. This is not rationalization but reinvention. The fabrication makes things up in order to weave a new narrative, one less indicting of and less costly to those making or defending the claims. Dread bubbles up in the cauldron of repeatedly not being taken seriously, of being denuded even of the terms of critical reproach.

Donald Trump and his defenders quickly turned to this "other," second practice of de-meaning. It allowed them to express themselves in racist, sexist, or gender-effacing fashion with political or personal impunity. They redirected the charge of racism at critics. "They are racist for calling me/him racist." This is not just clever. It is to remake the very notion at issue, to "re-mean" it. The point is to put critics on the defensive, to devalue any terms of critique. If all is racist, nothing counts. The logic at work, if that's what it can be called, applies and perfects the now well-trodden tactic to identify any criticism of the Israeli state or its policies and practices as anti-Semitic, as racist. In defending Trump, his political supporters both denied his racism and immediately charged the four Congresswomen with being "anti-Semitic" (or critics of Corbyn and the British Labour Party as failing to have faced up to charges of their anti-Semitism) because they criticized Israel's pernicious treatment of Palestinians. The focus is shifted from the initial criticism to the semantic slipperiness of the terms deployed.

Dread is forged on the sense, accordingly, that there is no truth in the matter, nothing to know or grasp. Dread trades on the reduction to absolute absence: no-knowledge, no-truth, non-relation, nothing left to lose. Dread, in short, is unspeakable. In J.M. Coetzee's novel *Foe* (1986), Friday is the figure of dread, his tongue cut out, bereft of speech. His forced silence renders him unapproachable, without meaning, incomprehensible in his insignificance. On the verge of incessant threat, even when minding his own business, or especially when in service. The illegibly unknown too close for comfort. Dread, then, is the urgent reach for a truth incessantly evaporating. Consider as a prime example here climate change denial. Dread is, to pick up on Virilio's compelling characterization, a "community of emotions," a "communism of affects" (Virilio 2012: 30) reduced to solipsism. In its most naked form, it is suffered alone, in silence. Where dread privatizes the affective, isolates it as a discrete individualized sensibility, all that is left to this communality of feeling is ever-expanding futility.

Modernity's drive to conquer the unknown as both an epistemological and political project has been displaced today by the reiterability of unknowability. Cartesian doubt or epistemological skepticism as the underpinning of modernity's epistemological drive has given way to proliferated doubt as political project: the *refusal* to know as power/ignorance. The power of ignorance is brandished as a blunt weapon, a refusal to know as a way of getting away with murder. Climate change. The actual consequences of Brexit. Foreign meddling in local elections. The costs of health care dis-insurance. The dramatic increase to the national debt resulting from tax reform overwhelmingly favoring the very wealthy. The social costs of spiraling inequality. The economic disbenefits of ending migration.

*

"Cruel optimism," Lauren Berlant (2011) has forcefully argued, is a pervasive, even national, attachment to dreams of the good life that the form and structure of living adopted render completely unachievable. Brexit, perhaps, is a reminder that this is more global than the American phenomenon to which Berlant's work understandably restricts itself. The social structures and ways of being with which social members surround themselves undermine realization of the Dream. It is the optimism of the fantasy promoted yet made impossible by the narrowing imperatives of social existence as presently structured.

Dread manifests as the sinking feeling that the fantasy is a cruel joke. This has been rendered all the more evident by the experience of COVID-19 (see Chapter 5). Dread is a driving social sense, prompted by the situated experiences of articulated structures, processes, and practices. Their impacts are expressed and experienced as a decomposing negativity, manifesting as an incipient clinical depression or anxiety. A psychoanalyst friend practicing in New York reported to me a surging workload in the wake of Trump's election to the US presidency, especially among politically targeted youth populations (women, people who are LGBTQI, migrants, recent immigrants). Psychiatrists likewise have reported historical levels of "burnout and depression" (Topol 2019). Dread manifests following from – even as the realization of – the intimated, the hinted at but to date held at bay. A similar trend has been informally reported in Britain in Brexit's wake. The mania of the social binge gives way to a depressive hangover when the bill comes due. It follows (from) the end of self-denial, the erosion and ultimately implosion of the social Dream. The cruelty in the impossibility of its realization can no longer be deemed someone else's problem. It is the comprehension, in the last analysis, that optimism here is tantamount to its contrary. Optimism fueled by the Dream, cruelly unrealizable, metamorphoses in dread's wake into social varieties and expressions of pessimism.

Platform capitalism (Srnicek 2016) necessitates being plugged in and networked just to negotiate the everyday, the effects of which further the surging power and profits of the few. The gig economy reduces responsibility for survival fully to the individual, diminishing time and energy for social commitment or contribution. Racisms are proliferating, authoritarianisms on the rise, freedoms threatened or curtailed, inequalities expanding. Homelessness, helplessness, and hopelessness interweave for many. All this is spurred along by indiscernibility and detachment, underpinning a generalized "zone of indifference" (Agamben 1998).

It is not without coincidence that opioid painkiller addiction has exploded as the pessimistically painful realization has set in that the taken-for-granted and socially promoted is unreachable. Economic deflation occurs when prices of goods across an economy fall. Social deflation sets in as the possibility of social growth is stunted and expectations for self- and social betterment evaporate or shatter. Children can no longer expect to be better off than their parents. Ecological thresholds evaporate with little or no effective political effort to address the widespread challenges or ameliorate their stifling effects.

All this involves a turning away, often the driving disposition of those few whose life circumstances have protected them from the challenging conditions facing the many. Those states that prematurely sought to reopen their economies from lockdown before COVID-19 data showed viral dissipation rationalized it as sacrificing the elderly and vulnerable for the economic viability of the majority.

Distraction is the cultural vehicle for avoidance and ignoring; detachment for the inflation of indifference; rationalization of cruelty for the protection and perpetuation of entitlement and privilege. Dread is "just another word" standing in for the gathering evaporation of the commons, the dissolution of the social, the severing of and turning away from the sometime social ties that bind. Demeaning racisms reinflate to cover for the insecurities inescapably materializing. Violent, even murderous, racisms erupt as a social prophylaxis against the paranoid projection of danger, invasion, and theft from the possessed by the dispossessed. These irruptions reinforce the longstanding futility and discontent, from creeping surrender to declaring that the racial chasm tearing apart the social is irreparable, a "natural" order of the racial state.

This irreparability underscores what Mbembe (2017: 79–84) characterizes as "racial pessimism," the claim that the racial order of things is inherent in the fabric of modern life and as such constitutive of it. It is taken consequently as unchangeable, unaddressable even. Dread here expresses the increasingly pervasive disenchantment seeping across polities. It is the incipient sensing, if not full realization, that the social, economic, and political arrangements are at irrecuperable odds with their subjects' collective and common – as opposed to some individuals' – interests.

Eugene Thacker (2012) characterizes this pervasive disenchantment as "cosmic pessimism." He identifies it in the expression, "We're doomed." Thinking has stopped, pessimism has us in its grip. But Thacker makes no attempt to spell out why "critical or philosophical thinking" might have been brought today to what he regards, debatably, as a standstill. There is no account of the voluminous mix of social, economic, political, technological, and now environmental conditions that has come to snuff out thinking, that has more or less completely instrumentalized life. Thacker offers no specificity as to why pessimism now. The pandemic and eco-anxieties creeping across the planet are due less to not knowing the causes than to not knowing or refusing what to do about the effective responses.

Dread and the pessimisms it reveals are invariably taken to be singularly stultifying. Bendell's projection that environmental collapse will likely strike us within the next decade threatens to have this effect. The associated sense of irreparability prompts the counter-call to "tear it down," to build the social anew, most notably without a set of ideals, principles, or even guidelines for what the "new man" and new social form might amount to. Afro-pessimism today perhaps most explicitly expresses this mode of negative discard.

The blues, rather than the religiously inspired compositions of Thacker's Bach, provide the playlist for the pervasive dread gripping the social. The blues express the existential pain of abandonment and disengagement by those with the power of refusal and disposal, turning those regarded as useless, as surplus, as burden, into the castaway. The blues lay down the soundtrack for the pain and suffering, the loss, rejection, loneliness, and alienation pervading social life. Muddy Waters' warning rings across this sense, the time of dread: you can't spend what's not in your pocket, and "You can't lose what you ain't never had" (Waters 1964); while Langston Hughes (1967) and Nina Simone (Olsen 2016) respond to the economic and physical violence, in the spirit of refusal, resistance, even reprisal, with "The Backlash Blues."

Dread, then, does not inevitably or only produce passivity or negativity, the fixed in place with little if any possibility of alternation and alteration, any cessation and transformation. Negativity is disposed to violent outburst as a lashing out or release. Tearing one's hair out, nevertheless, can also get one off one's derrière and, as witnessed repeatedly across the globe, into the streets collectively, to broadly common purpose.

Critical pessimism in a Nietzschean mode ignites the sense that there are no inevitably fixed limits to social engagement and the possibility of transformational social betterment. Where melancholia often leads to abrogating or evading responsibility, as Gilroy (2005) pointed out regarding Britain's dominant sensibility concerning its colonial history, dread is more ambivalent. For some, it freezes into a refusal to acknowledge let alone address the impacts of wrongdoing. For others, however, it can serve as prompt, a Sartrean ignition charge to get going. Even Kierkegaard was excited at the prospect that if there is no omnipotent force determining universal commands and obedience, individuals have license to design their own life paths for which no one but themselves in concert and collectively is responsible. If debilitating dread is the anticipation of stasis, the paranoia of end-days made palpable, this more liberating sense of pessimistic dread tends to an incisive analytic for the sake of a constructive, reparative, replacing transformation.

In his haunting song "Treaty," Leonard Cohen (2016) metaphorically captures something of the warring tensions between religious deceit and refusal, dread and exhausting anger. Cohen's "treaty" is the reach for the sort of reparative remaking it would take to turn around futureless futures, to reimagine and reinstall possible futures collectively made.

*

These tensions are being rewired and reconfigured, mediated and remixed by the revolution in digital technologies in a complex entanglement of dread-inducing and liberating ways. I turn in the following chapter to consider these developments.

3

Dread's Operating System

A faculty member of Tsinghua University in Beijing recently told me that while driving on campus she received a text message on her smart phone. It was accompanied by a real-time photograph of her car and license plate. The text message was auto-generated from the campus police. It informed her that she was driving at 33 km per hour in a 25 km speed zone. She was warned to slow down or risk a fine, hinting as well at the loss of social credit. What unnerved her more than the threat of a fine was the intrusiveness and immediacy of the tracking. It was as if her every move was being watched. It no doubt was.

It is now a cliché to point out that any person virtually anywhere today has the world at their fingertips. Technological connection through computers, tablets, or smart phones makes it possible to be globally plugged in at the press of a keystroke or two. The digital divide of course remains deep and serious, reinforcing and extending inequalities in a wide variety of ways. At the same time, many can connect instantaneously with people on the other side of the globe, know what is happening in the most distant places within seconds of its occurrence, and listen to music or watch videos produced half a world away. Mobile banking at considerable distance from the nearest bank has rendered life easier for those without easy access, from Bangladesh to Kenya. The reach of individuals has been made technologically almost limitless. Contemporary technologies reinforce Gayatri Spivak's insight that every place is the center of some(one's) world.

These extraordinary possibilities nevertheless are accompanied by equally compelling threats, as the Tsinghua experience exemplifies. Dread emerges as the anxiety that one's daily moves are being followed for the ends of commercialization or social control. This anxiety is exacerbated in equal force by the fact that the virtues of deep and abiding social relation, of the face-to-face, the one-to-one-to-one, so long a bedrock of social life, have been stretched beyond their elasticity. As the relational tautness slackens, the values and meanings associated with these once driving social relations ultimately begin to be lost too.   *Problem w social media*

Social media, so the worry goes, have become a pathway to the evacuation of sociality as such, or at least to prevailing sociality as we have come to know it. The presumed tightness of the one-to-one is undercut by loose ties of more readily substitutable many-to-many relations. Virtuality prompts virtual relation, distance more readily enabling distantiation. Social media, perhaps perversely, prompt the infrastructure of widening social alienation, if not social dissolution. While the worry may be overwrought, current conditions exacerbate rather than alleviate the concern. Wellbeing, whether economic, political, or social, is in danger of being reduced to the handheld device, and so to its invisible and troubled infrastructures of production, relation, and value entangled with their constant threat of disablement.

*

Algorithms furnish the operating logic of digital technology. Algorithmic logic frames, structures, and regulates the limits of the conceivable and doable regarding the subject (matter) of their address and reference point, if not more broadly. The algorithm molds the world according to its syntax. Algorithmic life is, in short, a lifeworld, life and world delimited by the reach of algorithmic reference. If the limit of the world is the limit of its language, then it could be said (riffing on Wittgenstein) that the limit of the world – in shape, formulation, reach, and temporality – is now the limit of the algorithmic (itself a linguistic product after all). "World-limit" (or world-possibility) is now more and less set by the scope and movements – the rhythm – of the algorithm (Pasquinelli 2014).

Predictions have always been made in the same way: analyzing data from the past or present to forecast futures. Predictions are not speculations. These techno-commanding instrumentalizations amount to the command of hypothetical imperatives, of the means–ends variety. We could push even further to say that the hypothetical has become categorical. Human subjects across a wide variety of domains are now techno-compelled to pursue nothing but the ends given to them by these instrumentations. These are the ends crafted by the technological of the kind by which human subjects are now being more or less universally networked. Algorithms give orders, commanding ways of doing and, by implication, ways of being. But they also create an order, even imposing it.

The algorithmic accordingly serves as "a process, a program with clearly defined limits, a finite instruction sequence" (Uricchio 2012: 21). Its repetitions structure the rhythm of lived experience. They shape sensibilities and affects rhythmed by – when not (occasionally) disrupting – the structures of social arrangement. Algorithms are patterned and patterning thought. What doesn't fit the pattern of their making is either correctable error or literally irrelevant, meaningless, counter-productive, mere noise or detritus. Dread is the unsettling sense of amounting to the misfit or the unfit in the shifting order of the system's commands.

The use of algorithms to make decisions is also increasingly widespread. VITAL is a product of Deep Knowledge Ventures. It surveys very large tranches of data to project the most profitable investments likely as a consequence of the patterns revealed in the reviewed data. A Hong Kong venture capital fund saw fit in 2014 to appoint VITAL nominally to its Board of Directors. The appointment has no legal status. It exists solely to advantage itself by VITAL's investment recommendations in the wake of repeated biotech investment failures (Wile 2014). The algorithm was accorded a veto-power vote on the Board applicable only in investment decisions. The experiment has proved sufficiently successful that VITAL is now being replaced by the advanced VITAL 2.0 (Finkel 2019).

Algorithmic or high-frequency trading is calculated and enacted on the basis of massive volumes of data, updated instantaneously with data about other trades, trends, earnings reports, the constantly shifting volatility index, breaking news about politics, takeovers, buyouts, and so on. The update necessitates the next trade, and then the next. When a large volume of stocks is sold, the algorithm will instantaneously recognize the resultant dip in the stock's price, issue a buy order in nano-seconds, and then, as the price rises as a result of the increased algo-demand, sell the stock microseconds later at the higher price. A penny increase in the price of a million shares will generate a techno-trading profit of $10,000 in seconds. A "flash crash" in 2010 led, again instantaneously, to the evaporation on US stock exchanges of upwards of a trillion dollars. The lag time between sell, buy, and sell is a function not of algorithmic application so much as of the relatively slow speed of real-world trading registration. There is no rest, either for the data inputs and outputs or for the generated trade. Conventionally set clocks are obsolete, overridden by the rhythms of data in, calculations, trades, data out, new data in . . . repeat . . . twenty-four/ seven. The world is awash not with crypto-currency so much as algorithmic virtual value, often cryptically veiled from ordinary view.

Algorithmic decision-making of these kinds is based, as with its predictiveness, on surface pattern recognition and the identification of regularities or irregularities. Ethical considerations about investing in a product because of, say, abusive labor practices, environmental pollution, or corruption would garner algorithmic attention only if impacting profitability, efficiency, or effectiveness. Instrumentalizing technologies recognize as relevant only those considerations that can factor into and impact the instrumental calculus. Non-instrumental ethical consideration on its own terms will be ignored.

instrumentism

Algorithmic temporality, thus, is teleological, reaching always for its immediate(d) end(s), only to be redirected instantaneously to a new end as soon as the previous one has been realized or data inputs alter. The effects tend to volatility, the giddiness of almost instantaneous trades producing profitability followed by dramatic losses. To date, the profits have far outstripped the losses. They are dramatically intensifying and deepening the wealth inequalities ripping apart the global landscape (Milanovic 2019; Piketty 2014).

This points to a deeper, even more unsettling, set of concerns. Algorithms increasingly interact among themselves. Trading algorithms interact with other trading algorithms, resulting in multitudes of transactions executed at speeds and in quantities never to be witnessed by or even made intelligible to humans. Even the most sophisticated quants have been at a loss to explain exactly how particular algo-trading decisions are arrived at. And those programming AlphaGo have been incapable of explaining the algo-generating strategies in the program's victories over the leading human experts in games of chess and Go. Trading decisions may be made by algorithmic computation with complete automation, or auto-generation, so that human intervention is further downplayed or excluded altogether. Thomas Bridle (2018) worries that "the machines are learning to keep their secrets." It is no stretch to imagine a day where we wake to momentous eventualities such as war upending the lives of multitudes across the globe brought about by decisions involving no human judgment or oversight at all. In the meantime, anxieties about these anticipated eventualities proliferate.

A number of jurisdictions in the United States have implemented an algorithm to determine bail eligibility on the basis of predictions about the accused's future. Based on inputted data about the accused, their past actions, financial records, and record of reliability, a calculation is made of the probability of them showing up to the required next court appearance or of jumping bail. Judges' experience and intuition, as well as their biases, are preempted from the decision-making. By all accounts to date, this has delimited personal bias as well as explicit racial and gendered slants (cf. Benthall and Haynes 2019; Siegel 2018; Srinivasan 2019). But it reintroduces new biases, notably weighting towards class determinations. These, of course, embed the original racial and gendered biases, if less overtly and in less easily recognizable forms. The lack of transport or funding to pay for a public transport ticket in order to show up for court hearings will translate – instantaneously, without the possibility of interpretation or mitigating circumstances – into bail denial. Algorithms have become the updated, mostly invisible, infrastructure of racially inscribed power.

*

In their computational composition, algorithms have sought to offer something of an order. But they do so only by insisting on an imposed structure, an imperialism of arrangement. They challenge our experience and understanding of the relationship of past and present to the future in really fundamental ways.

As self-generating, algorithms defy the historical, render the historical – history itself – beside the point. History, in contrast to the stored data points from the past, is erased as the next algorithmically produced instant is immediately created. Even historical data become the present the moment they are algorithmically invoked. Not the first time the end of history has been declared, to be sure, but perhaps the first more or less full enactment of perpetual motion technology. The algorithmically recognized past exists only as a present. Perpetual virtuality reaches for virtual perpetuity.

It follows that thinking, on this profile, has no temporality other than instantaneity (cf. Skow 2015). This structural prescription contours thinking. It is restricting as much in how thought and memory operate as in the formalistic delimiting of legitimate modes and, by implication, objects of critical thinking themselves. Anything can be thought so long as it fits the constricting profile of this prescriptively formalistic reasoning, of the temporality of instantaneity.

Anthropomorphic memory is made up of the recollection of pasts. While drawing on the bits of data in people's memory bank, such memory is not simply reducible to these data bits. It involves the recounting, the narratives composed to make sense of how those data fit together, re-membering the occurrence. Human memory threads together registers of the past with their being made present, often adding embellishment in their re-presentation to themselves and others. Memory in this mode, as Achille Mbembe (2020a) suggests, is constitutive of what makes the human. It involves the calling up and sharing of histories shaping time and place, such as slavery and colonialism, wars and genocides, without elevating any one in value over the others.

For algorithmic memory, by contrast, the data and their operationalization are all there is. There is but a singularity to the plane of data qua data. It is not coincidental that we speak of algorithmic memory only in the singular. Algorithms produce no traumatic or happy memories, no affective reminiscence or recollection of their own. Algorithmic memory operates only as perpetual presence. It may be tempting to suggest that human memory is a mode of interpretative mediation whereas algorithmic memory is not. It would be more accurate, however, to say that different modes of mediation operate for each: interpretational narration in the former instance, data match-mapping in the latter. (The composition of match-mapping obviously embeds interpretative assumptions.) Algorithmic memory consists not of memories produced by algorithms so much as the data bank, the cache, of algorithmically produced matches. It is no more nor less than buckets of coded information. Dread's seepage signals an anticipated loss in trading narrative richness and interpretative reach for the overwhelming volume of linear data points promised by machinic memory.

*

Algorithmic reasoning, in contrast to the slow(er) time of anthropomorphic memory, is constitutively disposed to futurity-made-present. The time of instantaneity, of time as instant, is the time for which the algorithmic reaches, its endpoint. It takes 250 microseconds to techno-read one megabyte of memory: that's 0.00025 seconds. If you can imagine this as speed, it means "reading" information approximately ten times the length of this entire book in less than the blink of an eye! It is almost unimaginably fast.

So, it is no longer adequate just to track the development of computational power. In other words, what the computer – or, more broadly, perhaps less materially, artificial intelligence – is capable of next in terms of how quickly and how comprehensively it can learn so as to respond intelligently to input is growing beyond the capacities of human reasoning. It is becoming pure potentiality. It is no longer that the limits of language are the limits of world-making. Rather, the limits of data processing have surpassed if not replaced natural language, hence interpretative variability, as the driving limit case of instantaneous worlding.

The world – one might better say worlds – is awash with data that algorithms are capable of processing at speeds and levels of sophistication far outstripping human capabilities. And, alongside this, even as a result, at least in part, there is an unpredictable, even ironically incalculable, potential of computer processing power due to computers' learning capabilities. The lag in moral and legal norms to take account of these deep and rapid shifts suggests the evasion of responsibility resulting from wrongdoings effected by machine learning and AI applications. It is fueling the culture of anxiety-producing social unsettlements. One could just as easily call this the "dread-machine."

The digitally inspired metamorphosis in social relation, the insistence on disruption of the established, on high-octane innovation, along with the encouragement of an unbridled imagination, have encouraged an unexpected social outcome. Fantasy has been unleashed, as evidenced especially in gaming culture but also in social platforms such as Second Life and now TikTok. Avatars emerged, so to speak, as (a) second nature. One could, at least in one's imagination, choose to be anything and everything, anyone if not quite everyone. The limit, if there was any, was simply in the framing of the item menus from which to choose. One's imagination, it turns out, is limited by that of the technological innovators. But this unleashing of the fantastic has had a larger ramification.

One may see this best, perhaps, in the tension between memory and make-believe, in the erasure of that distinction. History in the making has become make-believe in constant demand. Make-believe is different than mistaken memory, or than fantasy, for that matter. Make-believe amounts to fabrication, collapsing the distinctions between sewing together a fabric of narration, misleading oneself, and compelling others to believe the made-up account or representation. These digitally promoted developments and the remaking of thought, memory, order – and indeed of time they have encouraged – have unleashed a sociality of making it up, and luring others into believing the fabrications too. Maker culture has inadvertently prompted the culture of make-believe, of faking it. A group of computer-graphics programmers created Lil Miquela, a realistic CGI rendition of a nineteen-year-old Brazilian film actress, singer, and influencer. Seeing her as a starlet in the making, CAA – the Hollywood artists agency – signed her to a contract. It is as much the supporting culture and economy as the product that sustains the make-believe.

One of the most unnerving applications of this capacity to digitally fabricate came at the hands of Cambridge Analytica's undertaking to impact the outcome of political campaigns. These included, most notably, Donald Trump's 2016 election and the "Leave" campaign in Britain's Brexit initiative. Created by Breitbart's Steve Bannon, later Trump's campaign manager and White House advisor, Cambridge Analytica (CA) was funded by the deeply conservative computer science and hedge fund billionaire Robert Mercer. CA implausibly datamined 80 million US-based Facebook user accounts to manufacture political profiles from the expression of online "likes." These political profiles were then mobilized to target potential Hillary Clinton voters with fabricated political stories, especially in swing states like Pennsylvania, Michigan, and Wisconsin. The aim was to discourage support for Clinton. For African-American voters, polling of whom indicated strong Clinton support, the undertaking was to discourage them from voting at all. Forensic data indicate a strong correlation between the CA campaign and voting tendencies, including lower black turnout in key states. The swings were sufficient to turn the election in Trump's direction. A similar logic played out in the Brexit vote too.

Digital technology has more readily enabled the anonymizing of falsity-making. In doing so, it has magnified, as Nietzsche put it, the powers of the false. Radical indistinction and boundary blurring, in turn, have proliferated indifference. Even the once sacred is no more. Fabrications are proliferating, and not only among notable politicians seeking to control agendas, mislead the public about opponents, or elevate themselves. Fakery fuels appropriation, the disposition to lift unacknowledged whatever is at hand to advance an interest, or just because one can. Digital technology has made it increasingly easy to create convincing fakes (Satter 2020), to doctor résumés, to fabricate videos, to place people in degrading or uplifting situations, to accuse them of saying or doing things they haven't, for which there is no supporting evidence. Anything to get ahead, to project a desirable image, to advance less a cause than a career.

"Deepfakes" name this game (Rini 2019). Donald Trump's online ads gearing up for his 2020 reelection bid projected images of young white American hipsters supposedly endorsing what a good president he had been in his first term. The images, however, were stock photographs of people who were not American, with voices likely not those of the personalities in the images

(Mazza 2019). It would not be too misleading to call him the leading promoter of fakeworld. There is an online app to hire fake crowds to show up for a political event, which the Trump campaigns took to doing to ensure "the biggest crowds in history" (Schneider 2015). At least it offered out-of-work actors, the un- and underemployed both before and during pandemic times, opportunity for a modest paycheck. After the COVID lockdown was eased in summer 2020 and Trump tried going back on the stump, paid crowds of unemployed participants were easier to mobilize from those willing to risk infection for needed income.

Consider stereotypical rumors circulating on social media platforms: a Jewish banker exploited a community to increase the bank's profitability; a black man raped a young white woman; a US presidential candidate with a "strange" Muslim-sounding name was born elsewhere. Not surprisingly, given the extensive history of pernicious stereotypes like these, social media networks soon took up these reports, sharing them repeatedly, in turn algorithmically amplifying their circulation statistics. That would cause the algorithmic logic to keep sending out the messages to those consuming and especially responding to such posts, and to their social network circles of "followers" and "friends." Such views, circulating in increasingly wide and viral networking ripples, soon become entrenched enough in corners of the population to conjure the possibility of dangerous outbursts towards communities the "perpetrators" are taken to represent. Accelerated social network circulation challenges the possibility of a fair media hearing, and of socially just treatment as a consequence.

Footage of disasters can be altered to make them look less or more damaging (Marks 2018). Videos are created of racial attacks which, when revealed as fake, undermine the credibility of actual attacks. During the devastating Hurricane Dorian in August 2019, which wiped out significant swaths of some Bahamian islands, Trump personally altered with a sharpie the forecasted track of the storm to show it would include part of Alabama, in order to "justify" his gaffe that it would. In fact, there was almost no chance of Alabama being impacted, as officials in that state immediately had to point out to deter residents from panicking. The political point of these fabrications is to make anything believable because nothing is (Lusher 2017).

It should come as little surprise that a person who heeds no distinction between truth and lies today could be elected President of the United States, but deeply concerning that an electorate has become less capable of being able to discern the distinction. Deepening economic anxieties are sought to be undercut by stoking social media-inspired dread of foreign invasion and projected racial threat, in the dual figures of the "China virus" and "Black Lives Matter." These fabrications are characteristic not just of Trump and his supporters. A poll shortly after Boris Johnson assumed the premiership in Britain thought him an inveterate liar. Yet the majority seemed to care less. The Polish political leadership has made it illegal to claim that Poland or Poles assisted Nazi Germany in its genocidal practices in Poland during World War II. Cultural figures and public intellectuals are not above the practice, as evidenced when, in researching self-elevating biographical claims, no corroboration exists independent of the figure's self-originating statements. Denial is the highway to historical reinvention.

*

Facial recognition algorithms offer another way in which algorithmic subjectivity unsettles social trust while driving social policy formation. I take "algo-subjectivity" to be the "subject" formation of the algorithmic in its own terms, not the determination of human subjectivity by the algorithm nor the anthropomorphizing of algorithmic subject formation. Algorithms have no fingers to scald, no skin to pierce, no ears burning for gossip. This is not to say algorithmic logic cannot spread rumors or conspiracy theories. The more people receiving socially networked rumors express interest in or preference for such claims, the more algorithmic logic as currently encoded will be encouraged to continue circulating them. Algorithms drive the capacity of machines to learn, to create and compose, not just to optimize cost–benefit calculation but actually to engage in instrumentalizing decision-making.

The latest development and application of facial recognition technology involves hiring practices in major technology, health, and financial firms. The technology is applied to conduct first-order computer-controlled interviews of the large pool of applicants, often around a thousand people. The app has been known to select white-associated names over black ones. It screens interviewees for facial expression, linguistic pronunciation, hand gesture, and the like, judging for aggressivity, patience, personability, clarity, and so on. From this screening, the program recommends to the firm's hiring office the leading candidates most likely to succeed for an in-person interview. HireVue is the company first associated with this app. It admits to being unable to give an account of the decision process embedded within the program application, or of the embedded cultural biases associated with gesture or linguistic expression, regional or national.

Major corporations are being sold on the efficiency of the model, reducing hiring time by 85 percent. Gestures, facial expressions, pronunciation, and diction vary widely, and are unrelated to the capacity to work effectively. Candidates are at a loss about what is being assessed, and as a result feel incapable of preparing properly for the anonymity of an interview with a computer program. They report heightened anxiety and stress as a consequence. Corporate enamoredness with the "charisma of the algorithm" translates into alienation for those subjected to its application (Harwell 2019a). The unacknowledged social upshot is to reproduce novel forms of preferred social homogeneity, themselves embedded in and predicated upon deep-set, often pernicious, social presumptions.

Algorithmic memory is made up of myriad data points, latent until invoked, static until plugged into algorithmic movement, formulaically bounded. Computational memory is a virtual infrastructure, hosted in hardware, of course, for housing data. Algorithmically enacted memory involves a code-driven matching of current to saved data profiles in a queried domain. Algorithmic memory, then, is a data bank or structured storage of these encoded matches. Google Brain has trained itself, not inconsequentially, to recognize a cat on the basis of matching the image capture of a cat passing by with 10,000 stored cat images. Facial recognition technology on our smart devices is designed to operate exactly on this logic. Recognizability, as now generally acknowledged, is predicated on the existing database profiles. What falls outside these stored profiles – almost invariably those that are not racially white or light – will fail to be identified (Buolomwini 2018), or will be misidentified, for better and for worse.

Half the US states today make available driver license photographs and identifying data to local police to conduct algorithmically determined criminal identification. Criminal suspect images are "lined up" against the drivers' license photographic database, the facial recognition algorithm seeking to make a match. No policy protocols currently exist to oversee mismatches. Race and gender once again loom large here. Darker skin tones and their facial contours currently are less readily recognizable by the software, and the algorithm is incapable of controlling for facial cosmetics (Buolomwini 2018). The relative techno-incapacity to make fine-grained distinctions for darker skin tones or cosmetic-covered faces (overwhelmingly women) means mismatches for people of color and women are more likely. This heightens the probability of criminological misattribution. With human line-up error, defense lawyers can at least cross-examine both police and prosecutorial conduct regarding the line-up as well as the witness, seeking to establish faulty process and memory. With algorithmic identification, first-order cross-examination is rendered obsolete. First-person human witnesses will be dispensed with in favor of technological experts. The prosecution alienates the defense from one more avenue of interrogation. This, in turn, foreshortens the time of prosecution, the time to a (mis-)determination of guilt.

The FBI has a facial recognition database including facial images of 640 million people (almost double the amount living in the United States). Chinese companies claim to have developed the capacity to recognize masked faces with a high degree of accuracy. Police helmets in China are being outfitted with increasingly sophisticated facial recognition cameras. The aim is to connect police bodycams to centralized databases in policing interactions with people and sensor-fed urban movement information, in interceding in or investigating criminal activity. Alibaba is building an integrated info-platform, City Brain, for the Chinese state to extend its monitoring reach. This likely signals the "technoptical" social future far more broadly.

Facial recognition technology at present, then, is partially inaccurate, the more so for the darker hued and women. Unlike fingerprints, facial shape, texture, and features are not so unique to an individual they could not be mistaken for a lookalike, a facial double, a twinned character who may be biologically unrelated.

There is speculation, too, that the database may be made available to immigration authorities to determine genealogical authenticity. The opening to rampant ethnoracial abuse to increase arrest, conviction, expulsion, and repatriation rates seems currently underregulated and unimpeded. Facial recognition or matching software will not solve all mismatch determinations. In any case, what one does in the case of a match requires political and moral judgment – wise practical reasoning – not ceding the political and ethical to an autonomous techno-fix.

This governing through coded formulations anonymizes control, undercuts attributions of responsibility, and alienates those subjected to the outcomes from avenues of contestation and redress. Control is ceded to the machine, decision-making to the formulaic, resistance and the seeking of justice to abstractions. Dread builds up at the lack of access to a person with whom one can reason, implore, or just let off steam when the formulaic outcome fails to fit one's circumstance or personal profile. Over time it gunks up the machinic operation, grinding down not just the social machine but the people the machine is made to serve. Dread, you might say, is the ghost haunting the operating system that produces it.

*

Judgment itself is in the process of becoming functionally algorithmic, nothing but the determination of the decision by algorithmic computation. Judgment, here, is reducible to computationally recognized and computable data. For example, Google Assistant (Assist), a Siri on steroids, is intended to be the omniscient database of all and any information relevant to the decisions facing one, and to yield the optimal outcome based on the available information, including one's history of preferences regarding the matter at hand. Assume one wants to book an air ticket to a defined destination. Assist would search out and purchase the best flights based on its "knowledge" – the data inputs available to it – about one's flying preferences, including cost, route, airline, seating, timing, and so on. The decision would be a function of the decision algorithm and relevant data culled from Google's vast database of over a billion people, things, and practices. The purchase would be transacted simply by hitting "return." The algo-automated learning machine would "understand exactly what you mean and give you back exactly what you want," as Google's Larry Page has put it. If only you knew yourself!

What of the role of having a feeling or intuition about the data, taking into account the feelings or sensibilities of others or even the judgment options themselves? What of a choice in the moment that deviates from one your record strongly suggests you would make? I usually choose a particular seat in the plane. It is open now when I am booking my flight but has the seat next to it taken. The row behind is empty though it has slightly less leg-room. In the moment, I choose the empty row, chancing that it might not fill up. I wouldn't always make that choice. It would depend on data inputs, to be sure. But it might just as well turn on a feeling in the moment. It may be one I will regret or celebrate later, but it is emphatically one no auto-calculus would generate. Algorithms have no hunches.

That algorithms have no hunches means that their commitment to render human lives and living more efficient – the repeatedly stated utilitarian endgame – imposes order, as stated at the outset. But in doing so, they come at a profound discount to human being. Having a hunch is not just exercising an intuition on the basis of which I take a calculated gamble. The algo-evaporation of hunching and intuition actually makes life less interesting, sometimes even more dangerous. An asylum-seeking refugee might Google-map escape routes across a landscape from a country of residence, but then decide on "instinct" for a more circuitous route to avoid more obvious and so more policed crossings. The technological erasure of hunches means there are fewer stories to share, fewer lessons learned. At the very least, this sort of techno-determination, once generalized across all domains, narrows if not obliterates the range of possibilities for freedom to be exercised. Given that wisdom comes from experience, from learning from failure, a reduction of life to a series of algo-efficiencies is likely to lead to less self-reflection, to making the world less wise, to rendering the political less open and less free.

It is telling, then, that with the emergence of crypto-value and proliferating technologies of encryption, calls for transparency have grown louder. As processes of value creation, of intrusiveness, and the curtailment of privacy have become more coded and so less readily obvious, concerns about openness in decision-making have grown. And yet the speed with which these logics of cryptic social processes have taken hold have far outstripped general comprehension of their operational logics, their spiraling application across increasing dimensions of social life, and any sustainable sense of how to regulate or control their applicability and social impacts. The socio-logics of encryption have resulted in less direct impacts too. Policy-makers have felt emboldened by this expansive culture likewise to become more secretive, more cryptic and obscure, and less transparent in their decision-making. Hence the gathering concerns about corruption in electioneering, political self-dealing, global trade policies, and governance. And the sinking sense that the world one inhabits is anonymously structured and fueled by alien and opaque forces.

That anyone with access to such technological proficiency could benefit from its application, nevertheless, reveals the democratizing possibilities of these technological developments. This has been celebrated by many commentators and perhaps borne out by the information sharing of WikiLeaks, among others. But the obscuring possibilities the technology also enables quickly place in question any straightforward social benefits. The latter is borne out by the vast expanse of the Dark Web and sites such as InfoWars.

*

Consider one telling instance, among many, of algorithms' corrupting impact on social trust, political processes, and equity. In May 2016, laying the ground for Trump's Presidential election, Breitbart (the conservative news and commentary website) and InfoWars (the conspiracy theory and fake news website) pressured Facebook to replace human staff determining trending topics with an algorithm, based on clicks. From this moment on, driven by the acceleration of bot-circulated stories and clicks, fake news proliferated (actual fake news, not political accusations of it, which perhaps could be characterized as an extension of fake news itself). Recall the discouragement from voting of the African-American electorate in the 2016 US election, mentioned above. Some have argued that there is nothing in the nature, the being, of the algorithmic in and of itself to produce these discriminating trends. But then there is nothing inherent in algorithmic being to delimit them either.

This embedded algo-discrimination is proving unsurprising. A recent study (Obermeyer et al. 2019) found that a health care algorithm designed to target patients likely to have the highest future health care needs underestimated black patient needs by more than twice that of white patients. The algorithmic design was not inherently or "intentionally" racist. Indeed, race was purposely excised as an algorithmic variable. Race, it is well known, is coded into the realities of socio-economic disparities. Black people tend to be significantly less well off than whites, on average, and this translates into their seeking less health care than their white counterparts. Lacking insurance, they more readily avoid health care visits, save in emergencies. The algorithm translated fewer visits into significantly lower medical needs, with dramatic real-life implications. (To its credit, the company deploying this particular algorithm has worked with the researchers to rectify the problem, which, it projected, is much more widespread in health care technology applications [Johnson 2019].) In so far as algorithms tend invisibly to reify the given and established – a product of long-existing data feeds – they likely amplify ongoing discrimination. Algorithms, at the very least, are a discrimination-reifying machine.

There is of course nothing absolutizing in digital technology itself that is necessarily corrupting, or for that matter dread-inducing. Just as there is nothing inherent in it that makes it necessarily democratizing. At best, we could say that digital technology lends itself to dramatically exacerbating trends. After all, "trending" is a central feature of its culture. The presumptive surface neutrality of code, the fact that its specific operating logic tends to be relatively obtuse – lacking transparency to the general consumer of its output or product – tend to dispose application of its operating logic to corrupting ends of the kind characterized above.

*

Hacking is digitality's underground. Directed at large oppressing systems, hacking for justice seeks to uncover information regarding systemic indiscretions, indirections, injustices. Undertaken for self-advancement, however, hacking problematically advances self-interest and profit-making or undermines voter participation and outcomes for individual, corporate, or state gain. Identities are stolen, accounts invaded, information leaked, fake profiles publicized, self-serving outcomes engineered.

Similarly, online user profiles and information are repurposed for political or commercial gain. Identities and private information are stolen, traded, used for purposes of theft and extortion. Political targeting seeks to advance a cause like Brexit, candidates like Trump, interests like Putin's. Cambridge Analytica to date is the most notorious, if far from the only, example. While it existed, CA could be viewed as a behavior change agency for hire, largely to promote political ends. It weaponized psychographics, as Britney Kaiser, a key figure at the firm, has put it in the 2019 Netflix documentary *The Great Hack*. Data are turned into weapons-grade fuel. One's social media accounts, browsers, and inbox are metamorphosed into the grist for info-warfare. Anyone who browses the web, uses social media, has consumed, banked, or provided personal information either directly online or which has been loaded into an online system is at risk of being drawn into the web of cyber-warfare, from low grade to high stakes.

Neural networking, machine learning, AI, and the rule of the algorithmic elevate data as the coin of the realm. This in turn has prompted a steep discount in theory, in hunches, insight, ultimately in interpretation, analysis, and understanding. Jonathan Zittrain (2019) has argued that the creation and uptake of medical drugs increasingly are promoted by these new technologies without understanding how they work. While not new (aspirin was created in 1897 and only completely understood close to a century later), applying complex, potentially life-saving but also high-risk medicines such as immunotherapies raises risks that remain unaddressed until too late, at least for some. Digital technology has made it so easy and inexpensive now to create, splice, and print DNA sequences. This heightens the possibility of rogue production of viruses that, if unleashed, could decimate populations. dBridge's (2016) electronic dub mix "Digital Dread" captures in sound the anxiousness embedded in these seductions into algo-worlds and their cultures (the flip track is "Fashion Dread," a critique of Rastafari looks/locks without the living commitment of Rastafarianism).

*

This profound reconstitution of being in the world, of worlds and world-making, is in the process of becoming all-encompassing, of global engulfment. There seems no outside to, no taking leave from, the digital, at least not without having the world pass one by. The sense that control has been lost sits in stark contrast to the modernizing hubris that humans could and one day would exercise complete control over nature.

These rapid technological developments upending so much of our social lives are one of the key factors encouraging the general social unsettlements so characteristic of our current times. One way a significant number of people have been dealing with this has been to deny not just principles, policies, or even facts with which they constitutively disagree. It has been to deny the very principles and findings of science itself, with no reasonable grounds to support them. Nothing is incontestable, all is subject to challenge, supported, if at all, more often than not by questionable "facts," claims, ideas. Skepticism devolves into taken-for-granted denial. In the context of this culture, it is perhaps unsurprising that "fake news" has become the all-too-easy charge by those unconcerned with facts against anyone calling their claims into question.

I do not mean to suggest it is all terrifying. Far from it. Digital technology has brought enormous economic and social benefits. It has enabled otherwise unimaginable medical and product advances, scientific breakthroughs, widespread knowledge development. It has unleashed great pleasure. But all this, too, may be why many have been inclined to look past not just the profound associated flaws but also the pernicious social implications the digital at once enables, proliferates, and dramatically accelerates. Dread, it could be said, is its irrepressible social subtext.

Dread here lurks as the anxiety at the loss of control over large swaths if not all dimensions of our lives. Or, more subtly, the loss of control while seeming to drive one's own preference profile. Where contemporary technology erases (much in) the distinctions between surface and depth, between what I wish to hold discreet and widespread public availability, between truth and fakery, dread is bound to lurk in the shadows. It bursts into outraged and outrageous expression at the least expected prompt, or none at all. An incessant and proliferated anxiety is the accompaniment; social exhaustion the irremediable outcome.

*

Algorithmic being is akin to human subjectivity only in the sense that it reduces the latter to the computational surrogate of the former. Algo-being trades on the logic akin to behavioral positivism. Eschewing the metaphysical in favor of the behavioral directives of coding syntax, algorithmic being operates purely processually. Popular cultural projections of human affect onto algorithms and the robotic perhaps render the latter more approachable and less alien. But they confuse the operating logics of the one for the character of the other. They anthropomorphize and anthropologize the technomorphic and technological. Algorithms are enormously effective in enabling a considerable range of functionality. And yet they are disturbingly delimiting and constraining of vast arrays of otherwise "permissible" activity, relation, interaction, expression, and social movement (cf. Fuller and Harwood 2016).

Machine-embedded algorithms do not so much "listen to," "overhear," or "eavesdrop" on our conversations, "probe" our bodies, or "read" our minds. Instruments may do that, driven by algorithmic directions. Algorithms, at core, however, direct or command the machines and collect the resultant data. And they do so subject to the data structures already in place, into which they are plugged, which in fact they serve to extend (Dourish 2016). They make matches with existing database entries, make predictions, even spew out resultant directives or commands. And they do so only in contingently materialized or "embodied" ways. They can operate quite effectively without ears and eyes, *sans* sensors. It is *we* who may indeed be spooked by this. We may hanker for "machines like us" as well as those that like us. But at heart, in so far as the metaphor holds, algorithms as such are constitutively – ontologically – indifferent to anything but data. Algo-being, to push the point, is a being that ultimately may become a DIY producer. But while it represents structuring architecture and so conditions, it will do so with no disposition, no inclination, no desire to call its own.

Algorithms are meaning-less. They operate syntactically and phonetically, not sematically. Yuval Noah Harari (2018) goes so far as to insist they have no consciousness. This reduction of algo-worlds – and by extension the ordering of all worlds that they touch, including ours – to meaninglessness is surface-reinforcing, depth-denying. Dread accordingly is a register of the affective remainder to psychic life in the face or wake of algorithmically structured sociality.

Joi Ito (2019) insists on calling the algorithmic "extended intelligence," an enabling supplement to human thinking and production. He exhorts us, then, to "forget artificial intelligence." This, of course, takes for granted the centering of the human in all articulations. The implication of my argument, *au contraire*, is that it

DTG's relatively nuanced view

would be analytically more accurate neither to privilege the singularity of human intelligence nor to reduce the possibility of multiple, interacting intelligences simply to supplements or extensions of the human.

Techno structuring

Algorithmic culture structures environments, with behavioral effect. Brett Frischmann (2019) has argued that this is no different than large-scale technological developments more generally. Big technology alters social environments and reorders or regulates experience of space, in turn having a broader impact on individual and collective behavior and culture. The steam engine and railways had profound transformative impacts on industry and travel, not to mention their deleterious long-term environmental impacts. They dramatically shifted conceptions of spacetime. Television likewise altered life. The sitting room became central not just to home life but also to life more broadly, recreationally, politically, economically, and culturally. House design and furnishings became factored in part around the television room, also imitating the images television programming and advertising projected. Bars, restaurants, shops, waiting rooms, and so on, have images and sounds popping incessantly at people bound to their spaces. The window on the world became another sort of enclosure act. Digital technology is having that impact today.

Sensors and digital tools measuring fitness, heart rate, number of steps taken in a day, and so on, are ubiquitous, and increasingly bio-intrusive. Frischmann and Selinger (2018) argue that they ready the population for even more intrusive scrutiny. We are being made increasingly ripe for, by becoming increasingly used to, unimpeded surveillance, from the outside in. Along related lines, the widespread reliance on GPS is not only making people over-dependent on the technology for directions. We are also losing the capacity, as a consequence, to navigate without it. So much so that GPS is less and less working for us than we for it. We are given detour directions by the technology not to save us time or provide the most direct route but because the device is programmed to get us to collect traffic-flow data on its behalf. Crowd-sourced traffic data translate into invisible techno-directedness to service corporate interests.

*

The virtues of online and mobile technologies are considerable. They provide instantaneous access to vast databases embedding an incomparable range of knowledge, functionality, and possibility. Much of our banking and business, learning and laboring, recreation, communication, even personal interaction is conducted online. The more so in pandemic times. These virtues nevertheless are always shadowed by a less appealing, more disturbing set of prospects, as my Tsinghua colleague at the outset of this chapter discovered. The mobile technologies we carry with us, on our persons and in our automobiles, track our every move, pinpointing in real time our very location. Our credit card purchases indicate not only our patterns of consumption, but also our movements through the day, even our objects of desire. Technologies embedded in our bodies monitor our consumption patterns and habits, reporting to medical teams our due diligence or lack of it on the health of our lifestyles, with impacts on our insurance rates, mortgages, and automobile purchase prices. In reporting also to those in or on whose bodies they lie, they shape our behavior, ordering our lives. The contours between privacy and publicness, command and self-determination have significantly blurred.

Dread follows from the ensuing indetermination. It is fueled not simply by the sensed loss of control. It balloons as a consequence of losing where my sense of self begins and ends, where and how I am able to decide for myself and what is the force of a nebulous, largely invisible, algorithmic determination. With a commanding ruler, we at least know whom to blame, resist, fight back against. Algo-determination is more like the odorless foul air. One doesn't know if or when or how one is being poisoned or infected until the nefarious effects are felt invariably much later and so seemingly unconnected to the actual source. The poisonous pollution is both literal in its individual impacts and metaphorical in the marks it leaves on the body politic more generally.

The suggestion of pollution as analog raises more literally the environmental impacts of digital technology. The technology has enabled the collection of the crucial data over time, tracking and modeling large-scale environmental trends. Global warming and climate change as a consequence have centered on our collective radar, bringing home to us importantly the challenges we collectively face. But the technology has also added to our environmental and production woes. Booking flights online became so much easier, mostly cutting out the need for a travel agent. This helped to heighten demand for air travel, contributing considerably to carbon emissions, ozone depletion, global warming, and the threat to our planetary futures. COVID-19 at least momentarily turned all this upside down, as I will argue in Chapter 5. But the pandemic has also brought home how misleading messages – for example regarding the refusal to wear a mask or physically distance – are made technologically to go viral, with potentially widespread deadly consequences. Technological virality serves as fuel for pandemic virality too. Similarly, the materials necessary to manufacture the hardware enabling the technological applications have proved enormously challenging to dispose of, and deeply humanly and environmentally costly to produce, most notably to some of the world's most vulnerable populations.

The reliance of most work environments on digital technology may have increased work productivity. But it has come at costs of physical challenges (e.g. carpal tunnel syndrome), frustration at the rapidity of software renewal and replacement, hacked data, reduced facetime with all of its social virtues, and time lost on updates, upgrades, and installing new apps. The technological economy, for all its affordances, has us teetering incessantly on the brink of dread. We live with the gnawing anxiety we will fail to live up to the technology where the technology has not already failed us. We constantly worry about identity theft, phishing scams, abuse of our data, incessant surveillance, and that our search history and online expression may come back to haunt us. Dread is the abiding sense, as a result, that we are edging to the cliff of disaster, of irrecuperable loss, even extinction, at least of life as we know it.

*

I turn now to focus on the political economy inscribed in the digital turn. This includes the accompanying shifts in cultures of life, nature of work, and the politics of control in this rapidly transforming landscape. Beads of dread condense on the skin of the social as a consequence.

4

Tracking-Capitalism

The Political Economy of Dread

---

1) Automation & robotification

In January 2014, rapper Jay-Z played a gig in Toronto. By geo-tracking their smart phones a marketing and analytics company was able to determine that roughly 13,000 fans attended the show at the Air Canada Arena, how long they spent there, and most notably where they had been both before and after (Ligaya 2014). Across the 2010s, a significant shift was taking hold of social life.

Digital technology, as I have demonstrated in the preceding chapter, has dramatically transformed our worlds. Work, play, learning and education, politics, and recreation are all conducted differently in the wake of its development and almost universal adoption. We communicate, interact, consume, exercise, mind our health, bank, invest, and travel not just with greater speed but in significantly contrasting ways to the past. Even writing, reading, and cultural production more generally have altered as a consequence. Personal computing and mobile devices are within arms' reach through waking and sleeping hours. Life no longer turns off.

As the Jay-Z event signaled, all this was upending social, economic, political, and cultural life in completely unanticipated ways. The large-scale changes of this past decade have had less visible but equally telling implications for work profiles and positions, for who gets hired and for what functionality, as well as in assessing job performance. The digital has taken its disruptability as a definitive operating condition of its widespread application. It disrupts longstanding and taken-for-granted modes of production, work structures, and practices. Social relations and cultural expressions too. Conceptions like "the born digital" and "digital native" reveal a contrasting time and culture before and after.

A major factor spurring contemporary dread, especially in industrialized states, is intensifying concern over techno-replacement and irrelevance. Significant job loss in the foreseeable future has become a driving anxiety as robotification ramps up. This has certainly helped to generate sometimes seismic political shifts and outbursts in countries like Britain, the United States, and France. Political forces have emerged here and elsewhere in part promising to reinvent or return to a nationalist political status quo ante. The "return" is often to an imagined state of privileging "purity," the reinvention a tacit acknowledgment of the fabricated social tissue underpinning the projection. Foundational to this political promise has been a commitment to ensure that jobs remain in the seemingly abandoned workplaces while sustaining the welfare structure that together anchored especially white working- and middle-class life prospects and lifestyles for much of the last century.

The fog of unease descending recently, manifesting in dread as it spreads across life, is knotted with the creeping sense that this bubble of work and lifeline has burst. The rapid development of AI and machine learning that drives expanding robotification is projected to result in massive job disappearance over the next twenty-five years. The shop floor increasingly has become an awesome exhibit of computerized robots and machines. Predictions range anywhere from 30 to 60 percent job loss generally, most notably in manufacturing and repetitive rote work. Carl Frey and Michael Osborne (2013) estimate that approaching half of American jobs "are at risk," a McKinsey Report that as many as a third will be lost (McKinsey Global Institute 2017). We are already witnessing massive technicization in automobile, aircraft, computer, and other high-tech manufacturing and assembly. Given the increasingly integrated nature of the global economy and its supply, distribution, and consumption chains, robotification in one national site will impact work availability elsewhere, often in unpredictable ways. The disruptions caused by COVID-19 have accelerated these dynamics in real time.

One more sober analysis (Lardieri 2019; Oxford Economics 2019) projects that in the next decade a little less than 10 percent of manufacturing jobs – 20 million worldwide – will be automated. Nearly three-quarters will be in China, rapidly leading the world in replacing manufacturing workers with robots. One in three of the world's robots are being introduced into Chinese factories. In the past fifteen years, every robot introduced has displaced more than a worker and a half, a process fast accelerating. The Oxford Economics study predicts that throughout the 2020s, China will lose more than 12 million jobs to automation, the United States 1.5 million, the European Union 2 million, and South Korea 800,000 (for a more skeptical analysis, see Benanav 2020). Cities with more diversified economies will tend to be less impacted. In Britain, for example, manufacturing is located overwhelmingly in smaller cities, towns, and rural areas while London offers a more varied range of work. Disruption will dramatically affect those areas less well prepared for the transition. The political shift is well under way, with some impacted working-class groups gravitating to more conservative – and, by implication, more conventionally conserving – political commitments.

In the past five years, robots have become less expensive, now undercutting the manufacturing costs of human labor. Microchips process more powerfully, batteries have longer life spans, and networked operating systems have become significantly "smarter." Production line breakdowns are easier to track and fix, output has become faster, costs have reduced. These trends are translating into automation developments beyond manufacturing, from warehouse distribution to service and some office tasks. The rate and range of job losses are bound to increase too. Amazon's warehouses deploy small robots to pack its goods for shipping. These robots take a quarter or less of the time human packers require.

Robots have been designed to do the heavy lifting and repetitive functions in manufacturing and commerce more generally. They function faster and operate without incurring injuries. When they break down, they can be replaced by the next in line without worker compensation costs. As robots grow smarter, they will be able to take on more and more rote functions in offices too, such as filing, perhaps basic bookkeeping, composition, completing standardized regulatory forms, sending and tracking form correspondence, and the like.

In manufacturing, those most likely to be impacted by job loss, at least for the foreseeable future, are less well-off. Blacks pretty much everywhere and Latinos in the United States are significantly more likely than whites and Asians to occupy those positions affected by robotification (Daniels 2018). There is a long history of identifying technological innovation and development with whites, as well as their benefits. Digital technology is little different, especially if you include those historically designated "honorary whites" or "model minorities" (most notably Asians). The top lines of work to be impacted by automation include manufacturing production, office and administrative support, farming, fishing and forestry, transportation and moving. Those least likely range over domains requiring more agile reasoning and nuanced, intricate judgment, including business and financial operations, education and training (the likes of Udacity, Coursera, and Khan Academy notwithstanding), as well as architecture and engineering. Workers with lower levels of education will be far more readily impacted than those with graduate education. Automation clearly will exacerbate rather than narrow existing economic and, by extension, political and social inequalities (Molla 2019).

It turns out that robotification is having unexpected impacts on how work is done too. Robots operate so much faster on work activities involving rote manual but also increasingly cognitive functionality (Harari 2018). This is being used to pressure humans in the chain of production and delivery. Workers are being driven to speed up in order to enable the machines to fulfil their quota. Studies of turnaround and delivery commitments at Amazon warehouses reveal that company management requires much quickened work rates for human workers in the production chain so that the robots are able to function efficiently. Robotic time is prompting management to drive the human work pace. Amazon is tracking warehouse workers on their capacity to meet impossibly quickened turnaround times, as a consequence causing much faster human breakdown due to fatigue and injury. Failure even marginally to meet quotas is a cause for firing and replacing workers. Work under these conditions is less a site of self-providing dignity than the fuel for days of dread.

Similarly, employers are using an app on wearables like Fitbit and Apple Watch to track employee performance. The app monitors non-work-related time away from an employee's desk or office, time on the phone, quality of sleep at night, and so on, all of which demonstrably impact quality of work. The app's developers, researchers at Dartmouth College, claim 80 percent accuracy – which is to say, of the tracked relationality between more standardly assessed performance and the app's assessment (Holley 2019). Automation, both cases are suggesting, is reinforcing the inclination among corporate leaders, pressured by shareholders and venture funders, to robotify human functionality.

The steady decline of manufacturing positions in industrialized economies as the global economy has become deeply integrated and workplaces increasingly automated has resulted in concerns about social disruption more broadly. Where once reliable work could be counted on for career-long employment, especially by the white male working class, employment opportunities today might just evaporate tomorrow. In the United States, it is estimated that a person changes jobs every four years on average, most notably in the earlier part of adult work life. They shift professions approximately every decade. This perhaps signals less that work is disappearing than that it is changing in nature. Service work is increasingly replacing manufacturing work. The shift away from mall shopping to online consumption means that entry-level positions in retail stores are giving way to warehouse packing and distribution work. Robotification requires not only design and manufacture but also ongoing systems service and operations management. Someone has to make sure the machines run well, to service or replace them, to match their capabilities to the job required. The gig or "on demand" economy is offering a wide range of work, more flexible if less secure in terms of benefits and health care provision. The ground is rumbling beneath our feet.

Digitalization as constraint, data harvesting

The digital revolution, of course, has produced a good deal that is productive and beneficial. But digital technology has also made personal and private lives more available to observation and intrusion by those to whom we otherwise bear no relation. The hardware of all contemporary smart phones and mobile devices enables active monitoring of data generated from their use and location, Google's Android considerably more readily than Apple's iPhone (Aiello 2018; McNamee 2019). Android phones integrate the uploaded data they generate in an archive with the user's Gmail, Google search activity, and Google Docs. Google Assist enables recordings of conversations occurring within earshot of its microphone, adding these to the database too. This stream of data, in turn, more often than not is made available for purchase by third parties. Everyone is much more an open book than they may be comfortable with, were they aware of the full extent to which these technologies reveal their lives.

Speaking of books and other creative products, Digital Rights Management (DRM) is the legal regime promoted by large technology corporations such as Microsoft. DRM enables corporations to self-define and declare what of their product is copyright protected. This includes digital code and anything that code produces or circulation of which it enables, from text and music to still and moving images. DRM thus cedes to corporations determination over the individual or collective right to restrict access and sharing, even though permitted by law, and the right to delete code or applications from one's personal computer operating system (Doctorow 2014). It thus is profoundly anti-open sourcing, requiring ownership abrogation of digitally acquired product like Kindle or Amazon books by consumers who have purchased them. The digital book copy, for example, might be erased from one's device after a defined period. DRM likewise removes from the user control over operating mechanisms of one's own technological devices and their contents. When I purchase a hard copy of a book, it becomes my property. I have the right to share it with whom I please, to scribble in it, to destroy it even, preferably to donate it to a worthy recipient. Not so with DRM-driven digital product. It is less about managing than surreptitiously disowning one's rights over digital material.

Algorithms provide the operating logic for the software running digital devices. They feed the collected use data into machine learning tools capable of tracking our online habits. From the information users seek, their interpersonal interactions, interests, consumption patterns, likes and aversions, a personal profile is established for each individual. In turn, they are presented with options and targeted advertisements, on the basis of the data gathered from their online search and activity histories, projected to be of interest to them. This serves to streamline and amplify their consumptive patterns (Evans 2019) while reinforcing social, cultural, and political presumptions. The process makes actual – Shoshana Zuboff (2019) calls this "actuating" – the "personality" each is projected to embody, at least digitally, by encouraging if not expecting them to reproduce the preference schemes it presents to them. In turn, this reinforces the digital personality profile, invariably ethnoracially and gender coded, more or less naturalizing it as the subject's signature character.

Zuboff traces these developments in terms of the history of capitalist forms. Capitalism has scaled from the production line through mass production to sequenced waves of managerialism, service and financial capital. The latest and most dramatically profitable form she identifies is more intrusive by far than any previous mode. Online user data – "data surplus" – are collected on a massive scale through the ubiquitous embedding of cookies in browsers as well as sensors and monitors in the general landscape. Together they generate personal user and navigated activity profiles on the basis of which subjects will be targeted commercially, economically, politically, even criminologically. No internet user, generally no one connected to or navigating any grid, digital or infrastructural, is immune. Personal user and activity data are declared the private proprietary products of the corporations collecting them. Users cede the data on the basis of "user agreements" largely illegible and incomprehensible to all but the lawyers composing them. Users are merely one click away from "disowning" their user data and "disinheriting" – ceding to some anonymous corporate entity – their user profiles.

Zuboff characterizes this new form of political economy, of which DRM is one building block, as "surveillance capitalism." It is a capitalism that pries into and logs every porous activity of contemporary lives. Data are generated through the web browsers used, through smart phone and tablet usage and location, consumption and navigation, online and off. Surveillance is meant to capture the technological intrusiveness where nothing is off limits to data harvesting. Zuboff concludes that "autonomy," "free will," and "privacy" – those Enlightenment-produced values subsequently universalized and dehistoricized – are under unprecedented attack as a consequence.

Nevertheless, contemporary capitalism and the profiles it creates are more concerned with patterns of navigation than the content of consumption. This is not to say that surveillance and content concern are irrelevant. Rather, the emphasis has shifted. The title of a book one has called up on Amazon is of more immediate focus, its metadata more readily inscribed, than the contents between the covers. Tagged terms are more directly generative for harvesting than the political or philosophical argument a publication might be making. *The Communist Manifesto* is equal to *The Wealth of Nations*, on this account, in so far as the former sells as many copies as the latter, or leads to as many sales of related titles, or embeds a security threat. So, it may be

more accurate to name contemporary political economy
tracking-capitalism.

*

 Surveillance is the generic term for attending closely
to persons, monitoring their moves and thoughts.
Technologically enhanced surveillance is about a century old. Wire-tapping, for instance, took hold in the
1930s, targeting suspected criminals as well as labor
and political activists. Tracking has come more recently
to provide the precise means, the technologies, for this
micro-monitoring. A considerable network of digital
piracy sites and practices has emerged, devoted in the
name of a global commons to making freely available pretty much any publication or media product,
copyright be damned. Corporations holding ownership
rights seem less concerned about protecting the contents
of the products than, perhaps relatedly, about tracking
and restricting access to sustain demand and therefore
profitability. Those tracking the Jay-Z concertgoers
were less concerned with what they were thinking than
with what they were consuming. Similarly, the account
of the Tsinghua University police with which I opened
Chapter 3 suggests less concern about the single speeding violation than about a potential pattern of code
violations police tracing uncovers over time and the
subject profile it accordingly generates concerning anti-
social behavior.

The dread-inducing implications run far wider than
attending to anti-social speeding. Across many African
countries, South Africa most notably, individuated biometric profiles have been developed for many residents,
linking fingerprints to work, banking, loans, patterned
consumption, and other sources of personal data. The
data are accessible for any governing or commercial purpose by and shared between government, banks, loan,
mortgage, and other consumer corporations. India like-

wise has developed a form of what Keith Breckenridge (2016) has called "biometric capitalism."

More intrusively, some Chinese factories are embedding technology in their production-line workers, measuring their brain-wave activity to determine fluctuations in emotions, fatigue, and so productivity over the work day. Nothing seems off limits, the intrusive coursing through every fiber of being. A school in the Chinese city of Hangzhou recently installed classroom cameras recording images of student facial expressions every thirty seconds. The images are sorted according to expression type: neutral, angry, upset, happy, sad, surprised. The assessment serves not just to enable the teacher's in-time adjustment to maximize teaching success. It is simultaneously a form of minute-by-minute teacher assessment, associating student emotional responses to teacher effectiveness, student attentiveness, and potential success. A dread-prompting future of learning.

The entanglement of data information, managed if not manipulated consumption, embroidered if not crafted political commitments and choices sews together immense economic and political power. The rapid advancement of AI and machine learning technologies has centered tracking technologies in contemporary political economy. Biometrics is a growing but not singular form of this tracking and its capitalization. Google increased its already significant profitability from 2001 to 2004, the birth period of tracking-capitalism following the dot.com bust, by a touch shy of 4,000 percent. This staggering increase followed Google's conversion from search engine to advertising platform, from user data as exhaust fumes to the fuel of capitalism's new turbo-charged engine. At the outset, users searched with Google, engaging it as a platform for discovery. With the quickening transition to the pervasiveness of tracking-capitalism, Google and other search engines increasingly became the tracker, users the tracked. Search results became their means. The resultant profiles have advanced the profitability of individual consumptive practices and the accompanying technologies of social control. Creeping dread became the prevalent affective state, veiled behind the immediate convenience.

The techno-neutrality of the digital likewise offers the means to advance political interests and applications across all stripes. The populist democratizing possibilities of digital culture – in information, cultural production, and sharing, in learning, journalism, and politics – gave rise to an exuberant tone among its proponents in the first decade of this century (Benkler 2002; Jenkins 2006). This has since given way to a more troubled sense of the impacts and implications as the dominant means of production and application have become more closely and narrowly held (Kreiss et al. 2011).

Early digital tools were promoted in the interests of reinforcing their democratic impact. Social-media-enabled crowd-sourcing, flash-mobbing, and sophisticated encryption technologies like blockchain have served populist democratic initiatives, sometimes with enormous impact. Yet it has turned out to be no glitch in the system that authoritarianism is back in vogue with a vengeance (cf. Schradie 2019). It is being embedded by those with overriding means and inclination as a feature of the operating system, if masquerading as openness and transparency, not a bug; a viral condition, not an anomaly. Huawei has ratcheted up tracking's operating system, driven by the direction of China's state authoritarianism and drawing on the resources of state capitalism. Data are the new raw materials (Naughton 2019), data harvesting the tool set. What Yuval Noah Harari (2018) designates "digital dictatorship" – the capacity of the digital to dictate what to do in matters of life and death – is supplemented by data sovereignty.

Tracking-capitalism mobilizes and applies algorithmically driven technology to track the movements, virtual and physical, of almost everyone and everything, nearly everywhere. Real-time data are incessantly updated and related to the vast existing database to project movements, acts, desires, interests, commitments, possible acts, and their probability. The pressure to track has been dramatically heightened by the COVID-19 pandemic. It should come as no surprise that the large tech companies – those exactly that have been instrumental in institutionalizing the sociality of tracking – have also been so pandemically profitable.

Over thirty countries have introduced smart phone tracking, many without knowledge of their users, to follow the health, movements, infectability, and interactivity of populations. South Korea has introduced tracking perhaps most successfully. Most of its population agreed to use the national tracking system. In early May 2020, an infected man visited three nightclubs one Saturday evening in Seoul. Within a day, authorities had identified more than 100 infected people and warned over 1,500 club visitors that evening, requiring quarantine. In Australia, more than 2 million downloaded the virus tracking app within a day of its introduction. In the United States, by contrast, 60 percent of those surveyed would refuse to download such an app, though I suspect the number would more or less halve with appropriate restrictions and a public health campaign. There is reason to worry. An Israeli company renowned for surveillance tools deployed by authoritarian regimes to follow political critics and journalists is developing software to track people infected with coronavirus. It is in discussion with more than two dozen governments to adopt the software (Fahim et al. 2020), one viral takeover promoted to battle another.

What those driving the technological undertaking are slower if not loath to acknowledge are the presumptions, ideational slants, and stereotypes implicitly built into the technological apparatus. The result is that significant, often group-defined, populations are caught up in the web of political implication and application, often with deleterious impact. Tracking-capitalism accordingly liberates its enormous economic power, prowess, and profitability through incessantly tracked and followed life. The data sovereignty it licenses dictates what its socially profiled subjects can do, and what can be done to them in the name of sovereignty.

Surveillance proceeds by monitoring the content people are communicating. Tracking, by extension, plots movements and networks. Surveillance reads off threat, danger, and performance from the content of communication and interaction. Tracking reads off from people's activity, from their "metadata," likely future behavior – via prediction algorithms – from relational data about movement, networks, lines rather than content of communication. The data supposedly "dictate." Dread's intensification signals anticipation of the deepening erosion of self-direction.

Surveillance thus requires tracking; tracking presupposedly does not necessitate surveillance. Tracking seeks to evade the charge of privacy violations that surveillance perennially suffers by insisting it is content neutral. Tracking updates surveillance. The virtuality renders tracking's technology less visible, more anonymous, perversely less deeply intrusive while more pervasive and stealthy than surveillance. Tracking generalizes drone logic. It is the eye in our everyday technologies seeing everything, faint enough to overlook while perpetually in play. Posing as your friendly enabler to advance your interests – "accepting our cookies makes us work better for you" – tracking in fact is a declaration of war on all.

The Trump regime used an algorithm to track countries a traveler had visited, notably Iraq, Iran, Syria, Yemen, and Somalia, whom they were communicating with, speaking to, what hotels they were staying at. People and their family members thus algorithmically identified were tagged, and as a result their visas or visa applications to visit the United States were canceled or denied. Together with his family, Eyal Weizman, the notable British designer of "forensic architecture," was subjected to this political economy of algo-identification (Shaw 2020). In order to acquire reinstatement, he would have had to "name names." He rightly refused. Dread is the lingering aftertaste, the trepidation at future travel troubles as a result.

What this points to and reinforces is the fact that throughout its history of economic domination, capitalism in its various forms has relied closely on military research and development for its technological advances. Military discoveries and developments have often benefited social life more generally. The history of computerization is an obvious if far from isolated example. The dramatic progress of modern surfboard manufacture would not have been possible but for the development of materials for military application in the 1940s. The great Californian board innovator Bob Simmons adapted these materials to surfboard innovation, revolutionizing the fledgling industry. Underpinning the general social readiness to accept often nefarious applications of military innovations is the extraordinary impact they have on everyday life, from outsourced and auxiliary jobs to the pleasures of recreational culture.

Tracking technologies are the latest iteration of this logic. Every object, movement, relation, act, practice, and structure is a data source. Tracking-capitalism has defined the logic marrying an intensified political economy of control with round-the-clock global capital formation and enhancement. While expanding a capacity for state control, it has simultaneously produced the technological means for its evasion, from which it also profits politically and economically.

Webcams built into or attached to user devices are capable of watching and recording what their users do, even unbeknownst to them. Hackers delve into individuals' and institutional machines to glean valuable navigational data and access codes. Often this arrives in one's email inbox or social platform messenger as an innocuous-seeming spam suggesting one download an attachment. Hackers are also able quite easily to hijack the device webcam. The target, soon to be exposed, could be a perfect stranger, political or business competitor, a former lover or acquaintance, classmate or co-worker. Your personal web blackmailer or sextortionist is watching or feigning to watch "you" through your online connectivity and activity. Almost every profitable digital affordance comes with the threat of its widespread abuse.

Where technology once largely served human determination and decision-making, now human judgment is increasingly ceding to the projected "wisdom" of techno-determination. Advanced algorithms offer processing beyond human capabilities of almost inconceivably large quantities of data across nearly limitless quantifiable factors. As a result, techno-generated predictions are being fashioned about future events, such as market behavior, fraud, accidents, political preferences and voting, amidst an increasingly wide variety of human actions. These profiles and predictions, in turn, strongly encourage, and sometimes activate, practices with the view to benefiting from their projected outcomes. That there is always the possibility of turning away from – or turning off – one's devices, hacking them, or using them for progressive ends undercuts the too-easy accusation of technological determinism. The digital turn may bend strongly in that direction. Nevertheless, it far from completely eclipses the wide array of ways human agency is capable of responding, nor the responsibility regarding how the technology is taken up, individually and socially.

*

In their seminal work, economists Thomas Piketty and Emmanuel Saez (2003) demonstrated that inequalities in both wealth and income decreased between roughly the 1920s and the 1970s as a result of increasingly progressive taxes. Home ownership, and by extension equity and wealth, multiplied as a consequence. A broadened proportion of populations especially across the globally more prosperous north were drawn into the racial horizon of benefit. In the past thirty years, by contrast, as successful campaigns were launched to slash taxes, and waves of austerity have been required by the International Monetary Fund to secure state loans, inequalities have ballooned again (Cassidy 2014; Piketty 2014; Piketty et al. 2019). In France and Brazil, 10 percent of the population today own more than 50 percent of the wealth. (Part I of the *World Inequality Report 2018* [World Inequality Lab 2018] demonstrates compellingly how the proportion of US wealth held by the lower 90 percent of the population dropped from 33 to 23 percent.) Much of this rapidly expanding inequality is a function of the fact that the top 1 percent increased its share of wealth from 30 to 40 percent, a trend repeatable across a wide swath of societies. Even in China, as of 2015, 14 percent of annual income went to the top 1 percent. In Britain, 10 percent of the population today owns 44 percent of the wealth, five times more than the bottom half.

Over the past thirty years too, across finance capital economies, inflation-adjusted wages have been static. In the United States, the annual median income of the bottom *44 percent* of the workforce is $18,000 (Ross and Bateman 2019). The jobs held by these workers almost never include benefits such as social security, employer-provided health care, or retirement contributions. Nor do they likely include paid vacation or sick leave. At the same time, investment profit and capital income have soared. Conservative provincial governments throughout Canada have been dramatically cutting support for citizens with disabilities while slashing corporate taxes. Across large cosmopolitan cities worldwide, new home ownership has spun out of reach of all but the top income quartile. While conditions differ across societies, fewer can afford to own homes, especially in those urban centers and regions globally that have become major technology hubs and financial centers.

Income inequality as a result further magnifies into expanded wealth inequity, more often than not ethnoracially indexed. Aggregate wealth, after all untaxed, is rising annually at a far faster rate now than income. Approximately 75 percent of the world's forty wealthiest billionaires are white men along with a couple of women (whites constitute approximately 11.5 percent of the global population, white men half of that). The remainder are all East and South Asian men. In 2019, the five hundred wealthiest people in the world increased their net worth by $1.2 trillion, adding 25 percent to their collective wealth (Fernandez 2019). This more generally global pattern of spiraling inequality encapsulates in a nutshell the long historical underpinnings of ethnoracial and gendered wealth formation. It is not coincidental that South Africa and Namibia today remain the most unequal countries in the world by almost all relevant measures, from the Gini coefficient or tax data to consumption and lifestyle indices.

Conservative commentators have pushed back against progressive analysts like Piketty, arguing that overall conditions have improved globally for poorer populations, that the wealthy create extraordinary numbers of jobs for those without, and that state curtailment of wealth creation delimits freedom and economic growth (cf. Delsol et al. 2017). Conservatives often point to successful global poverty reduction as an argument against targeting national inequalities. Poverty, nevertheless, can decrease while inequalities soar when the growth in wealth of the wealthiest outstrips the reduction in poverty, as witnessed above. Two telling counterfactuals bear this out. First, much of global poverty reduction has taken place in Asia, notably for the world's most populous nations of China and India. This has meant that average global poverty has declined while most countries have seen internal increases. And second, since 1980, global income growth of the top 0.1 percent has been equal to that of the bottom 50 percent. As of 2019, India, despite its extraordinary economic development, remained mired at 102nd place (out of 117 countries listed) on the Global Poverty Index, below the significantly less economically advanced Nepal, Bangladesh, and Pakistan. Social programs to address distressed groups or to benefit all members work best when the commitment of society at large, increasingly globally, is not contingent upon the good will of this or that mega-rich person or well-meaning foundation.

Investment income is driving a considerable proportion of wealth generation today. The claim of trickle-down job creation, while a standard political talking point since the 1980s for tax reduction for the wealthy, largely lacks supporting evidence. And if one is to include in income government support for the poor, state privileges for the wealthy must be counted too. Tax policy, for example, tends overwhelmingly to favor the rich. Reports have Amazon paying no US federal taxes in 2018 on $11 billion-plus of profit, while receiving a tax rebate of $128 million. Donald Trump famously has paid no personal income taxes for almost all of the past twenty-plus years, and next to nothing when he has. By the same token, workers receiving government benefits are subsidizing their employers who fail to pay them a living wage. (In 2017, nearly a third of Amazon employees needed federal food assistance simply to survive on their Amazon wages.) The deepening inequality also fails to register the resulting cross-generational impacts on differential education opportunities and nutrition with long-term impacts on income, wealth, health, and enduring quality of life.

These summary patterns have now been extended and exacerbated by technological developments and cemented by growing global authoritarianisms. Rapid info-technological developments have enabled massively increased wealth while making it possible to narrow its control to fewer people. The technological capacity to track and profile almost everyone likewise concentrates political power much more narrowly. Population-wide biometrics introduced in countries such as India and South Africa in the name of centralizing state functionality render more efficient the social welfare or caretaking functions of the state like health care or pension support. And yet these technologies power governmental capacity to track almost every social member, from birth to burial. The technology extends centralized state power in an increasingly controlling and authoritarian direction. It "future-proofs" the tightening circle of the wealthy and powerful to the detriment of everyone else.

*

Algorithms and machine learning tools have placed the drive to predict on steroids: more data crunching, more patterns, more statistical application, more assurances not of some outcome per se but of the heightened probability of its likelihood. The dominance of algorithms in such predictive analytics creates a world of empirical measurement, tabulation, instrumentation and instrumentalization, statistical modeling, and utilitarian calculation. In short, it offers a contouring of the social that delimits the thinkable as much as it opens up to productive possibility. Subjects are increasingly rendered by the political economy of tracking-capitalism as nothing more than cogs in machine-driven circulation.

Zuboff names the general sociality produced by these mechanisms "instrumentarianism." She defines this as "the instrumentation and instrumentalization of behavior for the purposes of modification, prediction, monetization and control" (Zuboff 2019: 352). Focused more on the form of capitalism that information technologies have unleashed, Zuboff fails to devote much if any attention to the appeal digital instrumentalizing affords through the collective and shared activities it enables. It is both enormously useful and extraordinarily seductive. The technology has given rise to new practices of collective engagement, and novel communal formations. In her abidingly negative critique, Zuboff offers no reflection on the transformative forms of communal sociality-at-a-distance enabled by digital media and the shared information they make possible. One might dub these affordances "infomunitarianism," playing on the relation between information and communitarianism.

The digital, then, has provided a complex mix of productive and controlling possibilities. This mix, and the tensions entailed, is evidenced in the popular take-up of the term "hive." In contemporary technological contexts, its self-characterization has been meant to convey a worker-bee culture, the inordinately productive capacity from an interactive, shared, and distributed workload. The appeal to the "hive mind" – the greatest output of which perhaps is exemplified by Wikipedia's extraordinary reach – draws on the collective wisdom spread widely across networks to address local lack of knowledge or to solve otherwise intractable challenges. Yet embedded less visibly in the notion of the "hive" is also the presumption of a structured, quite hierarchical, and ordered environment in which power reigns. Violating a structured role in the hive comes with considerable peril, most extremely

excommunication, even (social) death. The technological hive is not so different.

Some, it follows at least implicitly, have dubbed the
mix afforded by digital technology as "info-power."
This conception is considered to supplement if not
replace biopower as the dominant articulation of our
time. Biopower, in the Foucauldian sense, seeks to
articulate the dynamic complex of enabling and commanding power, of discipline and regulation, conceived
and manifested around and through transforming bodily
conceptions, formations, and control. For Foucault, biopower is elaborated and institutionally applied from the
eighteenth through the twentieth centuries, assuming
ultimately power's dominant form. Info-power, for its
proponents, takes over as the driving mode of power's
definition and application, as productive and controlling force, with the dominance of the digital.

Info-power represents social relation constituted
by information profiling. It has increasingly outpaced
biopower, or at least combined with it, in a heightened form of regulative and disciplinary social order.
Where biopower tends to drive collective conception,
info-power operates through micro-individuations
that nevertheless often presuppose and by extension
reproduce collective attributions such as race and
gender. Countries increasingly are profiling visitors
at the point of entry in terms of an expanding biometric informational database of passport information,
fingerprints, photographs, and eye scans. It may not be
long before more countries also fully link one's social
security, employment, tax returns, and medical data.
Airlines have started the process of facial recognition
boarding, matching one's facial image or eye scan to
a background data profile as the latest iteration in
the security regimes of air travel and human flows.
Mid-pandemic, it is likely that temperature, medical
history, and ultimately vaccination data will be added

as well. Much of the world has made such info-power the driving logic of economic and social interaction and relation.

China has led the way in constituting its heightened, intensified, distributed mode of social regulation as a novel governmentality through the application of social and corporate metrics and credits. Every commercial transaction and most social interaction is conducted through citizens' smart phones, the data instantaneously available to and stored by the state. These activities, as well as ordinary daily activities like jaywalking, donating blood, interacting well or poorly with neighbors, are factored into one's algorithmically calculated social credit register. Citizens are effectively reduced to their credit score, their reputational capital, on this social metric. This determines whether they have access to better or worse health care, or travel opportunities, and whether their children attend better or worse schools.

China, however, is far from alone. Some insurance companies in the United States have taken to requiring as a condition of a homeowner insurance policy that sensors are placed in clients' homes. Homeowners accordingly are tracked for smoking or other hazardous household conditions or habits, the heightened risk resulting in increased insurance rates or policy cancelation if the actuarial risk is considered algorithmically to overstep a threshold. The social credit system is translated into market-impacting credit or reputational scores in tracking-capitalism.

Even more intrusively, parolees in the United States are being outfitted with GPS monitoring devices to track their location and movements, and by extension their interactions and networks, around the clock. Incarceration is being extended into what Michelle Alexander has called "e-carceration" (Alexander 2018; see also Arnett 2019), prisons into what other carceral critics have named "digital prisons." What this suggests is that as concerns are being raised about the runaway "prison industrial complex," tracking and its logics of info-power are enabling a less visible, more extensive and insidious mode of cyber-correction, digital regulation, and e-discipline. Black and brown people will once again bear the brunt of these now digitalizing infrastructures of racism.

The logic has been at work more broadly still. Pre-pandemically, an increasing range of universities across the United States introduced a "monitoring" system for their campuses. The app tracked classroom attendance or late arrivals via geo-location software linking to students' smart phones, often affecting their final course grade. It also recorded whether students were showing up to the library, whether they were eating regular meals, and the like. Colleges rationalized this data collection as a way to monitor student progress. The aim, not uncaringly, was to reduce drop-out rates, and ensure student health and safety. The app's developers sought explicitly "to change student behavior," presumably for some unstated betterment, registered once again in terms of a "social credit" accounting (Harwell 2019b).

However, college administrators do not consider the intrusion into private lives that their intervention represents. And they overlook the lasting impact on diminished student capacity to make wise decisions for themselves and society. Wise decision-making is often more likely to be driven by scorching hands than never being subjected to failure. Moreover, the data may be coded in racial or gendered terms, reproducing while reinforcing longstanding stereotypes (Benjamin 2019).

As online schooling and college courses have pandemically taken hold, it would be no surprise to find attention-tracking sensors embedded in courseware, as has eye-tracking exam surveillance. The techno-fix is often a troubling extension of the social conditions fueling the perceived need for the fix in the first place. After pandemic lockdown lifts, one can also envisage the technology being used for other extended monitoring purposes. Similarly, with the dramatic expansion of home-working in the wake of the COVID-19 outbreak, a new app, aptly named "Sneek," has been deployed by employers. It photographs workers at their home desks every five minutes, ensuring that their productivity is not lagging (Holmes 2020).

It is not just information driving this revolution in power's definition. More broadly, it is the technological machine's massively expanding capacity to collect, store in a memory bank, and be driven by this massive informational reach. Defining information surrounds and is taken up by us. We import it into our bodies through the techno-replacement of inserted devices that in turn dispose us towards certain sorts of behavior, while feeding instruments with behaviorally defining information. As the college tracking app explicitly admits, techno-power has updated the driving commitment to the social instrumentalization of behaviorism and behavioral modification. The undertaking of what I have characterized as info-power is to shift the dynamic from what Zuboff (2019: 8) characterizes as automating information *about* us to automating *us*. The *technopticon* primes dread's self-habituating operating system.

Capitalist modernity produced profit-making in large part through labor exploitation. Tracking-capitalism extends the profit-engendering exploitability from labor and finance capital to techno-generated information. This produces incessant revenue streams by circulating and repurposing user data for multiple consumptive purposes, mostly in ways invisible to the subjects from whom the information is being generated. It is not that labor exploitability has been cast aside. Tracking-capitalism makes for round-the-global-clock profit generation. This includes, though is far from limited to, the tracking of exploitable labor both as a means of squeezing more out of their workday and from their consumptive habits. Tracking-capitalism and the techno-power undergirding and reinforced by it thus contour the existing flows of capital, goods, and people. The ends are dramatically expanding profitability and inequality alongside intensified, technologically enabled if more or less masked, mediated, and distributed authoritarian control.

These factors in political economy prompt the spiral in contemporary anxiety, heightening a pervasive sense of uncertainty. Life-sustaining resources seem not to be readily available or to quickly evaporate. Unanticipated disasters, whether environmental or political, appear more dramatic and potentially deadly. One cannot know when next one might participate in taken-for-granted practices, from social gatherings to travel and attending crowded events. Invisibly tracked interactions by government, corporations, or hackers materialize almost daily. And private personal information threatens to crystallize when least expected. Dread is that seeping anxious sense of being in the grip of controlling social forces that just won't let up.

*

Promoters of digital technology and the systems of social interaction to which it has given rise claim that they render social life more efficient. They have enabled massive data collection that can be used to address social challenges and produce solutions. Implicit in their claims to provide innovative solutions, however, is the admission that digital technology has come laden with implicitly prescriptive social designs. Tracking-capitalism is profiteering from harnessing the attention of almost everyone (cf. Gilroy 2020). Alongside the endless warrant for collecting user profile and preference data is the massively escalating bureaucratization of everyday and especially work life. Almost every waking hour is incomplete without being urged to fill out some online form. To use a system or app. To make a purchase or enact a service. To fulfill a user agreement. To provide employee data, medical permission and insurance coverage, systems access at work, financial reports, copyright agreements, or building access. To complete satisfaction surveys after every purchase or experience. And on and on. One is but a step away from filling out a digital form to go to sleep. Or to wake up.

It is not that one cannot ignore many though far from all of these requests and demands. But the pressure is relentless, the culture of encouragement and seduction if not command ubiquitous. There is after all a benefit even to those ignoring the surveys. One can get quick reviews of restaurants, movies, or service providers, though the reliability and manipulability of crowd-sourced responses is always in question. To avail oneself of the benefits without contributing is to position oneself as a free rider. The reach of digital capacity and the affordances it offers run far wider, however.

Digitally monitoring the steps one takes in a day, one's heart rhythms, or breathing patterns during sleep is tantamount to clockworking one's life functions. Digitalization, not to put too fine a point on this, far from freeing us up, has turned out to be in danger of becoming a totalizing technological control machine, even if no single authority is the driving commander at the wheel. One's complete life-cycle, from genetic inheritance through daily functionality and consumption to life trajectories and transformations, is in the process of being tracked. The tracked subject, at the very best, is but half in control of what data about oneself gets to be collected, less so how, and almost not at all of the uses to which the data ultimately get put. If we are, or have become, nothing but the sum of our data, self-determination (such as it was) has slipped more and more out of control. Info-subjectivity dissolves the self into digital bits and pieces.

Techno-power underpins an extensive political regime of totalizing tracking. It makes it at least technically possible to keep track of virtually everyone round the clock. Subjects can be traced in their browsing habits, their movements, physical and virtual, in their consumption patterns, interactions and networks, in their sleeping culture and waking habits. Technoptical power, in short, enables "digital dictatorship," concentrating power in a narrow and increasingly powerful elite (cf. Klein 2020a). Digital dictatorship today can assume the older, more recognized, form, where a single political authority, an individual or collective ruling sovereign, overridingly determines the nature of possibility in society. But it can also, and today more likely does, assume newer modes. A globally dominant digital corporation – a Google or Facebook, Tencent or Huawei – may dominate economic, cultural, and political possibility for individuals and governments both within a society and across many. And it does so more seamlessly, less visibly to those going about their daily affairs.

The challenges far exceed individuation, as institutions have jumped on the bandwagon. Universities have doubled administrative and service positions in the last twenty-five years. Overhead costs and costs per student thus far exceed the rate of student growth. At the same time, full-time teaching faculty positions have increasingly been replaced with adjunctification. The growth in administrative positions no doubt has been fueled by the need to attend to the massive explosion in regulative regimes and student demands (New England Center for Investigative Reporting 2014). Arguably, both the surge in administration and the growth in student demands have a significant technological component, as the location tracking of students on campus attests.

Governments or institutions will regulate because they can. They are regulatory bodies, after all. And they now have the technological means and "space" – in short, the power, in all its expressions – to collect, store, analyze, and call up the data at will. Student demands, individually and family driven, by the same token, are fueled by the readily available online institutional comparison points no doubt shared on social media. In a telling turn of university self-defining phrase, students have become less learners of the considerable knowledge that faculty have to impart than consumers of university services.

Academic administrological multiplication of form filling, whether for everyday functionality, teaching, or research, exists to create and expand a record as a mode of control. It enacts a partially invisible hyper-governmentality, a digitally virtual, data-fueled pan-legibility. The exercise of power here is simultaneously at a distance and yet capable of immediately reminding the subject of a proliferated, internalized presence of technological insight and oversight.

In mass societies, as Max Weber (1921/2015) pointed out, bureaucracies help to apply resources equally across large population bodies, maximizing organizational and economic efficiency (see also Kreiss et al. 2011). Bureaucratic application tends to treat unequals equally, leaning in the name of fairness to extend the inequalities now considered justifiable. Yet it can discourage participation also. This, in turn, deprives decision-makers of access to the full range of research data.

David Graeber (2015) remarks in his book on runaway bureaucratization that any official undertaking to reduce red tape and unleash market forces, as the prevailing social rationalization goes, inevitably increases regulations. The self-fueling administrative mandate licenses platoons of bureaucrats to apply and enforce the regulatory explosion. And the administrative bloat, in turn, multiplies the total volume of form creation and filling to which we are subjected minute

by minute. In automating surveys, form-filling requirements, mandated employee training regarding issues
like cyber-security, sexual harassment, and implicit
bias, techno-bureaucratization has automated the uni-
versalizing of audit culture. Social subjects have become
so acculturated that they happily assess the restaurant
meal, the cab ride with Uber and Lyft, the consumer
experience, the movie, and so on, just completed.
Technoptical power has quietly folded audit power into
its operative application and appification.

Graeber puts these developments down to the massive growth of the imperial state. The rise of (wannabe)
authoritarian political figures globally is not unrelated.
Authoritarians today increasingly seek to rule through
ubiquitous info-control. Rampant bureaucratization is
also a mode of diversified social control. Nevertheless,
while the state has obviously played a key role, the
broadened reach and seeming independence of this
contemporary technicizing logic suggests that the political economy of tracking is socially ubiquitous. It spills
out far beyond formal state power and economic proficiency into all corners of the social.

*

In his *Lectures on Abnormality*, Foucault points to the
"Ubu-esque" character assumed by key forms of state
power and their exercise. Ubu-power is "grotesque."
The power is vulgar in its anonymous, affectless expression. It is exercised in the shadow of – perversely
through – being discredited as "odious" or "ridiculous"
(Foucault 1974–5/2003a: 12–13). Its expression of
power is absurd. The contradiction between its claims
and applications, the finery of its self-representation and
its self-projection as serving "the people," cover over
the grubbiness of its application. The qualities of the
person, bureaucracy, or technology enacting the power
accordingly disqualify them by the very nature of these

qualities from expressing such power. The wisdom of leadership, the abstract equality of bureaucratic application, the neutrality of technological application should "know" or be designed to preclude the inequitable exercise of this self-serving power.

With the digital, the ridicule falls on deaf ears. In being taken up by the powerful and the bureaucratic, the technology largely shields them from the derision. Technologically, the criticism is just an additional metadata point in the generation of another round of private preference schemes. Ridicule might likely result in a recommendation to one's inbox that one would "like" Trevor Noah on Comedy Central.

The prolific popularity of stand-up comedy in the era of digital culture perhaps exemplifies the salvific need to laugh in the face of the sensed absurdity of powerlessness. The system grinds on regardless. Emojis substitute for actual emotion. Info-subjects, on the other hand, complete the forms while deriding them, berate their demands but rue their lack of instantaneous availability. We rate the ride while watching the recommended joke show, readily fill out the surveys while making them the butt of online jokes. There is a populist appeal to its vulgarity, the creeping recognition that if everywhere is, bureaucratically, a "shithole place," one can dismiss all others oblivious to the charge that one's "own" is one too. The form of power at play is nothing less, but equally no more, than the "assholery" (James 2012) of contemporary social life. Like "bullshit," this, too, is now a term of critical thought. And yet in this expanding everyday intolerability, we put up with – we tolerate – the insufferable.

Until, perhaps, a growing number of us don't.

Dread, in this scheme of things, is the dawning recognition, one still inchoate, that my techno-replaced life is some public or private entity's form-filled data power. My life fuels the machine's force field utterly beyond my control. Hence the rage against the machine, even while deploying it. Techno-dread manifests not as some Luddite reaction but rather as the fog-filled (in)comprehension, apprehensively anticipated, of the reduction to being utterly socially and survival-dependent on it. The Toronto Jay-Z concert also hinted at the planetary techno-anxiety that would ratchet up in the wake of the info-power soon to envelop us all. We are, as the saying has it, "phenomenologically flipped off."

Some might suggest that if tracking-capitalism becomes ubiquitous, then the need for a regulative administrative state is obsolete. This, too, was claimed about expansive neoliberalism in the 1990s. Neoliberalization reshaped the state in its own image, to its own purposes. It downsized caretaking state functionality while dramatically upsizing commitments to state securitization. Regulations did not disappear, they got restructured, and intensified.

Just as neoliberalization did not forgo the need for the state, neither does tracking-capitalism. Here, the state leans towards authoritarian bureaucratization. The state is turned to by those corporate entities driving the economic agenda. State institutions seek to guarantee and protect the social infrastructure necessary to conduct and shield their activities from those human and ecological forces challenging or threatening their power to sustain, expand, and control the social life of their reproducibility and extensibility. Over the past century, state capitalism has shifted in form and practice from welfarism to neoliberalism (Goldberg 2009), and now to tracking-capitalism. Tracking-capitalism is driven by technoptical power. States are in the process of shaping the operative conditions, contouring reach, possibility, and socially ascribed limits of information-accumulating trackability and traceability. As with earlier state forms, the state of tracking-capitalism is punctured by internal tensions resulting from its contradictions of production, and from jockeying by factions and constituencies for state influence and impact.

In its first decades, cyberspace was deemed the new frontier of a radically unleashed freedom. State and corporate power, however, saw it, first, as a challenge to their respective domains, but then also as a power to be harnessed to their respective ends. Tracking-capitalism has emerged to reintegrate state and corporate power by quietly circumscribing collective freedom. Tracking as mode of social relation and control has become increasingly pervasive as the fragility of infrastructures supporting collective life (Bhan et al. 2020) has been rendered undeniable by the interactive challenges we face together today. The intensification of collective dread as a consequence serves as a gauge of both the perils we face and the resourcefulness of the responses.

Irritation erupts into social resistance, though never unidirectionally. Resistance may be fueled by and assume a variety of expressions across the global landscape. Even conventional political forces have started to push back. As 2020 rung in, California required all corporations to make available to their consumers details of their data being collected at the point of purchase, and the choice to opt out of the company's program to sell subjects' consumer data to third parties. In this, California is adopting European legislation but moving more quickly to implement it. Yet across a wide range of societies globally, youth today are coming to a digitally enabled and mediated understanding that the world they are inheriting is stacked against their widespread well-being, if not their extended survivability. Social dread today can be read as the register that the prevailing political economy is outputting nothing but futureless futures. The massive intensification of inequalities and their material conditions of substantiation, economically and socially licensed by tracking-capitalism, are prompting a politics of refusal (Honig 2021; Kafka

1920). It is a politics far more radically at odds with, even as it draws on, the technological means of the digital revolution.

*

Two inescapable and interactive social challenges currently threaten planetary life: the pandemic and climate change. Each factors significantly in tracking and resisting global economic, ecological, demographic, and migratory movements. These dread-driving concerns are the respective foci of the following two chapters.

5

Viral Dread

As COVID-19 began surging globally in February 2020, the pandemic produced state responses – and often non-responses – as terrifying as the worst effects of the condition. In April, Northern India's Uttar Pradesh turned hoses of chemical disinfectant intended for dousing buses onto migrant groups clamoring to leave the city for their countryside villages. With work fast disappearing, 100 million migrant workers and their families sought to avoid the pressed urban confines conducive to spreading the coronavirus. The dousing was reminiscent of the way Germans treated East European Jews fleeing pogroms in the 1890s. Trainloads of Jewish fugitives bound for Hamburg to board Baltic ships for new lives in Britain and beyond were side-railed outside Berlin. Passengers were disinfected and quarantined aboard the trains for two weeks. India, approaching 1.5 billion people, had registered 1,000 COVID-19 infections at the time of the migrant hosing. The Virus was a convenient vehicle to extend the exiling of Muslims, de-urbanize unemployed migrant village workers, and expel unwelcome foreigners. COVID-19 effectively updated social untouchability.

In late March 2020, the Florida Governor introduced a two-week quarantine for any traveler entering from states currently exhibiting high rates of coronavirus infection. This principally included those traveling from New York, New Jersey, Connecticut, and Louisiana. Florida state troopers were ordered to check incoming passengers and vehicles at borders, ports of entry, and on interstate highways in an effort to stop the viral spread. Those arriving from out of state who failed to self-quarantine would receive a sixty-day prison sentence. The focus solely on outsiders seemed misdirected. Floridians had spent warm days at packed beaches alongside partying spring-breakers. Like climatic conditions, the Virus knows no borders. At the time of instituting the restriction, nearly 4,000 infections and 54 deaths had already been recorded within Florida. In a state with a large retirement population, less than two weeks later infections had surged fourfold, deaths sixfold.

Uttar Pradesh's "disinfecting" and Florida's failing responses to the fearful seepage of coronavirus infection highlight numerous threads in contemporary social life. COVID-19 has brought into sharp relief the counter-pulls in decision-making between health provision (in short, matters of life and death), economic capacity and unbounded "liberty." The Virus spotlighted the tensions between globalization and nationalism, movements and borders, migration and walls. And it revealed abiding social stresses between competition and cooperation, viral infection and memic (mis)informational spread, privatization and the commons, lockdowns and lockups, freedom and safety or securitization.

*

SARS-CoV-2 is a virus of our time, one we all are involved in circulating if not feeding. It courses across and through populations, worldwide. Like popular music, it waxes and – eventually – wanes with global force and local accent. It is parasitic, exploitative, sucking life more readily from the vulnerable, the aged, the racial poor. It is a mirror reflecting what we have made of ourselves, our world, our ecoformation. The picture is far from pretty. Individual care, extraordinary in courage and contribution, has had to fill in, at considerable personal risk, for broad and deep politically shaped failings.

This is a migratory virus. SARS-CoV-2 seeks a host in order to survive and to pass along COVID-19, the disease it produces, replicating and mutating as it takes up compoundly in one host's cells after another. With no mitigation measures such as masking and physical distancing, each infected person initiates a spiral that will contaminate a lengthening string of people as it transmits from host to host: "the shadow of death" (Seghers 1944/2013: 4) wafting across worlds, elastically thickening and thinning as bodies press together or pull apart.

It has been a stunning turn. A world spun at the interface of the microbiome and the social so quickly driving itself to lockdown, supplemented to degrees by older governing technologies of locking out and locking up. Lockdowns have something of a history too. As Foucault (1974–5/2003a: 43–4) reminds us, lepers were expelled, exiled to external colonies, effectively locked out. Those suffering plagues, by contrast, were quarantined, containably locked into their homes to die or recover in silence, almost invisibly. Prisons in most countries today are overcrowded, unhygienic environments, people packed into infrastructures of infection. In the pandemic, dread plays out for the locked-down many differently than for the locked-up less fortunate and more vulnerable.

We have not come that far from earlier pandemic conditions, at least not in physical distancing and isolation. COVID-19ers are isolated, or expected to isolate themselves, making themselves at once prisoners and prison guards. Temporarily new untouchables, visibly invisible. Social distancing has become a more or less global self-sequestration. The panopticon has given way to a supplemental form, an introverting self-confinement. Evidence is exhibited to one's networks at a distance through social communications platforms and social media, instituted in waves across regions.

The deepening interruption of face-to-face social life, the ransoming of life predicated on mobility, incessant acceleration, immediacy, and instantaneity (Mbembe 2019), conjure the dread that sociality could end. Slamming on the social brakes, slumping with little warning into a counter-state of pervasive deceleration, has seemed to some tantamount to semi-social death: the demise of supply chains, shortages of everything, the drying up of markets, the shrinking horizon of demand. More deeply, the virtualizing of social intercourse has threatened to shred the relationality upon which social life is founded, suffering mostly in isolation, even as newfound intimacies are ignited.

Dread intensifies in the invisibility of transmission, the absolute anonymity of contraction, misinformational circulation as much as asymptomatic spread, and the anxious alienation of utter aloneness at the end of life. It expands and pervades in not knowing how one's constitution will respond in the face of infection, if not also social isolation. COVID-19 is dread's test-tube, its crucial experiment. It invades us, eats at the body from inside, initiates a struggle that can kill. Boundless unpredictability and unforeseeability signal loss of control. Infection is like racism, the scorpion sting of the new pariah, social paralysis in the seepage. Dread is fueled interactively as much by the imaginings about contagion as by both the drama and the mundanity of the experience.

As authorities have reacted, dispositions of enmity and rhetorics of warfare have taken hold. They are familiar, easy to mobilize. It's broadly comforting to know there is a playbook at hand, a tried-and-tested game plan on which to draw, a rhetoric to fall back on. "A few of us had resolved to clear out before the Last Judgment," Anna Seghers continues in her striking novel *Transit*. "But the commandant had set up machine guns in front of the camp gate" (Seghers 1944/2013: 5). War on the Virus soon slips into war on those made ill by it, those bearing it, even if asymptomatically and metaphorically its cause and carriers.

In the first weeks of the Virus reaching South African shores, the police presence in informal settlements dramatically increased to enforce mandated "stay-at-home" and distancing directives. Brazil's favelas fared similarly. Informal settlements are sprawling, compacted spaces of social life self-styled from found materials. More residents initially were killed by the enforcing police than by the Virus. COVID-19 has also assumed the memic mantle of "China virus" or "kung-fu virus" in the febrile minds of the conniving and confusing, of those invested in stoking the "(coming) China wars" (Navarro 2006). War talk fuels viral dread in the name of mobilization against it. This is a projected war that cannot be "won" because declaring a war against a virus is a category mistake.

The threat of war is the logic so often taken up in surges of human migration, a battle hymn of belligerence. It offers the comfort of self-assertion, the "do something, do anything" chorus in the face of otherwise pervasive shortcoming. Little matter that declaring war on a nebulous "enemy" – it is everywhere and nowhere at once – flails and fails every time. Aggression drowns out reports of the shortcomings, dread filling the seeping sense of nothingness in the wake. We have comforted ourselves that we have done all we can as the inevitable failings settle in. "Their" treatment is costing us "our" comfort, our discomfort is worthier than their lives, than the dignity of life as such. Power, as Foucault puts it, no longer "recognizes" but "ignores" death (Foucault 1974–5/2003a: 243). It is the mark of sovereignty, individual or collective, that it can do so. "Our" people are rendered strangers, beings made disposable objects. Dread is no longer of power itself, but of one's own diminishment in the face of others' death. To riff on Pastor Niemöller, when it comes for you, there will be no one left to care . . .

*

COVID-19 is the siren song of *neoliberal* capitalism. The Virus has called into question the contemporary state's cracked foundation on *economic* freedom, the deep paring back of the caretaking state. This includes undercutting viable access to necessary health care, the incessant attacks on "the deep state." The contours of those fracturing fissures have become undeniable. FDR's famous "four freedoms" – of speech and worship, from want and fear – have always been but *partially* exercised. Their securing and guaranteeing have not just been ignored but actively undercut – "drowned in a bathtub" – by neoliberal capitalism when convenient (Foucault 1978–9/2008: 102; Norquist 2001). Neoliberalism has privileged economic freedom, using it to trump or advance other liberties as economic interests and utility calculi dictate. Neoliberal capital has pushed freedom of movement, while calibrating it differently for financial capital, goods, and services than for people. COVID-19 has not so much undone capitalism, as some have bemoaned, others celebrated. Rather, it has dramatically mobilized paving the path from neoliberal capitalism to an intensification of another kind. I have called this new form tracking-capitalism.

For conventional *commodity capitalism*, value is principally extracted and profit produced at the point of consumption, the moment at which goods and services are purchased. Value changes hands, materially or increasingly virtually, with payment. As service capitalism expands into *experiential capitalism*, the production of value is radically extended into and throughout the experience. Witness cruise ships, fun parks, gaming, sports spectatorship, concerts, festivals, fairs, spectacles in the everyday, including mega-church services, fancy restaurants and expensive wines, and so on. The experience itself is stretched out to maximize profit-making via endless sharing in and after the moment. This includes experience-related merchandise, photos, recordings, reviews and newsletters, consulting, advice, gig offerings, even nostalgia-inducing social media anniversary reminders.

The experiential became capitalism's extended logic. Commodities themselves were advertised and sold through the experiential qualities they were made to represent and promise, including "value-added" servicing agreements and warranties. It is neither happenstance nor inconsequential that the experiential and its make-believe culture assumed the public face of neoliberal capitalism. This was coterminous with the exorbitant but far less evident, even grey rise of speculative finance, privatizing individualism, more or less anonymous virtuality, and boring back-end digitalization. The experiential is the loudspeaker of otherwise far less visible and celebrated success.

COVID-19 not so much momentarily ended as upended the conditions of possibility for experiential capitalism. It did so both by exhibiting their deadly impacts and by curtailing the broad range of experiential possibility. In the former case, cruises and large church services became ground zero for viral spread. In the latter, the lockdown requirements delimited the conditions of possibility for robust consumptive experiences. Already in the making, as I have argued, tracking-capitalism began to suffuse in the take-over.

The experiential both reveals and conceals. Value

reveals itself in the experience. Focus on the experiential conceals the circuits of capital, production, and delivery of the means to enable that experience. To take one example, consider the route "exotic" food takes on its way to the restaurant plate. And how the drug necessary to treat the pathogenic illnesses those exotic foods may unleash finds its way from a Chinese lab and factory, where it is likely produced, into my possession. What get tracked in tracking-capitalism are largely the experienced endpoints. Covered over are the circuits of capital and work leading both to the possibility of the experience and to the offshore capital movements extending the economy of experience and capital generation in its wake.

In March 2019, Italy was the first EU country to sign on to China's New Silk Road project, much to the chagrin of other driving member states. Chinese entrepreneurs quickly invested in Northern Italy's fashion industry. They brought with their capital a high number of Chinese migrant workers. Prato, a manufacturing center outside Florence, housed 60,000. Their comings and goings, alongside the fashion and cultural tourism both Italy and China promoted to the newly monied, experientially hungry Chinese middle classes, created the circuits for the ease with which the Virus circulated between Lombardy and Wuhan. By late February 2020, the first registered Italian cases began to flare, three months after China's. Pandemics globalize infection, diffusing them across space and time. But they concentrate their effects, intensifying their impacts from one place to another.

Experiential capitalism requires and promotes movement: travel to places far and wide for business and recreation; cruises and vacations to distant locations; explorations and expeditions testing limits of endurance and determination, not to mention local ecologies and older habitats. Pathogens once localized and so limited to usually remote rural biosystems find new life as they are carried by trade and travel to densely populated urban environments. There they swirl energetically through newfound peoples and places lacking any built-up immunity. Just as European diseases once decimated colonized populations, today something of the reverse is in process. The expansion of industrial food production, with closely quartered animal stocks and fast throughput, likewise extends the zoonotic life and circulation of viral pathogens (Wallace et al. 2020). Tracking-capitalism will eventually build up, if never quite catch up, to trace these cross-over circulations too. Dread leaks from the realization that the Virus is unleashing wide-reaching, aspirationally universal if never exhaustively accurate tracking with its associated economic and political capital.

Some tracking is visible, some more discreet, some again too late to be productively impactful, only to be added to a dormant database for future mobilization. Yuval Noah Harari (2018) concedes that a regime able to mandate, store, and analyze the genetic data of all its citizens will be better placed to address efficiently the medical challenges of diseases – or, for that matter, the health impacts of global warming. In 2017, a new medication came to market that included a "digital ingestion tracking system" enabling medical practitioners to determine if and when a patient properly imbibed their medicine (Goold 2019). In a free-market health system, the latter information no doubt will impact on insurability. As Harari quickly recognizes, these sorts of developments will likewise position the current medical regime to dominate in an increasingly unchallengeable way. The state will be able more readily to mandate who under its jurisdiction flourishes and languishes, cementing its unbridled power over life and death. We have already witnessed a calculation of coronavirus survivability, and by extension livability, from Italy to Britain, Texas to California.

The digital can wax dictatorial in two related ways. Digital profiling could soon inform dictation of life-forming decisions: not just what to study and which profession to pursue, or whom to marry, but who gets to live in a pandemic and who quickly to die. It can also provide the awesome technological apparatuses for rulers to tighten totalizingly authoritarian domination and control. Democracy is not so much abandoned in name as emptied of any recognizable processes and substantive commitments. These formations of "digital dictatorship" are already in process, from India to Hungary and Russia. Donald Trump, too, in claiming absolute presidential authority at every whimsical turn, danced with this devil.

Tracking-capitalism thus enables tracing global movements and networks of human capital, interests and consumptive demand, just-in-time delivery of labor and product, threats and disruptions. Tracking drives micro-targeting: of genes and proteins having a causative role in the disease; of people with the disease and those with whom they interact; of a health condition and when, if at all, to intervene with treatment. Tracking-capitalism, soft-pedaled as "tracing," fine-tunes when to keep those belonging locked down, while determining whom from places with high rates of incidence and undesirability to keep locked out. It is fine-tuning in real time the governing logics of securitization as the emerging technologies of domination programming our times.

*

The Virus has revealed in stark outlines the brittle social tissue holding together life today. For one, it has challenged uniquely and ubiquitously the unbridled emphasis over the past half-century on individualizing enterprise and disruptive innovation. The Trump administration used COVID-19 to intensify the logic. States were required to compete with each other for purchasing necessary health professional equipment to treat the disease, from masks and gloves to ventilators, just as individual consumers were fighting over the last remaining toilet paper roll in supermarkets. In refusing to coordinate national testing, Trump undercut the cohering power of the centralized state while asserting unbridled sovereign power. African countries like Tanzania depend on State Department funding to cover much of their health care costs. As the pandemic took hold there, they were warned not to use these funds for purchasing protective medical equipment to avoid competing on world markets for such materials with the United States.

Dread oozes from the realization that asserting sovereign authority undercuts the necessity of a sociality predicated on sustained cooperation, on a vibrant commons. It takes hold in sensing that the constitutive social threads necessary for sustained social cooperation are in tatters, if not completely shredded. By early July, the United States had double the number of coronavirus cases in the European Union. At the height of infection in New York City, in early April 2020, the city had more than any other *country* worldwide. Fever-ravaged people in their mid-seventies sat alone in emergency rooms for upwards of twenty-four hours awaiting an available bed. Dread proliferates and intensifies in having to compete, individually and socially, for necessary medical tests and treatment to address infection and the spread of life-threatening conditions. But it also clouds the collective capacity to test and count systematically, to reach consensus on comparable infections and mortality rates. The pandemic not only reduced us to what Lorraine Datson (2020) insightfully calls "ground-zero empiricism." It also infected us with the politics of knowledge and instrumentalized ignorance.

Neoliberalization has spectacularly failed the acid test of our time. Even the regimes most forcefully institutionalizing its mandates have fallen back, belatedly, on the fabric of the social it has insisted on denying to save them from complete implosion in the face of the viral deluge. The cost of the initial refusal and delay can be measured in the unnecessary extent of the suffering and lives lost as a consequence. Dread is the anxiety of dying completely in isolation, one's body merely a corpse disposed of anonymously. It is, relatedly, witness to the fact that there are people in charge who have thought 100,000 people dying in one country is "winning" the viral "war." Dread is the dawning realization that a past denied to the point of invisibility has been made the taken-for-granted deathly new normal. And that it is too late to stave off the worst of the effects.

The Virus has revealed, too, the radically uneven and unequal vulnerability to calamitous large-scale challenges, within and across societies. Viruses don't discriminate, as the saying goes, between the hosts in which they find an opening to settle. Once in, they replicate more or less readily according to the local conditions of vulnerability and immunological resistance. These conditions are a function of risk factors exacerbated by socio-economic standing, access to health care and education, nutrition and dignified livable conditions. People who have to work in public places, whose work is deemed "essential," who out of necessity have to share living quarters with larger numbers of age-distributed people, whether family or not, are the more vulnerable. They are multiplied by those not in a position to afford sufficient nutrition or sustaining rest, medicine, or health-enabling supplements.

Race, class, and their interface accordingly are indicators, among other variables, of health and vulnerability. US cities such as Milwaukee and New Orleans experienced a significantly larger proportion of coronaviral deaths among African-Americans than their proportion of the local population and than those not black

(Johnson and Buford 2020). In states with significant black populations, between 20 and 30 percent of infections and of COVID-19 deaths have been of black people, though making up just over 13 percent of the population. In Chicago, by May 2020, nearly 70 percent of US COVID-19 infections and deaths were among blacks, double the proportion of the city's population, and five times the mortality rate of whites. Of the initial 480 people infected in St. Louis, 12 died, all black people.

Native Americans living on rural reservations in crowded housing with lack of running water initially faced quickly rising death rates. Blacks, Native Americans, and Latinos have higher rates of high blood pressure and hypertension, diabetes, asthma, and cardiovascular disease, as well as significantly lower rates of health insurance than whites. Quick tribal government intervention to limit non-reservation interactions effectively leveled off Native American infection and death rates. The banlieues of France's large cities and the favelas of Bahia, Brazil, were not treated so carefully, and rates spiked in both. The latter, with a high black population, were targeted for early experimental vaccine trials, an awkward reminder of the Tuskegee experiments.

In Britain, black men were three times more likely than white men to die of COVID-19, the black death rate double that of the population at large. Roma across Europe and Palestinians in Israel-Palestine experience similarly health-compromising life conditions, with comparable viral vulnerability (Tanous 2020). Those with less ready access to clean running water are significantly more at risk. Those confined to the rightlessness of refugee camps, often invisible at the margins of contested jurisdiction, are the most vulnerable. Living in dense environments where physical distancing is impossible, they mostly lack adequate health care and are already undernourished and overstressed. In both these challenged conditions and many high-income countries, a growing ratio of frontline health workers are migrants, mostly people of color (Dempster and Smith 2020). Here death by COVID-19 is having a disproportionate racial impact on those most committed to stemming its tide for others.

At the same time, across sub-Saharan Africa, infection rates have mostly remained relatively low, despite initial predictions to the contrary by health modelers in the global north. Most African countries acted early to shut down before the spread could take hold, have existing networks of community health centers, and have populations that are relatively young. Senegal, for instance, ranks close to the top among countries that best managed the Virus, drawing on its experience with Ebola. That such African countries have fared significantly well in containing infection strongly suggests high black infection rates in numerous overdeveloped countries are a complex product of their deep racial histories and systemic racism.

Dread registers as the irrepressible reminder that much of the world was at least formally on lockdown for a few months except for those caring for those who were. In more overdeveloped economies, caretakers are disproportionately black and brown people. Viruses, in short, don't discriminate. We do. Sometimes a cough is just a cough. Societies discriminate in the everyday, but also in ways that become embedded and reproduced more or less silently through social structure, with fatal implication. The rate of premature death is an index of structural racisms, and of their deadly effects (Williams et al. 2019). No one is pandemically immune until all are.

The overdeveloped world has long tracked those whose lineage is taken not to be from, not to belong to, to be indecipherable to that world. Those deemed monstrous.

Techno-tracking today will only more deeply inscribe by making less readily visible the racial predispositions of tracking. As the operating logic of techno-tracking, the algorithmic is a hyper-discriminating machine. It is discriminating in both of its two driving senses. First, algorithms differentiate between relevant and irrelevant data, between what's of interest and what's not, based on past patterns that then don't just inform but drive relevance. It follows, second, that algorithms trade on and intensify discriminating trends, deepening the disadvantage of the already disadvantaged. They do so by making invisible – almost constituting as irrelevant because virtually untraceable – the grounds of the discrimination. The perverse logic at work is that one is rendered a social subject by being tracked, denied such subjectivity by not being. The course of technological developments will dramatically, and often imperceptibly, exacerbate these trends.

COVID-19 has faced medical decision-makers with determinations over life and death. In the face of medical resource availability short of widespread need, protocols were developed to guide decision-makers about who might more readily have access to life-saving technologies. Other considerations being equal, the presence of co-morbidities in one patient rather than another becomes a key factor in limiting access. A considerably higher rate of co-morbidities faces Black, Latino, and Native American than white patients. An otherwise neutral-seeming set of considerations with life-determining outcomes – like "saving the maximum amount of lives" – accordingly tends to get built into the algorithms on which medical decision-makers rely to guide them in determining the probable outcomes of pursuing one course over another (McLane 2020). Probabilities thus silently reinforce not just preexisting conditions but also preexisting racially indexed structural inequities and systematic prejudices.

The discriminatory inequalities extend into other areas of social life. The loan funds to support small businesses provided by the first US stimulus package in response to the economic disruptions of the Virus were cycled administratively through banks on the assumption that they already had existing relations with their small company clients. In the first round of loans, existing bank custom identified through their databases overwhelmingly favored white-owned businesses. As a consequence, 90 percent or more of Black, Latino, and Native American owners, and 75 percent of Asians, were precluded from the loans. Eighty percent of new US businesses are owned by women from these groups. Structural racisms reproduce existing inequalities.

Algorithms discriminate with utter indifference, without affect. The reproducing discriminations consequently become more or less naturalized, seemingly sewn into the condition of social being (and not just the social condition of being) itself. The algorithmic has no reflexive or reflective memory of the discrimination, only accumulated data bits about employment, residential address, education, or consumption. The algorithmic suffers no guilt or shame, no qualms or self-doubt. It is an entity of a different ontological register, especially conducive to social tracking. Algorithms constitute the perfect post-racial discriminating machine.

*

Self-protection is not just individual, nor narrowly local. One appealing if unexpected turn in the pandemic lockdown was that global air quality quite dramatically improved. It was especially pronounced in and around large cities, where polluting vehicular traffic dwindled considerably. This resulted, too, in far less seismic vibrating in these areas. Increased accuracy in seismic sensor readings of the earth's vibrations and tectonic movements followed from the reduction in seismic noise

(Gibney 2020). There seemed also to be a break, a half-time of sorts, in most wars. The planet, if for a brief interlude, was both a touch healthier and less eruptively violent as a result.

As China lifted lockdowns, it also reduced restrictions on carbon emissions, resulting in even higher pollution than before COVID-19. In ways likely to have much longer lingering impact, countries also used the viral moment to ramp up travel restrictions within but especially between them. Borders closed down, some more generally, others more discriminatingly. Those from foreign places of origin were pointedly kept out, the periods of closure and denial left unrestricted. The open-endedness of the closures suggests more discriminate reopenings once the viral dangers appear to wane. Access for some will be made more readily available than for those deemed perennial undesirables or risks. The list is long, shifting, virtually global (for an in-process time-stamp of April 2020, see Aljazeera 2020). COVID has made borders into metaphorical if not metaphysical walls (cf. Preciado 2020).

A world with less war seemed ill at ease without one. A global war declared against an enemy oblivious to the characterization seems like a losing proposition. Borne on the air breathed and surfaces touched, the Virus is more like an angel of death. Dread wafts off death's wand waving spasmodically through the world, no one sure they won't be touched by it. Like global warming, COVID-19 is a process rather than a person or event, seeping across and into everything. It is to be lived with manageably rather than fought, adapted to, accommodated, and worked around, habits altered to address the relational condition while delimiting the disruption.

Authoritarianisms (re)emerged and solidified through varieties of "coronavirus coups" (Weinstein 2020). New authority came to be licensed, repressive measures introduced or extended that will be likely to last well past the worst of the pandemic. The suspension of elections, and sometimes the insistence on holding them precisely because of the dangers, the capacity to repress and imprison dissidents – all ratcheted up. Not only critics but also scientific knowledge and accurate data were silenced, emergency powers and non-contestable sovereign power all too readily invoked. Application of tracking technologies was ubiquitously expanded, covering not just movement and networking but also social media use and free expression. The reach for dictatorial power has mixed the material with the digital, response to the Virus with the techno-viral.

Hungary's Viktor Orbán perhaps most quickly and baldly took advantage of the infectious upheaval. He grabbed what are likely lifelong powers. Before there was even a single COVID-19 case in Hungary, his regime was blaming migrants for infections. "We have observed a certain link between coronavirus and illegal migrants," Orbán's national security advisor insisted. The right to asylum in Hungary, an EU member, was abolished as a consequence (Monella and Palfi 2020), with barely a croak in outcry from the European Parliament. Just as migrants are made the medium of infection, infection is made to fuel dictatorship. Rodrigo Duterte in the Philippines ordered the shooting without questioning of anyone seen to be disobeying his viral stay-at-home order. India's Narendra Modi issued without notice a complete lockdown of all inhabitants, instantaneously shuttering even grocery stores and necessary medical device developers. Of India's nearly half-billion workers, only 19 percent enjoy social security. In the ensuing aid package, day laborers, street dwellers, and migrant workers were provided no relief. Lacking any perceived utility in the moment, it was as if they did not exist. The state of Kerala was the one notable hospitable contrast. Elsewhere, police especially targeted Muslim citizens for beatings. These developments built on already existing social closures, erosions of democratic freedoms, and targetings. Dictators rule through disease.

*

Over the past decade, starting slowly and gathering pace, biometric technologies have been applied increasingly broadly. These have been most notable at airport and immigration entry points. But they have been applied also to home security, building entry, even student tracking at schools and universities (see Chapter 4). Introduced in 2009, India's Aadhaar biometric system was the most ambitious. It sought to centralize comprehensive records of everyone in India, linking the data – birth certificate, bank accounts, employment, tax returns, health, and prison records – to individuated fingerprint and iris scans. A unique ID card and number provide proof of (social) existence. The numeric card is required for all interaction with the government, and ultimately for acquiring a bank account, loan, even to purchase a cell phone. (In 2018, the Indian Supreme Court ruled card requirement for commercial transactions unconstitutional.) The National Social Registry is supposed to end up tracking every element of citizens' lives deemed socially significant, from religion and caste to property purchases, moving to a new job or city, family, births, deaths, and marriages (Shrivastava 2020). Given the focus on citizenship, it also became the basis for extending discrimination. Discriminated against like the migrants doused with chemicals at the outset of this chapter, migrant children lacking birth certificates, and so biometric identification, have been denied school access. Biometrics instrumentalize the circumscribing of human rights to citizenship belonging.

Many have followed the Indian example, both for state security and for commercial purposes. Trump's

US Department of Homeland Security was planning by 2022 to complete comprehensive data collection on three-quarters of US residents. The data include "historical" and "projected" fingerprints, facial images, and iris scans. They incorporate also networks of relation to signal potential terrorist or criminal behavior (Rorlich 2019). Biometric ubiquity is only likely to be expanded and revised in the wake of the Virus, even as touchpad fingerprint identification is a surefire technology for viral circulation. In Wuhan, an initial outbreak epicenter of COVID-19, tracing contacts of those testing positive, updated temperature levels of all residents, even whether a person had shared a recent airline flight with an infected passenger, are gathered on all through their smart phones. Once a person tests positive, the phone app notifies all those with whom their phone has recently registered physical proximity. After the initial rollout of "TraceTogether" in Singapore, adoption of similar appifications followed in European countries. Bluetooth's digital footprint cuts a deep data scar.

These are, of course, potentially life-saving applications. But it is easy to project how tracking technologies are adaptable to even more controlling political ends (Harari 2020). Some US states deployed technology corporations to determine whether their citizens on aggregate were respecting physical distancing guidelines by smart-phone-tracking the distances each kept from others around them (Fowler 2020). The tracked were unaware of the practice until they received a warning. Google and Apple developed an app for Android and iPhone devices respectively able, ironically, to "handshake" as evidence of co-location. The Italian government adapted this for its tracing app, "Immuni." In Israel, technologies designed for counter-terrorism purposes were adapted to tracing those with whom a COVID-infected person had come in contact (Landau 2020; Tanous 2020). The resulting app, perhaps predictably, is called "The Shield." Security technology firms more generally have pitched their tracking technologies to governments for contact tracing. South Korea, Pakistan, Ecuador, and South Africa have already adopted such technologies. European, Asian, and Latin American countries worked to take them up too (Schechtman et al. 2020).

Technology has enforced the "great apartness." COVID-19 licensed the universal experiment in "social distancing" (which had to be 2020's term of the year). This, in turn, further advanced technological escalation (cf. Mbembe 2020b), and diffused social discomfort in the interests of biopolitical securitization.

E-securitization is fast trumping freedoms. The digital today above all tracks movement: physical and virtual movements, their interactive networking circuits, linking locations, places, spaces, people, things. Across boundaries and borders, past gates, across walls, into and out of buildings, through websites and databases. Where bodies are showing up, leaving traces. Where they are "dis-appearing" – from and to, vacating one site only to show up elsewhere and otherwise (Abbas 1997). Biometric traces are more difficult to leave behind, even when changing what was worn and borne. Their sensed and "sensored" states of being stick to them. The "sensorious" has acquired new functionality, ascribing novel meaning.

This regime of almost ubiquitous tracking reinforces the reach for states of totalizing control. Control exercises itself over what it is able to identify, pin down, at least to shape and contour. It seeks to monitor flows and movements, long conditions more or less evasive of surveillance. States of control reach their limits, become paranoid, with deepening shadow spaces, the unseen, the less trackable. There the bombing takes over. Perhaps the operative logic drives states inevitably to this condition. Hence the still early but gathering

effort to supplement if not shift from sensors monitoring spaces to sensors placed (permanently) on and
ultimately *in* subjects. There is a movement in process
today from all social subjects having displayed logos of
corporate masters to carrying built-in self-tracking technology. Cyborgs may escape easy ascription of identity.
Techno-subjectivity is fast making evasion of technoptical identification more challenging.

*

Borders have become the conventional modern political technology for controlling transnational movement.
They are both inscribed around ethnonationalities and
key in (re)producing the ethnonational identities around
which such boundaries are materialized. Borders are
mobile, always porous. They are technologies of administrative power and ordering control. They can be shifted
in shape and purpose, to exercise control over territory in response to the "conflict shorelines" of arable,
defensible, or settleable drives (Weizman and Sheikh
2015). Colonial, postcolonial, and globalizing political economies, interspersed with local and global wars
and environmental events, increased the movements
of people across borders, alongside financial capital.
Technologies to shape, monitor, and police flows were
developed to supplement physical borders. Labor needs
and politics internal to economically developed states
pulled people in, temporarily or more permanently.
As those economic pulls unsettled taken-for-granted
cultural homogeneity, political power, and familiar
ethnoracial comfort, resistances to the supposedly non-
belonging almost always quickly spiraled. Tracking has
now emerged as a convenient techno-fix for the tension
between economic need and cultural discomfort, historical relation and political refusal.

We find ourselves today – as the very outcome if not
condition of the processes marked as globalization –

historically at a demographic flex point. As with global warming and climate change, we are deeply into the transformations – demographic, cultural, economic, technological – of which these population shifts serve as the more visible edges. The demographic flex point conjuring such deep anxiety is that of proliferation itself, of what it is taken to entail. These are anxieties about mixtures and their manifestations, entanglements and their entailments. In short, about purity and pollution. Their transformative intensifications erupt where borders, boundaries, walls, and divisions harden as impossible resistances to the processes deeper and more profound than they are able to hold off.

As COVID-19 demonstrated, aging populations across the global north see themselves as needing younger people to fill the roles of "essential workers" for pretty much all the registers that this newly valued "pandem(ocrat)ic" concept references. Essential workers are caregivers and providers of the baseline needs to survive. They are far more diverse than the newly vulnerable populations whose lives they visibly enable. Twenty percent of African-American and 17 percent of Latino workers are in jobs that can be done from home (in contrast with 30 percent of whites and 37 percent of Asians). Caregivers have often emerged out of cultures with more diverse, non-nuclear family forms. Here respect and care for elders resonate more deeply than within nuclear and self-interestedly competitive "modernizing" social traditions.

There is a violent irony, consequently, in French commentator Alain de Benoist, an intellectual progenitor of today's white nationalism, denouncing "left-racism" as leading to the "homogenization of the world." De-emphasizing ethnic differences, he charges with no argument or evidence, would lead to "ethnocide," the killing off of "ethnic groups as ethnic groups." His worry, the worry of white nationalists, is the obliteration "of the right to difference." His implication is not to defend all difference. Quite the contrary. It is to ensure the "right to live with one's own ethnic kind." In Benoist's case, this is to consort only with "Europeans" or whites, the rest to be kept beyond borders, or eliminated (Feder and Buet 2017). Difference, in short, is invoked to rationalize homogenization. The paranoia represented by this "ethno-differentialism" develops out of the anxiety of losing the familiar, of what might become of one's life once control is lost, power forgone or foreclosed. The dis-ease about a future "overrun" and "infected" by those taken to be "not-us," those not sharing a way of life, "common" values, "common sense." The ill-at-ease with a world Benoist won't recognize by looking in the mirror.

Underlying this viral irony of nationalizing racism is another. The claim to ancestral birthright belonging pretty much wherever it occurs must be read against the historical record that every nation-state has no ancestral purity. All states are multiplicitously constituted. Old and newer groups move into and out of territory. The artifices of bordering, settlement and abandonment, wars and colonizations, ecological disruptions and disease, economic opportunity and destruction all contribute to these movements. We are all more diversely made up than we tend to recognize. As Bob Dylan recently sang, referencing Walt Whitman, "I contain multitudes."

Just as biodiversity is being threatened, quickening violence is eating away at the soil cultivating heterogenizing cultural life too. Saskia Sassen (2014) has written of land made barren across Africa, Latin America, and parts of Asia. Multinational corporations have bought up vast tracts of territory for cheap biofuel and food production as well as for mining. Sprawling new gated cities and corporate parks have sprung up. "Networks of extractive and predatory" practices

(Mbembe 2019) rapaciously exhaust natural materials as a result of drive-through exploitation of labor and resources. Long-suffering local inhabitants are driven off the land to which they have no formal title with less and less to cultivate and from which to feed themselves. As climate change has made small-scale agriculture more challenging, drug trading and turf wars have made life less livable. Migrants into cities and across borders are made by the very conditions overdeveloped economies produce expropriatively at a distance.

It is the migratory effects, disconnected from their causal conditions, that the beneficiaries of those economies bemoan. "Build the wall," "Send them back," "Britain is fed up and full up," "Lock the gates" echo across the hollow divides, ringing out to farms and mines of the new extractivisms. "Now we are asking you to get yourselves killed," Michel Foucault mimicked, "but we promise you that when you have done this, you will keep your jobs until the end of your lives' (Foucault 1978–9/2008: 216). Ethnic cleansing is enacted explicitly in the likes of Poland and Hungary, ethnic paring and pruning in Turkey and Israel-Palestine, immigrant lockouts in the United States to secure the "naturalization" of ethno-homogeneous states (Gattrell 2019). Their waves ripple, sometimes crash, across borders into neighboring states.

"You" can die to ensure "our" wealth and wellbeing, just don't dare seek to settle in the homeland. Pandem(ocrat)ic prophylaxis just took a deadly viral turn.

*

Dread is not immune to political division. Some are less in fear than in dread of whole populations socially demonized to the point of dehumanized unrecognizability. "The dread of the Negro," as James Baldwin famously wrote in his notes on Medgar, Martin, and

Malcolm, or the dread of Palestinians by Israel and its supporters. Not of any specific person, nor any actual acts of identified people, but abstractly of *the* Black or Palestinian, Arab or Muslim, Chinese or Asian. Here dreading drips from the illegibility prompted in the dehumanization, the consequent incapacity to recognize shared value and virtue. This perhaps is even more dangerous as violence is licensed, encouraged, enacted. Not against any recognizable person but against a faceless phantom. A figure made to carry all the burdens of an imagined suffering scrubbed of any coherent facticity.

COVID-19 has shaped a "structure of reality" (Critchley 2020, channeling Raymond Williams), heightening concern, even paranoia, about porosity. The Virus has intensified worry about the leakages, microbial comings and goings, between human, animal, and genetically modified organisms. Over the past century, more than 80,000 new molecules have been introduced into the biosystem. These anthromes – humanly crafted genetic entities, often for profitable purpose – are altering the biocene in real time (Mendes 2018). This further blurring of the lines between human and natural worlds and their respective conditions of conception and possibility has deepened concerns about the porosity across seemingly cemented but ever-shifting geopolitical borders.

COVID-19 has undercut confidence in the technologies of walling out as the Virus seeps undetected aboard atmospheric droplets through, under, across, and around all fixed structures of securitization (Simone 2020). There is no closing of borders to molecular flotsam. The vacuum cleaner for microbes is called an immunity system. Its fortitude actually requires viral presence in one way or another. Viralities and dis-ease are taken inevitably to accompany the unaccompanied, the unidentified if not unidentifiable, the incomprehension at the incomprehensible language(s). "You speak

[English] with an accent." And you don't? Paranoia about contagion by the "China virus" seems as much anxiety about economic, political, and cultural takeover as about immunological infection. The meme may be as deathly potent as the gene in viral spread.

Now, the collapsing of boundaries between the human and natural, the social and biogenetic further undercuts any naturalization upon which the concept of race has rested. Bodies are today less "finite unities" than "distributed networks." Life is a "non-linear," even "chaotic open system," as Margerida Mendes (2018: 129, 134) puts it. Any differentiations in health, now attendant on traditional racial distinction, accordingly, can be seen more readily as a function of economic, social, and political power and standing than some putatively natural group-inherited condition.

Paranoiac dread has manifested, then, in the perceived or projected loss of racial control, the fantasized theft of social standing. Presumptive power is accusatorially stolen by the invading hordes from under those taking themselves to have (had) racial privilege. The power can't have been too secure if so easily spirited away. The social unsettlements produced by waves of disruptive financialization, globalizing hyper-competition, job-erasing automation, intrusive digitalization, and viral death-threats have been displaced onto the not-from-here, the not-like-us. Any discernible Asian, in the United States and to lesser but recognizable degree in Canada and Europe, has been in danger of being publicly vilified or, worse yet, spat upon and physically attacked because taken to have brought the viral woe upon the unsuspecting host. Public protests across parts of the United States by overwhelmingly white groups, some menacingly armed with automatic weapons, were prompted and funded by wealthy conservative political action committees and presidentially encouraged to break out at the height of more or less enforced social distancing. Protesting signs equated "social distancing" with "communism," imploring "no foreign vaccines." At the time of the protests, three months after the outbreak, the US government was still refusing to coordinate coronavirus tests for more than 1 percent of the population. There is no recognition of an "us" in "them" because there is no collective self-recognition in the cracked mirror.

Heightened concerns over loss – of work, of property and life, of social power, however tenuous – are displaced onto the phantasmatic figure symbolic of that threat of loss. The individuating address of micro-targeting is helping to spur an insistent reinforcement and extension of a destructive, deadly politics of demographic and cultural homogeneity. Homogeneity is almost invariably purchased with the coin of repression. Nearly 50 percent of white Americans polled in 2019 expressed concern that American "customs and values" would be significantly weakened if – not when! – the country became a "majority nonwhite nation" (Miller 2019). "Herd immunity" is the development of anti-viral immunity *through* viral spread of infection widely across the community. Transliterated into immunity *from* the foreign herd, it is taken to need a little political help.

As viral infection and death were hitting their first-wave peaks in the United States, President Trump announced halting almost all immigration. Vernon Reid, the founder of the great mid-1980s metal funk group Living Color, recently observed that blacks have always been identified, in life and culture, as the figure of the Monster. The Monster, Reid suggested, is made up of different parts, and is usually nameless (Smithsonian 2019). Blacks have long been positioned as the dominant cultural object of white American dread. This is a dread expressing itself resentfully, and turned to violent outburst. The pandemic has widened this field of the

Monster, the Moloch, if temporarily as it does from time to time, to that of the racially identified migrant too (cf. Baldwin 2017).

Black, brown, and Asian figures, unknown and fantasized in the real, are transformed into these phantom bearers of threatened disinheritance. Given the ethnoracial impacts the biosocial Virus has extended, white nationalists are lauding the projected eugenicist implications. Some white nationalist groups have advocated for using COVID infection as a bioweapon to naturalize their commitments to "cull" the population. Resentment, the manifestation of unresolved dread turned to vicious deadly anger, grips those who feel the world they owned and entitlements they possessed have been wrongfully wrenched from them by some alien force, experienced as the dreaded.

Another, counter-strain of dread has seeped coterminously across social and political life. Here, the sense of possibility and aspiration to a better world in common is felt to be ebbing away, slipping from grasp. The undermining of widespread collective cooperation in the form of physical distancing alongside the devastating revelation of inequality, unfairness, and injustice across life and in death conjures a forlornness, a helplessness prompted more politically and socially than bio-virally. This dread manifests more readily in despair, loathing, loss of hope in being able to repair the ripped fabric of life. It is more readily an anxiety about the lives of others than one's own. Resentment and forlornness, then, have come to make up the atmospherics of disaster in the viral wake as the expression and experience of the everyday.

*

There are, thus, multiple debilitating costs to tracking. One is technical. If life is an open "exponentially chaotic" network (Mendes 2018: 134), the algorithmic undertaking to reduce it to its inevitably linear calculus (Goldberg 2019) significantly delimits comprehension and possibility. It renders invisible what is not legible to the logic of the calculus. Another debilitation is the devaluation of privacy. Commercial tracking of one's web footprint has already placed privacy under considerable pressure. Data privacy – one's control over the data about oneself – has been further eroded by the significant danger to life the Virus has threatened. Techno-tracking of person-to-person interactions for health purposes encourages concerns about data privacy to be checked almost literally at the door.

The messy merger of biosocial- with techno-capitalism tends to embed the unilinear and homogenizing forces into the economic infrastructure. This in turn reinforces the forms of social ordering legible to it, and the outcomes it is able to produce. The algorithmic is its operating system. Tracking is its techno-social application. Monoculturalism is its technopolitical design, in its biological and social applications and reach.

The attendant worries, if not dreads, have long found cultural expression in monsters, from the creature in Mary Shelley's *Frankenstein* and its renewed spin-offs since to Ian McEwan's robotic "Adam." "Adam," as the name suggests in McEwan's ambiguously titled *Machines Like Me* (2019), threatens the genesis of a new order in which robots rule the home and bedroom, in both reproduction and profitable production. David Mackenzie's film *Perfect Sense* (2011), more prescient than its projected characterization as "dramatic science fiction" suggests, traces the coursing trajectory of a virus causing serial loss of each human sense, starting with taste and smell, through hearing and touch, and ending with sight. All that is left holding life and hope hanging by a thread as the Virus closes them down is an aspirational politics predicated on human care, concern, and consideration for another.

Bio-systems are complex interactive formations which exist and thrive not competitively but cooperatively, in ways that self-regulate. Microbiomes "colonize" bodies in settling into them. When bearing viruses, they may take over in infecting and ruling the body they "bio-colonize." This draws into sharper relation the biological with the more familiar and less value-neutral conception of "colonizing." SARS-CoV-2 is one such viral infection, introducing a competition for bio-control rather than just systemic co-presence, neutralization, or in some sense cooperation.

The Virus has stopped the world short. It has worked to take our breath away. The costs and impacts of practices bringing us to this point have been thrown into sharp relief. The viral shutdown momentarily cleaned the air and water, brought animals to their old habitats now largely untroubled by human presence. But the consequent reduction in emissions turns out to be about a quarter of what is needed to reverse furnace-like temperatures and their effects. The destructive conditions have been underpinned by deeper cultures more difficult to forgo. Velocity and volatility, speed and movement, discardability and waste, obscene wealth and instantaneous vulnerability, privilege and disposability, disinformation and make-believe. The constitutive conditions of viral sociality.

Against the backdrop of this culture of vulture consumption and furious circulation of disinformation, the Virus can only be read as ecological. We have run out of breath. The Virus manifests most catastrophically by closing down the lungs. And its global unsettlement, infectious swiftness, and anonymity have left us collectively gasping. The Virus has attacked the organs of human life, in turn upending sociality. It serves as a reminder that the capacity to breathe and breathable air are inseparable conditions of living. Bodily and climatic health are mutually reinforcing.

Together they ensure that the next breath is not the last.

Ground almost to a standstill, the planet's inhabitants are collectively, if unevenly, faced by the large looming question, the challenge of our time: what is the future to be made together to survive, and thrive? Wanting to get back to "normal," to pre-pandemic time, is implicitly to seek to return to the very conditions that produced those through which we are now collectively clawing. Ecoformatively, economically, existentially. Cut-throat competition between individuals and states for resources and comforts undercuts exactly the cooperative tissue necessary to survive the far-reaching threat to life and its fabric posed by a spiraling pandemic.

Those best addressing the pandemic challenges have resorted to deeply cooperative engagement, mutually supportive endeavor, and collaborative problem-solving to advance collective interests. As frontline doctors watched the most breath-distressed patients perishing as ventilators forced air into virally compacted lungs, trans-national experiential knowledge flowed from Lombardy to Long Island, from sites earlier to those later infected. Put aside the technologies of ventilation. Turn patients at the earliest signs of distress on their sides or stomachs, taking compressing pressure off their lungs. The caring touch turned asphyxiation and breathlessness to lifesaving relief, almost instantaneously.

So, it has taken a challenge of unrivaled planetary proportion to reveal what is effective in managing the intense upending of local and global life. It is precisely the contrary to cut-throat competition and sovereign authority, as states like South Korea, Taiwan, Senegal, and New Zealand have demonstrated: deep social connectivity, courageous contributions in the face of personal risk, the reliability of supply chains and dependable coordination of resources, not least the open sharing of reliable, trustworthy information. Key are the grounding of socialities and solidarities of trust in community relation and care. These virtues cannot simply end at the border. As a global disease, an all-encompassing pandemic, the Virus reminds us we inhabit worlds. Our own, those larger than us, those we don't even know. The more readily these virtues are relationally available and applied, the better societies – worlds, our world – have fared.

What vision of future survivability faces us, then, together even as we have been torn apart? On one side, a mash-up Redditt image post of a white woman, social distancing protestor, holding up a sign reading "Barack-6, Hussein-7, Obama-5 = COVID-19." The image doesn't quite add up, to take a dig at Trumpetarianism. On another, an exhausted emergency room doctor in Brooklyn, New York, movingly acknowledging the global appreciation of ER staff as a consequence of the pandemic rather than the culturally more usual New York abuse. The appreciative generosity showered upon them by their Park Slope neighbors materialized in mounds of caloric food being gifted to the ER. The running joke among staff was that they would be "gaining 'the COVID-15'" (Voorhees 2020: 13).

The driving question is whether the conditions can be sustained to produce and extend such bountiful offerings making generosity like this possible.

6

Ecoforming Dread

Fires scorching large swaths of Australia roared out 2019. Smoke billowed nine miles high. A young man in rural New South Wales spent six weeks as a volunteer firefighter. He came home as much emotionally as physically exhausted, unable to go on. What had done him in, he told his mother, a farmer, was not the relentless march of the firescape, as devastating as it was (Lynch 2020; Moir et al 2020). He was haunted by the incessant screams of the koala bears devoured by the flames.

This perhaps is as powerful an image as there is of the planet's current ecological plight. Bears only by metaphor, koalas are actually marsupials, pouched mammals. Adored for their baby-like seductive cuddliness and seeming approachability, they occupy the ambiguous netherworld between outback and backyard, the wild and domesticity. They represent with their human co-residents that co-constitution and co-habitation of nature and culture I will call, analogously to "terraforming," the process of *ecoforming* (Haraway, 2008, terms this "natureculture"; Latour, 2018, "geo-social"). Like koalas, humans shape the ecology forming both.

Koalas move more slowly than most non-human animals. Their only refuge from daily danger is to climb the very trees feeding the fast and furious fires. While not yet close to extinction, a significant portion of their habitat is threatened by land development. This comes with increased automobiles and dogs, deepening drought – "the Big Dry" – and resultant degradation of the food supply as fast-rising carbon dioxide levels decrease the nutritional value of the eucalyptus leaves on which koalas have thrived. Port Macquarie north of Sydney harbors a Koala Hospital dedicated to rescuing and nursing the fire-damaged marsupials. We clearly share eco-systems. Koala demise is our doing, and relatedly our undoing. Their dreadful and dread-filling screams are our screams. As koalas go, it could be said, so go we.

*

Weather is the blood of the environment. It colors life, contouring possibilities and limits. But weather can ruin it too: a day, a life, lives. Until recently, weather has largely been taken to have a forceful agency, a character, all its "own." Most have thought about weather as they rose to face the day, but as a purely natural condition, the product of only physical forces outside all but its self-determination. Many mostly still do, until it reminds us that humans have a heavy hand in the destruction it – and then most still like to think only it – is dealing us. Denial of human implication is refusal of our own responsibility in the ruin. We dread the delivery, even the threat of ruin, but ignore any hand in the conditions of its possibility. The huffing and puffing that blows the house down, drowns multitudes in the storm's wake, is, most imagine, all nature's doing.

But the denial can no longer be plausibly extended. As Sonali Deraniyagala's excruciating account of the 2004 Sri Lankan tsunami attests, nightmarish eco-stories will increasingly proliferate, haunting more and more among us (Deraniyagala 2013; cf. Wark 2020).

Prompted by profit, prestige, and pleasure, homes are built too close to the water. On eroding cliffs, shifting sands, crumbling banks. Nuclear power plants are

placed at the water's edge, for cooling or waste purposes, in the obvious path of surging waters. Homes
hover over and in the sea itself, repeatedly replaced after
the last one is washed away in the surging storm swells.
And the commons is expected silently to subsidize the
clean-up and repetitions. Reparations of a hidden history. Pity turns to dread. Those poor people have lost
their homes. There but for the grace – of God, the insurance company, the mortgage provider, the deep state,
goddammit – go I. Those corporate entities lacking all
evidence of a history of grace. Grace is dread's state of
perpetual denial. Anxiety is its muted expression; anger,
turned to fury, its outlet.

Humans not only aid in the destruction. We are now
driving elements, mostly unknowingly, inattentively, or
uncaringly, in making the weather and its impacts what
they are today too. Weather dictates and metaphorically characterizes mood: he looks like thunder; she has
a sunny disposition. When we ask about the weather,
pretty much anywhere, whether it is "angry" or "calm,"
we are in principle asking about the sea somewhere,
not to mention our own moods. Weather-volatile archi-
pelagos like Haida Gwaii off northern British Columbia
know this so well they speak not of weather but of sea-
borne winds. And when we ask about the sea, we are
querying the state of the planet. It is key.

*

The sea is a crucial vector in global warming, in climate
change, and accordingly in unpredictable weather.
Water – seas, oceans – makes up two-thirds of the
earth's surface. The water is rising, alongside creeping
desertification. The ocean is unpredictable, its contours,
surfaces, and boundaries constantly shifting in response
to celestial, atmospheric, and anthropogenic forces.
Our oceans and seas are increasingly polluted, fished
out, bleached. Once average atmospheric temperature

increases by 2.7°F/1.5°C above pre-industrial or early nineteenth-century levels – the increase today is already at 2°F/1.1°C – 70 percent of the planet's coral reefs will be dead, as if scalded by hot water. At 3.6°F/2°C, coral destruction will rise to 90 percent. Oceans hit their warmest temperatures in recorded history in 2019, increasing at a rate faster than in *any* previously recorded year.

Ocean warming is critical to global over-heating and its devastating impacts. Oceans absorb upwards of 90 percent of the excess heat trapped in the atmosphere by carbon dioxide and methane (Cheng et al. 2020). They are being de-oxygenated and acidified. Oceans have an accelerating inability to reproduce and cleanse. In the past fifty years, low-oxygen ocean sites have risen twenty-fold. Coral reefs harbor the greatest biodiversity of any earth eco-system. They reproduce subsistence food for fish and other species in the oceanic food chain. There is no healthy planet without a healthy ocean ecology.

Water temperatures in the eastern Pacific Ocean reached 11°F/6°C above average between summer 2015 and spring 2016 as an El Niño cycle warmed the water. In Southern California, we surfed that entire summer with no wetsuits, as highly unusual as it was momentarily welcome. None of that thick neoprene to hamper movement, or swollen feet from the freeze. Yet had we peered northwards, we would have seen evidence, if too late to prevent, that approximately a million common murres, a seabird abundant along the northeastern Pacific seaboard, were perishing. They likely starved to death as the warm water killed off their sources of food. Other sea life died too, including sea lions and baleen whales, though not to the same extent. Tens of thousands of murres washed ashore, from Central California to Alaska. Their breeding pods were largely destroyed too, many failing to reproduce. It is unclear how readily the stock will replenish. The same is true more recently of the second-largest colony of emperor penguin chicks, most of which were drowned as a major Antarctic ice shelf melted quickly in spring 2019.

This century has seen eighteen of the hottest nineteen years on record since record-keeping began in 1880. As global temperatures have warmed, snow and ice caps across land and sea have melted. On February 6, 2020, Antarctica reached 65°F/18.3°C, its highest temperature ever recorded. On August 23, the Mojave Desert in California experienced a high of 130°F/54.4°C, the highest in over a century. The global temperature in January 2020 averaged its monthly highest ever. Surface sea temperatures have heated up and sea levels have risen. Canada's ice shelves have reduced to just 10 percent of their volume a century ago. Greenland's dramatic ice-melt in 2019, now irreversible, added 2.2 millimeters to global sea levels. The Arctic is warming faster than elsewhere, hitting 80°F/26.6°C in May 2020. Unusual fires have broken out as a consequence. As major storm systems develop and intensify across the wide expanses of oceans, they now pick up more warm water. Wind velocity intensifies, in turn producing significantly more precipitation once the storms make land. Gale-force wind and flooding destruction invariably follow.

The destruction has grown in scale not just because storm power has exploded but because of the built environment too. Houses, apartments, and hotel buildings line long, unsteady coastlines, eroding cliffsides and river banks, dotting thick forests the uncleared bedding of which is tinder for fast-spreading fires. "Modernization" increasingly produces the conditions for uncontrollable consequences (cf. Beck 2011). But the effects are less obvious and more widespread too. Temperatures within US cities can vary by as much as 20°F/6.7°C. Hotter neighborhoods have less greenery, especially trees, and are covered with more cement and bricks. In 101 of 108 cities examined in a recent study, these less profitable and revenue-generating "heat islands" or "heat domes" have been more readily abandoned by municipal services, often the legacy of racial redlining. Here the soaring heat has increased illness and death, especially for the elderly and children. They are, in short, poorer neighborhoods to which black and brown people have mostly been circumscribed (Lakhani 2020). A similar logic marks the Cape Flats shantytowns and government cement block housing of often drought-stricken Cape Town.

Violent weather has surged as inequalities, individual and national, have soared. This wave of inequality, discussed in the previous chapter, is a function of what Bernard Stiegler identifies as "algorithmic governmentality," the engine of "24/7 capitalism" (Stiegler 2018). While income and wealth inequalities underpin differential vulnerabilities, environmental forces strike all in their paths. But the racially and class vulnerable, the old and infirm, the poor and the very young have been positioned by political economy, advanced by earlier forms and enhanced now by tracking-capitalism, to inherit greater vulnerability than their better-off peers. They are situated in and often confined to sites that are denser, more concentrated, lower lying, and accordingly less able to avoid the destruction (cf. Hage 2017).

If drawing relevant distinctions is the first capacity to think critically, the algorithmic is the demise of such reasoning. Algorithmic automaticity and neo-mobility multiply while masking the power of rupture as the disruptive. The changing of the rules algorithmic sociality produces is magnifying the wrenching tears in the social fabric. Wealthier, increasingly capitalist nations use more resources and by extension emit more pollutants. As wealth in countries like China, India, and Brazil has surged, so have their polluting and global warming impacts (Amazonian fires, Chinese coal pollution, asthmatic suffocation in polluted Indian cities, more automobiles everywhere). They join the club of major culprits such as the United States. But global warming and unpredictable weather do not abide by national boundaries. Smaller economies across every continent suffer at least as much as North America, Northern Europe, China, or Brazil. There is no outside, as Ackbar Abbas comments in his reflections on critical theory and the weather (Abbas 2012). Relatedness means the interconnectivity and overlap of effect and impact.

The conditions of possibility are systemic, for which no single individual is or can be held responsible. The generalized system elevates, as Ulrich Beck puts it, a structure of collective irresponsibility (Beck 2011). Tracking-capitalism may operate to mitigate risk for individuals by pre-tracking and so projecting their movements and actions. Capitalism accordingly is less the absolute privatization of all risk, vulnerability, and ultimately attention than their redistribution. If individual risk is privatized, risk associated with too-reliant-to-fail institutions such as banks and utilities is socialized. Tracking, however, has its inevitable, dread-inducing blind spots, its *unheimlich* forces or dynamics it is incapable of seeing, predicting, or identifying. Things (like COVID-19), as the saying goes, that come out of nowhere.

Weather has become increasingly volatile because of the ocean. Or more accurately because of an exploitative eco-system that seas and oceans anchor. If the sea has produced storm and flooding destruction of biblical proportions, the dramatic temperature increases – weeks of 120°F/50°C plus in recent Delhi summers; record temperatures along Australia's east coast, approaching 120°F in Sydney; seemingly endless droughts in the Western Cape and Southern Africa more broadly (Comaroff and Comaroff 2001) – are associated with furious fires. In the last four months of 2019, Australia

watched 38,000 square miles (61,000 sq. km) inciner-
ated, a larger area than all of Ireland, including the
North. The fires released more carbon dioxide into the
atmosphere than all of Australia's annual emissions.
Australian annual temperatures were 2.7°F/1.5°C above
late twentieth-century levels, and 3.6°F/2°C higher than
levels a century or more ago. A recent study predicted
that for every 1.8F°/1°C increase another one billion people will live in intolerable habitats, equal to
the Sahara Desert's hottest areas (Xu et al. 2020). In
Siberia, Alaska, and Western Canada, fires in 2019
each burned close to half Australia's destroyed acre-
age, and in Indonesia 10,000 square miles (25,000 sq.
km) (Gardiner 2019). Anthropocenic climate change,
in short, is transforming environmental and geological
time into historical time, just as humans must be understood as a natural force (cf. Chakrabarty 2009).

Some have said the heating up has to do with the sun
burning hotter. This is but a manner of speaking, mis-
understanding, or the intentional mis-stating of climate
change deniers. The sun radiates heat at a steady temperature, at least across astronomically extended time
periods. The earth's heating up is not the sun's fault.
It is a function of the fact that we have rendered toxic
the earth's own sunscreen. Soaring carbon monoxide
emittance ringing the earth's surface – the highest levels
registered in over 800,000 years, at no point higher
in human evolution – absorbs more infrared sun rays,
radiating them earthwards as heat. The human response
has been to add coolant to the air conditioning. The life
support system further fuels the conditions pumping up
the heat, much as laying desperately ill COVID patients
on their backs may hasten their demise. As the earth
grows hotter, recent climate models are predicting that
the lower-lying marine stratus and stratocumulus clouds
keeping especially oceans cooler by refracting the sun's
heat will thin out or evaporate completely. The planet

will end up even hotter during the day, and cooler at night as clouds also trap heat beneath them. The effects of climate change and range, in short, will be dramatically amplified (Pearce 2020b). We are and will grow hotter as a direct effect of our exhaustion.

*

Land-produced pollution, from fossil fuel production to plastic discards and swarming fires decimating swaths of the planet, is throttling maritime ecologies. Our cast-off culture is killing the life these ecologies support. Oceans absorb 8 million tonnes of plastics each year, now totaling in the tens of trillion pieces. By mid-century, there will be more plastic in oceans than fish. It kills birds and mammals, polluting the marine life other species consume. The disintegrating plastic particles, suffocating sea life, are nearly impossible to absorb or remove. A "hydrocolonial" quality characterizes these practices, to bend Isabel Hofmeyr's (2019) term. The landbound exploitatively pillage oceanic resources while caring less about the health of oceans as long as they keep on giving.

There should be no expectation these trends will be easily reversed, notwithstanding gathering efforts to increase the economic and moral costs of using plastic bags, packaging, bottles, and straws. Some small retail stores use no plastic containers or packaging, requiring customers to bring their own. In the United States in 2019, however, less than 9 percent of plastic bags were recycled. Gestural changes seem symbolic in the face of apocalyptic threats.

With a half-eye on the horizon of diminishing resources and gathering climate change activism, the major petrochemical companies are preparing to shift the balance of investments from oil extraction and delivery to increased plastic production. Plastic compounds suffuse contemporary economic culture. They fashion clothes, shape the bodies of cars, furnish countertops and the outer bodies – the skin – of our technological devices. They significantly lighten vehicles, from automobiles to aircraft, making them more energy efficient. In the next thirty years, plastics will rise to 50 percent of the increase in US oil demand. (They now constitute just 14 percent.) Plastics production plants churning out materials for manufacturing are mushrooming in oil-reliant states like Texas and Louisiana, but also in Pennsylvania, Ohio, and West Virginia. A Shell plant outside Pittsburgh has acquired an emissions permit for as much carbon monoxide as emitted by nearly a half million cars! Similarly, that airplane bodies are lighter and so energy efficient in turn has led to many more flights globally. Energy savings are offset by industry growth.

The plastic plants bring jobs welcome in the poorer communities in which they are placed, but at a cost. While plastics subjected to intense and lasting sunlight biodegrade faster, they leave behind toxic chemical components absorbed by fish and sea life. In 2019, Texas saw four major fires in facilities producing petrochemical plastic ingredients, causing evacuations of many tens of thousands because of carcinogenic fumes (Gardiner 2019). Plastics are in the business of suffocation.

Human bodies and almost all animals are sustained by the air breathed, which nevertheless can kill when toxin-bearing. The air supply has grown increasingly polluted since the onset of the Industrial Revolution. Vertebrates are largely defenseless in the face of their need to breathe. Coal underpinned much of the energy demands of industrialization. It has been supplemented since the late nineteenth century by other fossil fuels, but has proved the most toxic. London's Great Smog of 1952 led to the deaths of over 4,000 people in less than a week as a result of factory and home fireplace pollutants. Automobile exhaust emissions, especially from diesel-burning engines, have added to significantly worsened air quality worldwide. In the first decade of this century, nearly half the population of the United States lived in areas designated by the American Lung Association as suffering from unhealthy levels of particle or ozone pollution, effects of largely human-produced ash, soot, diesel exhaust, aerosols, and chemicals. Australia's ongoing fires have turned the bright blue light of day to a blazing orange grey, blotting out all daylight. The foundation of Australia's economy today, between fires, remains vested in coal production and use.

Fifteen years ago, Beijing notoriously was suffocating itself. I recall driving to Beijing airport as the sun was rising. A dirty orange ball pushed eerily against the thick grey air enveloping the city from surrounding coal-burning plants and factories. Prompted by the Beijing Olympics, the city has since reduced airborne pollutants by 35 percent, to more livable if not exactly healthy levels. As COVID-19 spiked in early 2020 across cities worldwide, greenhouse emissions dropped another 25–50 percent but have rebounded as economic activity has reignited.

Face masks, on the other hand, have become a familiar sight across a broad swath of societies and cultures. Governmental warnings to stay indoors or not exercise outdoors ring with growing frequency. Degrees of asphyxiation threaten collective futures. That the weather knows no human boundaries entails that the large-scale changes being experienced are planetarily produced. A massive Saharan dust storm in late June 2020 was carried by west-bound winds across the Atlantic, through Caribbean islands, into southern US states. The impacts of such events nevertheless are more or less unpredictably local, though not unusually with transnational effects and implications. This is Dante's inferno but not in some netherworld. Cycles of drought, fires, dust storms, snow blizzards, and floods are our fast-approaching everyday. A silent purgatory is becoming our ecoformed lived experience in the now.

*

Dread-inducing considerations invariably have a human dimension underlying them. In older ways of relating, indigenous people lived with the knowledge of unpredictable environmental challenges as part of life, mostly not in dread of them. It is not that they didn't face challenging environmental conditions, even existentially threatening ones. The Sinagua's extraordinary cliff-embedded homes at Montezuma's Castle in Arizona were abandoned in the fifteenth century due to drought and resource depletion. And Mesoamericans lived with a deeply lingering anxiety that their existing world, the one of the fifth sun, would end catastrophically, as had the four sun worlds previously. Yet indigenous peoples took on their environmental challenges mainly as elements to work with rather than against, ordinary life conditions rather than objects of conquest or control (cf. Diamond 2011; Jones 2020; Scott 2017). Their history is one of burning more field fires but on much smaller, controlled scales, and so far less destructively. Every firefighter knows that firewalls constructed by controlled burning reduce the number and extent of devastating wild fires. That is the ancient wisdom of eco-management (Pearce 2020a). Only those continuing to deny climate change today think they know better.

Over the past two centuries, capitalism – its structure, practices, and effects – has formed the principal object of critique, and so necessarily also colonialism and slavery. Now it has become climate change and global warming. The latter implicate capital in our pressing existential threat, along with the ethnoracially discriminating effects. Some scientists are predicting the early onset of the "sixth extinction," the killing off of at least 75 percent of species' life. The 2019–20 string of Australian wild fires wiped out nearly 3 *billion* animals. Our koala screams echo far and wide.

It was with industrialization, and in particular development of the steam engine, that the environmental impacts dramatically heightened. China had already been burning coal since the eleventh century, as Amitav Ghosh reminds us, piping steam into homes, and Burma used oil in the eighteenth century (Ghosh 2016a). In any case, the steam engine and the technological and production developments it spawned led to a surge in coal consumption and the spewing of carbon emissions into the atmosphere. Coal mining scarred landscapes. Steam engines quickly caught on across the colonies as railway tracks were laid. Local rulers recognized the convenience of train-traveling across large stretches of their countries, and colonial officials sought the advantages of techno-control through military mobility. Steamships likewise expanded the reach of economic colonization as well as global warring, expanding the ecological impacts of each in then unprecedented and accelerating ways.

Some key captains of contemporary capital and their political representatives are in denial of the threat, or at least of its extent. Indeed, neoliberalizing austerity has worsened matters dramatically. The culture of the incessantly new – of seeking new experiences, products, places – fuels the gorging and exhausting of resources, adding to the environmental pressures. While promising and predicting to line public coffers, the practices identified with neoliberalization have deeply depleted them. Wealth accordingly has been transferred to a small sliver of increasingly powerful and self-serving individuals and the corporations they control. Debt and then austerity are proposed for everyone else to offset the public revenue shortfalls. These shifts likely exacerbate rather than alleviate the ecological challenges currently faced, at collective peril.

AccuWeather is a US-based corporation founded more than fifty years ago by Joel Myers, a meteorology student and then faculty at Pennsylvania State University. Starting out as a weather prediction company nationally and growing globally, it morphed under the leadership of Myers's brother Barry into a media company. The company has depended for its source of business on the free data provided by the National Weather Service as the basis for corporate profitability. In 2017, Donald Trump nominated Barry Myers to head the National Oceanic and Atmospheric Association, administrative home to the National Weather Service. While the nomination stalled in the US Senate, AccuWeather's lobbying successfully continued to restrict the National Weather Service from making its data publicly and freely available. AccuWeather bundles the data into fee-driven commercial services and sells them on the open market while providing a fee-free weather prediction website profitably sponsored by advertising (Lewis 2018). Weather tracking is the work of the public treasury. Weather reporting based on public works is the product of privatized endeavors, made available by the sponsorship of tracking-capitalism. This has repeatedly placed lives at risk.

*

Water's liquidity both sustains and destroys. There is no life without it. We can't drink too little for want of avoiding dehydration, but consuming too much can drown our organs, causing damage and demise. Water can seep into everything. Transparent until it stains, unremarked and taken for granted until it rusts or dries up, its uncared-for economy and infrastructures increasingly deliver too much or too little. The less attentive we are to its infrastructures of storage, delivery, maintenance, and management, use and abuse, the more devastation it will likely leave in its wake. Water bears life, and it can carry death.

The possibility of effective social action to the benefit of the commons is deeply compromised. Public goods have been curtailed, the resources needed to support them shifted to private benefit and protecting privatizing power. Most important and direct is the failure, even refusal, to invest in upgrading any public-serving infrastructure other than what serves commercializing info-power such as laying fiber-optic cable (Khalili 2020). Social infrastructure – water delivery, drainage and sewerage pipes, potable water, electrical grids, public transport, bridges, and so on – accordingly is far more vulnerable to rapidly intensifying weather, pretty much everywhere. Flint, Michigan, is best known for its toxic water as a result of aged and decaying lead piping. Its municipal water utility had to cease for approximately five years to provide water to its majority black population for both drinking and washing.

Coastal areas along Florida or the Gulf of Mexico may be used to flooding from increasingly volatile Atlantic storms, if one can ever get used to drowning. But the US Midwest and Midlands Britain, central Germany, Venice, and elsewhere have been suffering their versions of the Great Flood too. Yorkshire and contiguous districts in Britain had historic floods with comparable consequences in 2015, repeated in 2019 and again in 2020. The amount of British land given over in flood-prone zones to new housing development more than doubled in 2019. The damage is not just the result of water and low-lying land, nor only of the failure or lack of levees, viable routes and destinations for run-off. It is also a result of ignoring the warning signs regarding where building is permitted and indeed encouraged.

The Mississippi River slicing vertically across the center of the United States regularly overflows its banks. The flatlands of Davenport, Iowa, were swamped in 2019, homes and businesses wiped out by meters-high water levels. Centreville, Illinois, south of East St. Louis, floods with almost any rainfall. The African-American inhabitants, having sought relief from urban abandonment in East St. Louis, have seen their town stricken by decaying water and sewerage pipes, incessantly potholed roads, and feces-laden flood waters filling fields and homes (Johnson 2020). Governments failing to invest in upgraded infrastructure, flood-water divergence, drought and fire-fighting preparation have a fast-expanding array of examples of the dread-filled futures most all face, the (racially) impoverished more so than the economically better off.

*

Weather is the sign of these unsettling shifts resulting from humans "interfer[ing] with natural causation" (Jaspers 1933: 1). That the distinction between the human and natural is no longer tenable reinforces Dipesh Chakrabarty's observations that "[h]umans . . . have become a natural condition," a "geological agent" (Chakrabarty 2009: 214, 218). The unpredictability consequently leaves no one immune, untouched, above or beyond, even if its effects will be differentially experienced and borne. The everyday has become the uncommon, the uncommon all but the everyday. All that is solid melts, well, today more readily into water. Unpredictability is a turning away from the expected. Almost everywhere there is fast developing a diminished capacity to read the signs, to know how to react, to weather the weather.

There has always been a degree of unpredictability to the weather. The definite article – *the* weather – indicates that there is weather even when ignored, taken for granted. But the hint of the definitive this carries suggests misleadingly that the weather is singular. Proliferating unpredictability, however, is the new normal. Even "normal" weather can come to seem unexpected, embedding a degree of exceptionality as storms grow dramatically more severe, temperatures more searing, droughts extended from months to years to a decade, floods of biblical proportion more frequent. A once-in-a-century weather event is fast becoming all but the lived everyday somewhere.

The Victoria Falls, in Zimbabwe's north, is best known as a mile-wide vista of cascading water funneled majestically by the Zambezi River over its jagged cliffs. Its cavernous roar still rings in my ears sixty years later. The thick spray bouncing off the base has incessantly soaked the adjacent rain forest century after century. Until now. The Falls today is but a trickle a few feet wide, dwarfed by the daunting black rockface. Drought has dried up not just the awesome river but also the ecologies and economies of life it has supported for eons. If this is what David Livingstone had stumbled upon in 1855, there would have been no "smoke that thunders," no incessantly roaring "Mosi ao Tunya" to have made sufficient impression imperiously to snatch its indigenous name for the sake of her majesty's. Ecological tragedy only now seems to have forsaken that of colonial conquest.

Disasters have not only multiplied but also cata-strophically intensified with little limit. They surge past the boundedness of space and time, defying dimension-ality (Beck 2011). The unpredictability, if not always of the event but of its intensity, is magnifying uncertainty. Dread fills the vacuum this uncertainty reinforces. Unpredictable weather is not just experienced but exer-cised by us, collectively. It is the cumulative and repeated outcomes of our individuated actions, oversights, inat-tention, self-denyingly destructive action and blindingly arrogant inaction.

On standard moral accounts, one is responsible only for one's own actions, not for those of others one per-haps does not even know. As we steadily tolerate the expanding intolerability of the everyday, however, I cannot evade responsibility for the collectively destructive effects. My failure to do my own little bit adds to or fails to help in reversing those effects, symbolic gestures notwithstanding. There is no more living as if aside of, against, or apart from nature, to refuse to see the outcomes. Bernard Stiegler suggests that the condition of the Anthropocene, that time of "Man's" making of (geologic) nature, has already slipped by. He baptizes the moment we now inhabit, rather, the "Entropocene" (Stiegler 2018).

Nature today is "being corpsed," as Samuel Beckett (1958: 35) evocatively declares (Abbas 2012). But not nature alone. It is the collective world that faces our Endgame. We are decomposing, "intoxicating on carbon dioxide" (Latour 2018), and, I might add, on methane too. Undertaking to colonize another planet, to launch our innovative industrial production into space beyond the blue horizon, as some billionaires with too much spare cash to burn are propelling forward, will just hasten the demise, bring on the cremation. As Jenny Offill has a character remark in her novel *Weather*, "These people long for immortality but can't wait ten minutes for a cup of coffee" (Offill 2020: 39). The Entropocene also names the new planetary political economy.

There are antinomies of knowledge and action at work in all of this, and in the accompanying unpredictability. By definition, one cannot know of the pending occurrence of an unpredictable event. Its unpredictability entails the impossibility of seeing it coming. But we do know today that because of collective irresponsibility destructive events will occur, unpredictably, with intensifying frequency, only not their exact nature, timing, or geographical occurrence. Their unpredictability has become less a predicate of their occurrence than their spacetime character. The less we do, the more likely we will have to endure extended droughts and weather storms swirling about more uncontrollably than projected. Expectation of the unpredictable becomes dread at the nagging premonition.

Antinomies are embedded in our political economies of action and inaction, and in our click-bait culture of updated gratification. Take one example, among many. Surfers (like me) see themselves as curators of the ocean. They are invested in beach and water clean-up; it is after all in their health and aesthetic interests. It is also in their surfing interests. At current rates of sea level rise, two-thirds of Southern California's surf breaks are predicted to disappear by century's close. Surfers have started globally successful programs to develop and deliver water pumps and clean drinking water facilities to globally remote communities who otherwise would go without potable water sources. They have taken the lead in closing down seaside nuclear power facilities, and preventing coastal highway expansion. But surfers travel incessantly in search of better waves, invariably in jet-fueled aircraft. Surfing death-defying giant waves, the product of these massive storms, has become increasingly popular, aided by polluting jet-skis and fuel-guzzling boats. And though ecologically friendly materials are on the rise, the dominant ones out of which most surfing equipment continues to be made are oil derivative and toxic. Surfboards, many readily snapped and discarded by the very waves for which they are designed, are mostly made with polyurethane foam and polyester resin. Wetsuits cover bodies in neoprene rubber. Increasingly necessary sunscreens are mostly composed of toxic, coral-poisoning chemicals. And swimwear is manufactured with petroleum-derivative synthetics the production of which emits large doses of carbon dioxide.

Surfing is far from the exception. The completely comprehensible drive to pursue satisfying lives is contributing significantly to the conditions of its ultimate impossibility. Consider the ecological resources it takes to build and maintain all those global golf courses, and how relatively few they serve. Despite the growing efforts by states to cut carbon emissions, in 2017 state subsidies to fossil fuel producers totaled 85 percent of all state subsidies globally. They add significantly to the consequent health hazards and deaths as a result of the air pollution fostered. And they serve as an overall brake on national revenues (by 3.8 percent on average) as a result of reducing fiscal support for other local economic activity, education, and renewable energy technologies.

The Texas oil industry is encouraging the federal government to subsidize sea wall construction along its Gulf coast. The aim is not to keep out Latin American migrants, who often provide the unskilled labor in the area, not least in construction. It is to protect local residential and business areas, and by extension the oil and refinery plants, from the storm surges and flooding the oil industry is a significant player in producing (CBS News 2018). Up to 80 percent of energy needs could be provided today by renewable sources (Ellsmoor 2019). It is not for want of technological know-how; it is for want of wealth, inconvenience, and will. Those koala screams echo hauntingly from the burning tree tops.

*

The dread swirling all about today is an anxiousness fed also by how readily the sometimes calamitous ecological conditions can upend lives. They now threaten species' life generally, all bio-reproductive or "zoe-centric" and not just human or "homocentric" life, to use Chakrabarty's (2015) terms. The anxiety abounds as a consequence of catastrophic local events (fires, floods) alongside the more readily circulating global facts associated with climate change (rising carbon emissions, temperatures, sea levels, troublingly fast rates of bio-diversity shrinkage, even rapidly circulating viruses). It should come as little surprise that the dominant responses to this represent flip sides of the same coin. On one side, a significant proportion of iGen youth can envisage scant futures for themselves (Ray 2020). On the other, the pursuit of extreme sports has ramped up dramatically as catastrophic events proliferate, amplified by the incessant, attention-grabbing news cycle. Opportunities are readily available to offset apprehension. If life "returns" to a state of nastiness and shortness, we might as well go out pushing the adventurous, adrenaline-priming limits.

Dread is the emergent inkling that a future has closed down but the terms are lacking for expressing, assessing, and addressing the condition. Industrialization accelerated entropy, dissipating energy with little if any concern for its replenishment or ultimate decay, as Stiegler (Sloterdijk and Stiegler 2016) and Bendell (2018) both suggest. Digitalization, in turn, dramatically hastens the rate at which available resources are entropically exhausted, celebrating it as "disruption." While disruption is promoted as opening up new possibilities, it has helped to hasten the under-appreciated existential threats. "Extinction event" is now the go-to term. Yet that, too, indicates the groping for conceptual comprehension as the world crumbles while it smolders, survivors shuffle through the charred ruins of fire-ravaged landscapes, claw back after the tsunami, rebuild tottering lives following the floods.

Eventfulness suggests discrete happenings rather than an incessant process of erasing the ecology of life we inhabit. One with which we have become comfortable. On which we now fully rely. Each happening extends the lineage, unsettling the comfort and upending the reliance. A bleaker landscape of being and (un)becoming seeps beneath our feet, our footing less and less secure. A zeitgeist is taking hold, an unnerving sense of a future with no future, predicated on a history of the present with nothing but algorithmic memory.

The non-stop, paradoxically, is effecting a dance not only with the incessant but also with the end-point, the nihilistic. Thinking is the vestigial power to produce interventions, breaks, ruptures in the taken-for-granted repetitivity, likewise operating at breakneck speed just to keep up. The circulating dread assumes a logic of its own, pumped up by "fake truths," mad fantasies, outlandish conspiracies, wild prediction, paranoia, and projection. The outbreak of COVID-19 and the rapacious pandemic spread conjure urban myths of cause and effect. Its mushrooming, one Hong Kong version goes, was moved massively along by wind-borne germs carried into apartment building air ducts to infect people in their homes. Another was that it circulated through subterranean drain pipes, requiring citizens to pour *plastic* containers of bleach into street gutters and drains. The weather assumes satanic power.

Satanic climate conduct sounds like ripe material for novelistic expression. Climate deniers battle eco-warriors, worse yet, at family gatherings. Or, more mutedly, families reminisce about forgotten pasts as they rescue heirlooms from flooded homes. Amitav Ghosh (2016a) has complained that the relative dearth of novels with climate change as the central figure, outside dystopian sci-fi and cli-fi writing, has disabled developing a hybrid genre for coming to terms with the constitutive conditions of our time. Perhaps science fiction's distantiation or fantasizing horror stories more readily enable negotiation of "the great [climatic] derangement" and pain in the face of an "unthinkable" passing of species' life itself. Ghosh (2016b) characterizes this as novelistic "concealment." Or, perhaps too, the widespread fictions sprouted by celebrity climate deniers exhaust attentiveness. Yogita Goyal has suggested to me, by contrast, that not much if anything is likely to change with the zombie apocalypse. Things will be largely as they are, mundane and banal. Not a whole lot of fictive fuel for mining serious storytelling in those grounds.

Without reducing dread to melancholia, there are numerous cultural works displaying pervasive disquiet in witnessing the apocalypse in motion and realizing there is nothing to reverse it or hold it at bay. The recent French television mini-series *L'Effondrement* (Collapse) (2019), inspired by the doctrine of *"collapsologie,"* addresses survival in the face of breakdown. Dread follows not quite knowing what it is we are witnessing, what comes after the sense of impending doom. Cultural projection here offers itself as palliative, a painkiller in the face of seemingly inevitable demise, a sharing of irrecoverable earthly loss. Narrativity holds personal or social pain momentarily at arm's length, or provides a salve for those subjected to similar suffering. The pain rests between pages or on screen after all, and viewers can tune out in a way we can't shut out the coming apocalypse.

Dread, however, has a way of escaping the covers. It bristles from the print proffered by any climatic analog to nuclear novels like Nevil Shute's *On the Beach* (1957). Ghosh's own novel *The Hungry Tide* (2004) qualifies as one instance. Dread's language here may emulate fiction about pandemics or plagues (Simon 2020), written for readers no longer alive. One driving distinction is that a nuclear explosion or the plague kills people. Climate destruction undercuts the conditions of possibility for life as such, the existential kindling fluttering into darkness after midnight. Washing hands, actually or metaphorically, won't help. Allen Ginsberg's *Kaddish* (1957–9/1984) is chanted for no one left to lose, Mother Earth in the death throes of self-destruction: "Dreaming back thru life, Your time – and mine accelerating toward Apocalypse."

*

The rampant anxiety washing over us in waves today is mediated, nevertheless, by two interactive "offsets" to the psychic distress. The first, as I have mentioned, is denial. Many go about their daily lives refusing to attend to both the events and their underlying global causes. And second, perhaps more broadly appealing, is the turn to technology as the inevitable fix. As it has in the past, the quieting projection goes, technology will save us. The never-stated implication is that the saving is from ourselves!

This supposed fix includes not just policy reversals. Microsoft and Ikea have committed to carbon-negative rollback of their own carbon footprint legacies, and Germany has declared itself the first country to end in the foreseeable future both nuclear power plants and brown-coal-fueled plants. Delta Airlines announced, pre-COVIDalypse, that it was committing $1 billion over the next decade in a bid to offset its carbon footprint. Technologies have already been designed to scrape up larger pieces of plastic floating in the ocean while popcorn-sized flying and diving bots are gobbling up the micro-plastics too small for the scraper.

The question is whether the proposed technological fix of the day can keep up with the technologically enabled and enhanced waste run-off. Conservative politicians are declaring proposals to plant trillions of trees to suck carbon out of the atmosphere. This is an encouraging start. Yet widespread forestation alone is more panacea than solution. Forests, it is now evident, require ongoing management, from clearing incessant growth of ground cover to controlled fires as breaks should uncontrolled fires spread.

Technology, no doubt, is having an impact. Critics of "degrowth" like to cite the advances of techno-solutions (Roulet and Bothello 2020). While a "soft power" mediation of more extreme manifestations of dread, however, technology is hardly a global solution. For one, the remit of the technological fix undercuts the responsibility of each, individually and collectively, to change their ecologically impactful ways. Technology, after all, has played a significant role in the challenging elemental changes now placing zoetic life at risk. Far less needs to be consumed, and so exhausted, in a dramatically narrowing temporal window.

Digital technology has made it more possible to track, map, data source, and data bank massive quantities of information about climatic conditions, causes, effects, and variable implications, close to real time. Its material conditions of production and application, however, eat up energy resources. This includes the surging heat generated by huge server requirements for cloud computing, the cooling necessary to keep the machines running resulting from the heat generated. Energy resources to mine bitcoin invisibly equal the entire energy consumption of the Czech Republic, a population exceeding 10 million. Digital application generates, proliferates, and intensifies the very conditions it tracks. Electrical cars are well and good, but short of extensively greening energy supplies, the environmental impacts of electricity production are rendered less visible. Our rapidly increasing technological take-up, the very technological fix to which we so readily turn as the foremost way to repair the shattered ecoform, is a major contributor to eco-exhaustion (cf. Chakrabarty 2009: 211–12; Moore 2020). The fix is also at fault.

The steam engine offers the precedent here. The marvel of technology in terms of transforming and expanding industrial production turns out to be – in Peter Sloterdijk's incomparable characterization – modernity's original monster (Sloterdijk and Stiegler 2016). The effect has been repeatedly and renewably to expand and exacerbate social grostequerie. Happy-making technology evaporates the more deleterious traces of its conditions of production. The medium is the misery.

More growth requires more resources. This, in turn, prompts the drive to control more territory. In its reach for ceaseless expansion, modernity is exhausting its conditions of possibility. Anirban Gupta-Nigam (2020) argues compellingly that the push for resources has fueled this reach for ever-new frontiers to conquer, whether for raw materials like cotton, wool, and furs, for oil, for food and water, for the technologically necessary materials like cobalt and lithium, or for natural pharmaceuticals, increasingly for breathable air and clean water. Implicit if never acknowledged in this imperial reach is that there are inevitably resource limits. The four core elements identified by classical Greek thinkers – earth, air, water, and fire – may once have seemed infinite, the material being of life itself. Those paying any attention, however, are coming to understand that these core elements interact relationally. They have limits too. With scant care, things not only fall apart but also run out or turn deadly destructive.

The fire season might linger, even when starting earlier and ending later, just as floods recede. Life picks up, at least what is there in the tatters. It goes on, as it must, remakes itself. There's the Australian Open to watch, amidst the clearing smoke and athletic shallowness of breath. There's life to live, the world not likely to end tomorrow, and even if it does. Fires and floods change our lives, as do street protests and boycotts, but do they change the way we live?

Learning to live within these limits, fast approaching and becoming increasingly evident, requires not just consuming less but also redirecting our collective aspirational lifestyle. These limits, Brazilian anthropologist and public intellectual Eduardo Viveiros de Castro (2019) warns, "will probably force us to adopt less comfortable forms of life – less comfortable from a certain point of view, determined by the social mode of production of today's dominant life. Today it's impossible to think of life without a cell phone. But we'll have to reinvent life without [one]." Perhaps technology has a fix for its own toxicity too. A lithium-free phone? And yet that dreaded ringing refuses to cease. The extinction event is calling. This time there's no hanging up.

Heightened ecoforming acceleration of burning, flooding, and asphyxiation conjures dread from the not knowing how fast it will descend, what unforeseen storm, poison, or resulting virus lurks just beyond the visible. We come to know of events in close to real time, in their unfolding, as if we are in the midst while half a world away. A premonition is almost immediately prescience. The speed at which contemporary technology encourages us to exist unleashes in turn anxiety about, of, for the hidden, the out of focus, the half-envisaged pixelated outline in the blur. Out of sight is no longer out of mind but larger than life. We are fast entering the spacetime in which there is no unseen, unheard (of), untouched, no distantiating relief or release. The seen unseen, the imagined over there being right here is the most dread inducing. As Latour and Foucault repeatedly remind us, the anxiety may be mobilized or mitigated by the discursive terms ordering what and how we see things, comprehended as given or manufactured. And yet there are material limits to the conditions of possibility. The demise of plausible deniability is the cruel justice we have brought collectively upon ourselves.

*

Dread fixates on the impossibility of any path ahead, a point about which the "collapsologists" make much (Servigne and Stevens 2020). Dread is reactive, ambivalent about acknowledging the dire future on the current trajectory. The contradictions, as I have made clear above, cut deep. National governments, and by extension the general populations they serve, are expected to shoulder the costs of the environmental and subsequent health and safety impacts that fossil fuel industries and interests are in the business of generating. Lifestyle cultures of driving, flying, plastic and carbon consumption (Mitchell 2011) are sponsoring the extensive wealth of a small cabal of oil oligarchs and their circle, those Douglas Kahn (2020) calls "ecopaths." The opportunity costs and externalities of sustaining fossil fuel industrialization are steeply discounted if not completely washed away behind the treacly dark grime. Everyone pays the piper.

An increasingly fractious political struggle has broken out between the carry-on-regardless crowd and those committed to addressing the pressing ecological concerns. It is, at the limit case the horizon of which seems daily to creep closer, a struggle not over-dramatically between a passive mass stumbling into an ecology of extinction and the drive to sustain life. Those now at the frontline barricades are millennials and Gen-Zers. After all, their futures are those being threatened, made increasingly less livable, more unrecognizable. Senior citizens will mostly not be around thirty years from now when all the tenable projections have the rubber literally *not* hitting the road. Dread serves sometimes and for some as brake; for others as the do-nothing of cynical denial; and for a growing constituency as accelerator, the necessitation to pilot driving action now.

Dramatic carbonization has accelerated rather than decreased, nearly two-thirds higher than it was thirty years ago. Emissions are rising by 1 to 2 percent per year, rather than decreasing by the 8 percent necessary to hold warming's increase below 2.7°F/1.5°C. Emissions currently are 120 percent more than the baseline level requires. Global temperatures will more likely soar past 3.6°F/2°C, requiring 50 percent less fossil fuel production. They could reach more than 5.4°F/3°C, magnifying the disastrous impact. Collective action for "deep decarbonization" and "deep adaptation" necessitates transnational engagement with local commitment, and sector-specific policies and goals. It will require near-universal on-the-ground (and across-the-seas) efforts (Bendell 2018; Cassidy 2020; Victor 2020).

The Convention on Biodiversity hosted the UN Biodiversity Conference in Kunming, China, in October 2020 to adopt a ten-year biodiversity plan. Environmental and climate scientists and activists worked in the lead-up to protect up to 50 percent of marine and land areas, seeking for the Conference to make steadfast commitments to these ends. Some governments have not only resisted but actually countered such efforts, deriding them as cataclysmic pandering. The United States is sacrificing approximately 6,000 square yards (5,017 sq. m) of wilds to clearing, fracking, and development every 30 seconds. Brazil is currently burning or clearing 10 square miles (16 sq. km) of Amazon forests and plains daily.

Preserving land and sea underpins the necessity not just to protect planetary biodiversity but also to maintain the biosystems that clean water and air today demand. The damage from air pollution caused by fossil fuel emissions totals $8 billion per day, about 10 percent of annual GDP in the United States, approximately 17 percent in China, and 6.8 percent globally, due to missed work, lower productivity, medical treatment, and premature deaths. The impact is highest in China, India, and the United States (amounting to $900, $150, and $600 billion respectively [Mittelman 2020]). There is a significant cost of pursuing the proposed biodiversity protections. There is a far greater cost of not (Klein 2014; Robbins 2020).

This cost of doing nothing of course is economic. But it is more deeply also existential. The erosion of biodiversity threatens species' life, including that of *Homo sapiens*. This is neither something being done *to* humans nor just a case of humans killing nature. The very biosystem that enables much of planetary life is being undermined. There are temperature parameters within which our planetary existence has been made possible (Chakrabarty 2009: 218). These are now being undermined at the upper limit. Bees, butterflies, and small flies pollinate most plant and food seeds. All are showing signs of significant depletion resulting from pesticide use, increase in invasive species, and rising temperatures.

If dread mostly represents a politics of despair, an antidote is neither denial nor distraction – after all, similar psychic reactions – but digging in at all scales to counter the direction of demise. This is both a top-down and bottom-up struggle, sometimes pulling in different directions. Youth and millennials, of necessity, are leading the charge. They are, increasingly, not white. It is their lives, after all, which most certainly will be – already are being – disrupted, foreshortened, subject to food insecurity and asphyxiating premature death. The racially impactful foreshortening of life is the very definition of racism, as Ruth Wilson Gilmore (2007) compellingly characterizes it.

To say we are doomed, as a growing number now do (Thacker 2015), is to give in to this dread. Greek Cynics advocated ascetic commitment to forgo wealth and worldly comforts while living at one with nature. Philosophically cousins of skepticism, Cynics were deeply doubtful of human and moral goodness. Cynicism subsequently has come to express abiding disenchantment, dread perhaps its preface, a stepping-stone. Anticipated doom is the dread of foreclosure, ultimately of annihilation. The Venezuelan thrash metal band Stormthrash broadcast this sensibility in their 2017 album *Systematic Annihilation*, with songs like "Dark Days," "Life of

Suffering," "The End is Imminent," and "Don't Learn to be a Corpse."

The driving responses are, again, overwhelmingly bivalent. A recuperation of Malthusianism is festering, waiting to explode. The racial casuistry rationalizes that a significant cause of planetary threat is overpopulation. The deaths from global warming, chillingly on this account, will "naturally" cull the population to a planetarily manageable proportion. Those more readily left to the racially eliminationist culling machine, history has taught us, will be the most vulnerable, those historically racially identified as poorer and not white. COVID-19 serves as a prelude.

Ecofascism projects the most extreme eliminationist version. Proponents advocate for a white ethnostate, a racially homogeneous, ecologically pristine and pure set-aside for an "ecofascist order." The commitment is to help along the culling, to advance elimination by wiping out, sending away, or preventing the immigration of the racially "unbelonging," the stranger within or trying to enter. Ecofascists are wedded to what they insist is *their* national land, decrying the spoiling of the national natural beauty by industrialization, the built urban environment, the unwelcome. Green here is bleached white, soaked in the red blood of others. Blood and soil, race and nature: the battle cry of the ecofascists.

Dread, then, emerges out of some of the conditions and politics it helps to reinforce. Ecofascist groups like "Northwestern Front," active in the Pacific Northwest, may be politically marginal but seed such ideas for mainstream politicians. While President, Trump spoke metaphorically of plastic dumped in the Pacific by Asian nations floating towards America to pollute the homeland landscape, and by implication Asian migration the body politic. Marine Le Pen castigated "nomadic migrants" for not caring about the national (French) environment. Dread is an affect of apprehension, a bracing for the worst. A pessimism less of intellect than of predisposition, the apprehension nevertheless freezes feet in place.

The compelling counter is being led by the courageous activism of mostly young women across all continents and many countries, caring deeply about life. They are working to transform relationally local and global comprehension, commitments, and practices. Dominant capitalist practice seeks to amortize consumption goods, literally to bury them once their depreciated value has expired and can no longer be written off. By contrast, castaways are being repurposed to repair and sustain ecologies of life, long a tradition of postcolonized societies (Mbembe 2017). Decarbonized energy sources are being developed and deployed, if too slowly replacing those dominantly relied upon today. The city of Seoul's quite comprehensive composting from food waste and local eco-food growth programs exemplify what can be done at scale when citizens non-exclusionarily take the lead.

Underpinning the activism is an emerging theoretical articulation now best known as "degrowth." Ecological economist Giorgos Kallis is a leading proponent, far more insightful and nuanced than the too easily dismissed clichéd characterization. Perpetual economic growth at 2 to 3 percent annually, Kallis argues, is no longer environmentally feasible. (Contending economists suggest that low growth is a predictable function of historically successful economies with now aging workforces.) Economic growth through endless cycles of increasing production and consumption, degrowthers insist, entails a spiraling tax on the environment. Unlimited GDP growth is tightly related to economic dominance of nature, and in the past 150 years with compounded carbon emissions. The politically challenging undertaking of divesting from dirty industries means balancing carbon-free energy sources at comparable cost and efficiency to current sources, maintaining stability with reasonable if lower levels of prosperity, while ensuring significantly less inequality (Kallis 2018; Kallis et al., 2020).

If ecofascists purport to protect the nature of the "homeland" to save those they take to be their ethnonationally own, "degrowthers" seek to scale back sufficiently to save all. Where the former tend to be narrow-minded, ethnonationally insular, and dispositionally violent, the latter have a planetary vision and aspiration. Environmental protections within borders alone will have relatively little internal climatic impact, given the globally relational quality of climate. Under neoliberalism, there has been a steady shift from governments to billionaires funding the solutions to pressing social problems. Unsuccessful US 2020 Democratic presidential candidates Tom Steyer and Michael Bloomberg have both contributed significantly to addressing climate change. Swiss billionaire Hansjorg Wyss is spending close to $1.5 billion to this end too. Recently, Amazon founder Jeff Bezos pledged $10 billion. They recognize the necessity of a healthy planet to both wellbeing and wealth. Yet the neoliberal stress on individuated wealth has come at significant cost to the commons and the conditions of collective response to global challenges. COVID-19 has proved the point.

Eco-rightsizing entails a smaller, slower, more equitable steady-state economic environment both locally and globally planned (Klein 2011) through low-carbon green technologies and reduced environmental impact. The decelerated carbon emissions necessary for degrowth are revealed, if all too temporarily, by the precipitous drop resulting from the sudden COVID-19 economic slowdown. Shrinking the "Great Acceleration" necessitates carefully targeted, coordinated, and sustained degrowth of carbon-impactful sources, technologies, and products alongside alternative energy sources such as locally networked solar micro-grids. Kallis stresses the immediate need for creative and resourceful ways collectively to consume less while promoting equitably living well. How are habits to alter to ensure all are reasonably fed and hydrated? Our collective challenge, then, is livability: how to remake a planetary commons (cf. Chakrabarty 2015), loco- and cosmopolitically, inhabitable by kids and koalas co-constitutively?

*

Calling climate change a "hyperobject," as Timothy Morton (2013) has done, tends to objectify and singularize it, setting it apart from its co-constitution through the sorts of lived processes, relations, and interactions characterized above. Climate change is not so much a hyperobject as heightened – hyper – conditions, actions, processes, and experiences the interaction between which intensifies and magnifies each element. Out of these intensifications and interactions perhaps an analytic "hyperobject" – the ecoform – emerges, taking on a life of its own. Notions like this, then, serve at best as shorthand for the relational interactivities and their effects, not a "thing" or even "event" as such but the eco-transforming processes for which they stand.

Dread fills the gap between being driven by outrage to do something, do anything – as Günter Grass's (1965) poem famously remarked half-skeptically in the mid-1960s – to address the condition and being at a complete loss about where to begin. It seeps in where one has no account, or no adequate one, of what uncannily is prompting the anxiety. Dread balloons without a compelling theory of the background or underlying conditions, the prodding concerns in turn running rampant. Dread expresses a sense of hopelessness. It fills the deepening chasm between obliviousness to the conditions of destruction, a carrying on in denial as if the problem is others' misinformation, and the commitment to start where one is to address what one can of the challenges in whatever constructive ways reasonably possible. The pollution at issue is ecological through and through, as much about the framing of information as it is environmental.

Dread fills the nebulous gap between the inability to put our finger on the problem and the evident inadequacy of any proposed or activated response. It is the sense of being overwhelmed, of not knowing where to turn between the bad faith of obliviousness and the inability to see or accept that even the smallest individuated if not collectively coordinated efforts and contributions, multiplied across many, add up. It incessantly delays closing the gap between denying responsibility and weighing up anything resembling adequate responses.

None alone could bring about these outsized ecoformational effects, which nevertheless could not happen without cumulative individual effort. So too with the emergency redirection necessary. Free riding is transforming from an abstract technical quandary for professional philosophy into a collective suicide march. The grotesquerie at work does not just concern the impact of effects from microform action and inaction but also exercises a power which, but for the magnifying collective outcome, no one has a warrant to authorize. Slow violence has exploded into a rapidly foreshortening demise.

Acting in calculated collaboration may be infinitely more difficult, as the all too partial Paris Climate Accords bear out. The scale of the challenges of "deep adaptation" (Bendell 2018) calls for efforts to face down the feet-dragging skeptics. But if there is any chance of reversing the destruction collectively wrought, it also requires adding all shoulders to the wheel of this daunting task. The politics in play cannot just be locally environmental. It is the very ecoforming fabric that is in question.

*

Climatically driven processes are destroying habitats. They are adding surges and unseasonal shifts in "zoetic" climate migrations. The magnitude of refugee and migrant circulations and social incorporation renews questions of social unsettlement and dread-inducing despair. These questions are threaded with those of heterogeneity and hospitality, ecoforming and eco-transforming dis-ease, civil wars within and across borders. As these contrasting responses reveal, the pressing question is whether to return, as a result, to an emptied-out future of social separation. Or whether to remake and repair the world in-common – as a commons – with compelling lessons drawn from the dark side of the looking glass.

7

Civil War

We inhabit an Age of Dread. It is not that of 1918. Nor 1929 and the early years of the 1930s. It is not just the repressions identified with the 1950s. Nor, again, 1968, which countered repression, war, and death with aspiration and hopefulness, if often readily dashed. Today we find elements of all these periods rolled into one. And then some.

The operative conditions interacting to produce a generalized social condition of dread have thickened the fog engulfing us. These operators have each worked to unsettle domains of social life and relation. They have prompted feelings of unease and anxiety more or less manageable where the pressures are discrete. Where they interface, the social anguish intensifies, the fog thickens. Interactively, these operative drivers magnify the social disruption and multiply the unsettling impacts and sensibilities. The feeling of anomie, loss of a map and often direction, confusing control for power, become overwhelming.

Dread's dynamic operators include not just the technological revolution, Bernard Stiegler's (2019) computational capitalism, altering so much of how we engage with each other. Modes of work and consumption have shifted, relationship making and managing becoming more challenging; even memory and temporality are transformed. The familiar has been made strange, disenchanting all aspects of the social, seemingly rendering the settled more uncertain, the controllable more out of our hands. Social and political control, once targeted overwhelmingly at the bodily, has been supplemented, initially by surveillance and self-checking and now increasingly by tracking. Tracking-capitalism is in the process of being instituted as the driving political economy, the resulting technopticon its mode of social control and raison d'état for these times.

As production is being automated step by step, consumption is driven by preference-defining algorithms. Human labor is steered increasingly to servicing, where labor time and conduct are tracked too. Tracking tightens control, camouflaged behind a veneer of self-determination and expressed personal preference. It has enabled sovereign authority to veer towards the authoritarian, with disclosure transformed to closure, practices veiled to the point of invisibility, and democracy increasingly hollowed out. The neoliberalization dominating the past fifty years is transforming into digitally enabled and enhanced "neuroliberalization" (Thaler and Sunstein 2008; Whitehead 2020). Just as architecture shapes our experience of space and place, the technological design and architecture of tracking are shaping "our" preference schemes, ordering and reinforcing choices economically, politically, and culturally, as if solely our own.

Tracking-capitalism offers an affectation of certainty in the face of dis-ease. It gestures at securitization in a time when existential threat has deepened, becoming less easily deniable. Tracking-capitalism increasingly took hold as worries about the impacts of climate change became evident but could still be repressed, dismissed, or proclaimed manageable. The Virus rendered the worries irrepressible, immediately coming atop the surging hurricane and fire seasons of late 2019, continuously

soaring global temperatures, growing economic migrations, and war-dislocated refugees. Labor migrants are
considered temporarily necessary in wealthier countries with aging populations. Climate and war refugees
nevertheless are deemed economic and social burdens.
They are marked as monstrous, identified with the troubled conditions causing them to flee their homelands
(Baldwin 2017), closed down by COVID.

Tracking stands today for social inscrutability in the
name of transparency. It is accompanied by proliferated
paranoia, unsafety, and the spreading of anxiety in the
service of the techno-logics of securitization. Tracking
operates as an insurance policy to address the human
carnage in the wake of globalizing neoliberalization,
the securitizing clean-up act. The capacity to know (or
pretend to know) where everyone is, who is interacting
with and doing what to whom, the traceability – at least
in principle – of all and everything has offered comfort,
if colder than expected. Tracking fills in quietly where
politicians fear to tread volubly.

Facilitated by the intrusive pace of digital development, these transformations have been hastened along
first by climate change and at present by the pandemic
experience. We will live and love, interact and intercourse, create and consume, socialize and politicize
significantly differently tomorrow than we did a few
yesterdays ago. In the year before COVID-19, international airports in China had introduced thermal imaging
technology to auto-screen temperatures of all arriving
travelers. In the Year of the Virus, Amazon warehouses
quickly shifted from staff greeting workers with temperature guns at the outset of their shifts to thermal
imaging auto-measurement.

With the Technological Turn over the past three
decades, economic inequality has been promoted as
the product of unlimited opportunity. Social freedoms
have been eroded in the name of liberty. Political par-

ticipation through voting, speech, and protest has been undercut as the expression of democracy. Safety has been threatened for the sake of security. It's as if we have nothing left to dread surrendering but the resultant dread itself. Dread hides the repressible, the uncomfortable, from (self-)view. It seemingly has made more palatable alienation of the strange, while rendering the strange less threatening, apparently more under control. Dread masks the seeping anonymity of evil.

*

Génération Identitaire (GI) is a French millennial youth organization initiated in 2012. It grew out of a larger political group, *Les Identitaires*. *GI* shares with its parent organization the drive "to protect" European identity as white and Christian, implicitly Catholic, targeting especially Islam and migration as twin threats. Both organizations feed the homeless, but only those identified, racially, as European and, religiously, as Christian. The youth group is more vehement, strident, and disposed to violence than its parent organization. *GI* partner groups have developed in Britain, Italy, Germany, and Austria, with smaller offshoots across central Europe.

In 2017, *GI* issued a public "Declaration of War." The Declaration is paranoid, explicitly racist, dismissively traditionalist, authoritarian. The video statement, the English version of which was removed by YouTube for "violating its terms of service," is pan-Europeanist (a re-uploaded French video in 2020 with English subtitles remains available):

> We are *Génération Identitaire*. We are the generation that get killed for glancing at the wrong person, for refusing someone a cigarette, or having an "attitude" that annoys someone. We are the generation of ethnic fracture, total failure of coexistence, and forced mixing

of the races. We are the generation doubly punished: forced to pay into a social system so generous with strangers it becomes unsustainable for our own people. Our generation are the victims and the May '68'ers who wanted to liberate themselves from tradition, from knowledge and authority in education. But they only accomplished to liberate themselves from their responsibilities. We reject your history books to re-gather our memories. We no longer believe that "Khader" could ever be our brother, we have stopped believing in a "Global Village" or the "Family of Man." We have discovered that we have roots, ancestry, and therefore a future. Our heritage is our land, our blood, our identity. We are the heirs to our own future. We turned off the tv to march in the streets. We painted slogans on the walls, cried through loudspeakers for "youth in power" and flew our Lambda flags high. The Lambda, painted on proud Spartans' shields, is our symbol. Don't you understand what this means? We will not back down, we will not give in. We are sick and tired of your cowardice. You are from the years of post-war prosperity, retirement benefits, S.O.S. Racism, "diversity," sexual liberation and a bag of rice from Bernard Kouchner [co-founder of *Médecins Sans Frontières*]. We are 25 percent unemployment, social debt, multicultural collapse, and an explosion of anti-white racism. We are broken families, and young French soldiers dying in Afghanistan. You won't buy us with a condescending look, a state paid job of misery and a pat on the shoulder. We don't need youth policies. Youth *is* our policy. Don't think this is simply a manifesto. It is a declaration of war. You are of yesterday, we are of tomorrow. We are *Génération Identitaire*. (*Génération Identitaire* 2020)

The declaration is dramatic by design, unapologetically suggesting violence. It chains together a sense of generational alienation, class dismissal, economic failure, and paternalism with bald nationalistic racism, Islamophobia, and strident identitarianism. The declaration of war is against what *GI* sees as the socialist political tradition within France and the threat of migratory invasion to national identity from without. The symbol of Lambda is adopted to signal the fight against Muslim invasion. It represents a commemoration of the Battle of Thermopylae (480 BCE, well before Islam, or Europe, for that matter), in which the Greek city states successfully allied to resist Persian invasion. *GI* accordingly connects its movement to the mythical creation of a European tradition more broadly. It self-consciously inhabits and redirects the street tactics of its "leftist" opponents, much as the insurgent right almost everywhere has done since the 1980s. It refashions a political temporality by wedding a nostalgic, retrospective reclamation project with a vanguardist cultural futurism in the Euro-fascist tradition.

Across Europe, the reach for fascism has become noisier, more belligerent. In Germany, ecofascism pulls for environmentally friendly policies but in the name of the sanctity of the father*land*, of reclaiming the unpolluted purity of the soil as national treasure. Here, the imperative is to preserve the land itself, the Heideggerian home (*Heimat*) of the body politic. These are views promoted by a new publication, *Die Kehre* (Magazine for the Protection of Nature), produced by a member of Germany's Identitarian movement and politically supported by the far-right party *Alternative für Deutschland* (Göpffarth 2020). The homeland is to be guarded against foreign invasion, considered to carry infectants, the bearers of foreign culture and religion, dis-ease, germs, vermin, and pollutants.

In the United States a comparable surge was exemplified by the forces elevating Trump to the White House in 2016, which his presidency subsequently unleashed nationally and fueled globally. The violent invasions of

Berkeley in 2017 and Charlottesville in 2018 under the banner of resisting "the Great Replacement" (a notion pointedly inherited from the French far right) by the ethnoracially "non-belonging" exemplifies the surge. Performative resistance to enforced COVID lockdowns dramatized the politics.

In May 2020, in the midst of the pandemic, tensions visibly erupted at the Michigan state legislature. The state of Michigan at the time ranked high in the national number of viral cases and deaths. It had played a key role in Trump's 2016 election victory. The more recently elected Governor, a Democrat, imposed strong stay-at-home measures to combat viral spread. The day the Legislature gathered in session to consider extending these measures, white armed militia in combat gear and very visibly bearing high-powered semi-automatic firearms forced their way into the Capitol building to protest what they characterized as "tyranny." Mostly unmasked and from rural Michigan or out of state, some screamed in the face of state police assembled to prevent them from entering the legislative chambers. Democratic lawmakers, including Sarah Anthony, a black woman, donned bullet-proof vests in fear for their lives.

Days later, Rep. Anthony was accompanied to another legislative session by a half-dozen masked, legally armed black volunteers who had co-organized to ensure her wellbeing. The protesting militia had been provocatively intimidating, visibly spewing spit in the faces of police lined up to prevent the protestors from advancing. The volunteer group, recalling Black Panther leaders on the Sacramento steps of California's Capitol in May 1967, were purposeful, quiet, peaceful. The white militia was secretly formed and funded by well-heeled Republican operatives. They threatened to impose their way through violent intimidation. The small black group, by contrast, was self-organized and self-funded, respectful if overtly signaling self-defense. Black gun rights self-defense groups have sprung up nationally. Legislator Anthony's safety detail and the black gun owner groups are exercising *armed civic non-violence*. Call this a newly proposed political concept for these times.

Donald Trump held his first political rally in Tulsa after the pandemic lockdown was initially lifted, site of the 1919 riotous razing of Black Wall Street and massacre of its residents. A thousand black gun owners proposed marching in Tulsa on Trump's rally day to signal that blacks were armed to defend themselves if attacked by white supremacists who supported him as their presidential surrogate. A week later, an unarmed racially mixed civil rights group marched through an upscale residential street in St. Louis en route to protest the Mayor at home. They were threatened by a white couple, both tort lawyers owning a mansion on the block. The couple aimed a semi-automatic rifle and handgun at the passing parade.

The contrasts between the groups are emblematic of the broader social conflict currently ripping apart social worlds. Before the pandemic, the set of social conflicts was shaping up broadly around climate concerns and immigration, health care and freedom of expression, underpinned by spiraling inequality. In the wake of the pandemic, these concerns have been revealed in sharper, more magnified, relief. The abilities to work, to play, to travel, to gather, to pray or party together have become contesting concerns of liberty and rights, health and safety. Who are defined as essential and non-essential workers? Which are essential or non-essential activities? Who wields class power? Who has social standing? Who defines and controls public and private space? Whose interests does the state serve? All is being remade, in short, as matters of life and death.

The Michigan and St. Louis events signaled a deeper

unsettlement, less an outburst than a blowup in waiting. As the pandemic lockdown was beginning to lift, if not fray at the edges, an explosive video rocked the world. In Minneapolis in late May 2020, George Floyd was an unarmed man suspected of passing a forged $20 bill at a local grocery store. He took his last breath with a white police officer's knee callously bearing down his full weight on Mr. Floyd's neck for nearly nine minutes. Like Eric Garner in New York in July 2014, Floyd repeatedly gasped to the officer that he couldn't breathe. Two other police officers held down his body, another keeping away protesting witnesses urging the cop to let up. A seventeen-year-old black girl caught the death on her smart phone camera. It immediately went viral. All four officers were fired within hours. Following three angry nights of the fire *this* time in Minneapolis, Derek Chauvin, the police officer who so casually throttled Floyd with his knee, was charged first with third-degree murder and manslaughter. Upon review, Chauvin's charges were upped to second-degree murder. Indictments were added for the three additional officers.

These events came in the immediate wake of two other cold-blooded killings of unarmed young African-Americans. Breonna Taylor was an emergency medical first responder. She was summarily shot dead at home in March 2020 when police forces in Lexington, Kentucky, conducting a mistaken address "no-knock" drug-enforcement exercise burst into her apartment without warning. The second case of concern was the bumpy prosecution of the Ahmaud Arbery case. A young black man jogging one afternoon in February 2020 in a Georgia suburb, Arbery was pursued and accosted by white neighborhood vigilantes, a retired law enforcement officer and his son. He was shot dead by the father when Mr. Arbery, in desperate self-defense, tried wrestling a rifle away from the son.

The day following viral circulation of the George Floyd murder, the country erupted. Protests in solidarity with black lives and against racism and police brutality followed in cities around the world.

*

Politics today has become nothing short of civil war.

Wars over resources and power differ from wars about forms of life. Many wars of course involve an interactive dynamic about both. Civil wars tend to be thought of generally as internal to states. They combine the drive to exercise control over resources and how to be in the world. And yet, like climate change and viral pandemics, civil wars don't simply stop at the border, as Hannah Arendt (1966–7/2017) recognized. Civil war has morphed from the politics of extreme exception or occasional outburst to that of the commonplace, virtually the everyday. It is the point at which politics and war are indistinguishable, a generalized combative enmitification (Mbembe 2016). There is a reason that the notion is now so readily invoked, even by elected politicians, as much to characterize political and economic polarization as cultural or ideological tensions. Civil war is no longer the end of politics but its normalized expression.

A National Rifle Association commercial in 2017 declared, "The only way we stop this, the only way we save our country and our freedom, is to fight this violence of lies with the clenched fist of truth" (Beauchamp 2017). The self-serving power of truth-fashioning requires armed compulsions to make the doubting believe. The armed invasion of Michigan's Capitol three years later was a direct effect of this sort of call to arms. As resistance to COVID closures spread in the United States, the husband of the NC (North Carolina) Reopen leader, a Marine Corp veteran, posted a live Facebook recording. "I am willing to kill," he declared, to end "the New World Order" promoting lockdowns and stay-at-home orders. In 2019, a Georgetown University poll concluded that two-thirds of Americans are at "the edge of civil war." And in the lead-up to his impeachment that year Trump declared, without irony, that his congressional persecution was creating a Civil War-like rift that would permanently scar the country.

Trump's declaration signaled not just his but his die-hard supporters' commitments. Following his re-election loss in November 2020 and his numerous failures to reverse the outcome in state and federal courts, his most rabid white supremacist and Christian identity fans stormed the Capitol on January 6, 2021, as a joint session of Congress was seeking to certify the electoral victory of Joe Biden as the 46th President of the United States. The building and its House and Senate chambers were breached, some leaders' offices mildly ransacked, and a handful of lives lost before the insurgents retreated. The sound of civil war reverberated from the Capitol across the country, and the world.

These examples all suggest that civil war is no longer just the fight of an insurrectionary group against a government found to be repressive. It is now invoked also to signal an intensifying battle between private groups, whether over the state and representation each would prefer or over the form of national culture. An example of the latter includes the call by groups like the English Defence League for a European "Counter-Jihad" against perceived "Islamification" of Britain and Europe (Meleagrou-Hitchens and Brun 2013). If there is anything that "unites" Europe, keeping out its "constitutive outsiders" continues to offer the fuel it did with modern European self-coherence circa 1500. Marine Le Pen accordingly characterized the 2017 French presidential election she ended up losing to Emmanuel Macron as "the choice about civilization."

The sensibility sewing together Christianity, culture, social self-containment, and armed self-defense takes on a hue of beleaguered whiteness. One Nevada assemblywoman – an elected official, after all – sent out a Christmas card of her family standing in casually innocent holiday attire, parents, children, and grandchildren all bearing high-powered firearms (Berardi 2016). They were signaling, in the name of a muscular Christianity, that they are armed to take law into their own hands to defend against perceived lawlessness. In announcing the bombing of a Syrian air force base in the wake of a chemical attack by Syria's Assad, Donald Trump did so explicitly in the name of "calling on all civilized nations" of the world, in short, those rejecting "Islamification." The culture wars of the 1980s, followed by the attacks on multiculturalisms across the next two decades, have taken on civil warring declarations today.

The driving question, then, is no longer so much whether this conflict or that is a civil war (Armitage 2017) but what work the notion of "civil war" is being politically invoked to do. States descend into civil wars when contrasting conceptions of life within them are deemed irreconcilable. Living for a considerable proportion of the state's inhabitants is made unbearable. Those at least nominally controlling the state apparatus insist on obedience and deference to its way of being, on pain of erasure for refusal or resistance. Civil wars are struggles over contesting ways of being in the world. They are struggles over their underlying conceptions, and over exercising or extending control of the state and its apparatuses to materialize and advance these commitments.

At the outset and in the end, civil wars are not foremost about resorting to arms, even as they may quickly gear up to blows. For the struggle to be deemed blowworthy, the contrast must be considered palpable and pressing. Civil war now has taken on something like the generalized expression of the unsettled, contesting not so much political or social ideas but the form the political and social themselves should take. It manifests as forced appeals to a contrasting set of commitments. These oppositional contrasts include appeals to the command of authority against accountability vested in constitutionality. The claims are embedded in a broader set of assumptions about "worldliness," expressed as a narrowed, inward-looking hypernationalism pushing against a planetary – global or transnational – humanism (Gilroy 2019) or cosmopolitanism. The tensions are played out as commitment to the homogeneities of fixed – "given" – identities while refusing the messy heterogeneities of relational, co-making *trans*formations. They materialize in solipsistic, self-interested, assertive, and often violent expressions of power over and against the reach for dignified, respectful, celebrated co-habitation by and among the heterogeneous. The St. Louis stand-off offers a microcosmic image. The bald contrast is between two ways of being: demanding conversion to one's singular way of being, doing, and living, on pain ultimately of excommunication or death if resisting, on one side; and co-habiting – whether itchily, indifferently, or intoxicatingly – with dissimilitude, divergence, and distinction, on the other.

There are underlying values in contestation too. Fabulation, fabrication, and make-believe are thrown in the face of evidence and science. Conspiracy theories like those of QAnon and Infowars are licentiously circulated. Self-promoting fictions are virally promoted in the face of facts. Insistence on the comforts of homogenizing sameness is mobilized against projections of discomforting challenges from heterogeneous difference. Securitizing states are structured to lock out and lock up, undercutting the possibility of advancing the interests of the commons. A nostalgic politics of the dreaded loss of a fantasized past, in summary, faces off against the dread of foreclosed possibilities of futures lived in common.

Force is always at work in these contestations. But it is invariably one-sided, in a doubled sense. One-sided in forcing one's commitments onto those uninterested in (even indifferent to), disagreeing with, and especially resisting them. But one-sided in the even more pressed sense that the force is almost invariably the product of the homogenizing commitment. It is the inevitable effect of the fixation on curtailed homogeneity (on authority, command, contempt, fixity), and on its conditions of reproduction. Where heterogeneity flourishes if left to its own powers, homogeneity is inevitably an imposition, as much epistemologically as politically, requiring always repression and sustained effort to establish and sustain.

The struggle, in short, comes down to that between manipulated control, at any and all cost, and co-constitutive, interactive engagement. Civil struggles that blow up into full-fledged wars (whether conceptually, materially, culturally, or politico-economically) require of people to declare their commitments. We are encouraged, if not forced, to take sides. This is demanded of both social members and distant observers. Neutrality in the face of impending death and destruction in the final analysis is itself side-taking. This extended sense of civil war is less one segment of society at increasingly dissonant odds with another. It is the society as such at war with itself, an allergic condition of civil society eating at itself from the inside out. COVID-19 is perhaps the perfect metaphor: the immune system attacks itself, fueling its own atrophy. Immunological interventions are just more grist for the mill, feeding the disinformation machine of the alien within devouring the body (politic) (Virilio 1983/2008).

*

It should be obvious that race-making shapes all the driving modes of civil warring constituting modern polities today. Race-making helps both to shape and to sharpen them. It reflects and animates, at least partly constitutes and exacerbates these conditions. Race is extended to all those taken not to belong, to sully or soil the projected purity of national belonging. Today those will be marked as "minorities," who are identified with accountability, responsibility, respect, and dignity for all; with the transnational and transitive; with heterogeneities, co-habitation and co-composed futures, fairness and equality – in short, with a robust commons. *They* will be equated with (if not straightforwardly as) the (ethno)racially marked alien. They will be taken to be aligned with or maligned as the (ethno)racially distinct, equated with or as the non-belonging, the not-white. "If you don't like it here, if you have nothing but criticisms, you can go back to where you came from." Even wayward supporters, those otherwise presumed white, will be treated by equation with the less than.

Race, then, is the cement in the architecture of modern sociality. It is a prompt and product of social warring, its medium and outcome. It is a deeply relational condition: racism – and the racial configurations to which racisms give rise – anywhere is sustained and sustainable only by racisms elsewhere. It is violence in the waiting, in the making, offense and defense, embodied and enacted.

It is telling that J.M. Coetzee's observation about late apartheid South Africa applies so generally today:

> South Africa is not formally in a state of war, but it might as well be. As resistance has grown, the rule of law step by step has been suspended. The police and the people who run the police (as hunters run packs of dogs) are by now more or less unconstrained. In the guise of news, radio and television relay the official lies. Yet over the whole sorry, murderous show there hangs an air of staleness. The old rallying cries – *Uphold white Christian*

civilization! Honour the sacrifices of the forefathers! – lack all force. We, or they, or we and they both, have moved into the endgame, and everyone knows it.

   Yet while the chess players manoeuvre for advantage, human lives are still being consumed – consumed and shat out. As it is the fate of some generations to be destroyed by war, so it seems the fate of the present one to be ground down by politics. (Coetzee 2009: 12)

It is telling, because after apartheid formally came to a close ("racism's last word," Derrida [1985] famously characterized it), the struggle to establish and maintain social "purity" and the "segregations" Lacan recognized as underpinning all racisms (Khan 2018) has continued to proliferate and morph.

A civil war, then, immediately draws a sharp line. The shifting conflict line in the dust-up. On one side: those committing to the state or status quo, of law and order or established arrangements, no matter how forced and unjust. On the other: those for whom the powers and social arrangements the state or status quo represents fall critically short and in defense of which the enforcing power resorts to repressive violence. Those outside the territorial border, those marked for and by preclusion, more often than not are those characterized as unbelonging and undeserving. They will be cast out as outsiders within. They are politically "tarred" with the brush of racial differentiation.

Anti-Semitic, anti-Black, and Islamophobic attacks have proliferated throughout Europe, connected to similar surges in the United States. As noted in Chapter 3, in 2018, Poland outlawed any claim it was complicit in producing the Holocaust. Use of "Polish death camps" to refer to Holocaust concentration camps may now be punished by up to three years in prison. A Polish nationalist newspaper published a front-page article on "how to recognize a Jew" – by names, character traits, behavior, and so on. Until a public and international outcry led to its removal, that newspaper issue was on sale in parliamentary building kiosks.

During pandemic restrictions, contentious debate cut like a knife across German media outlets. Mainstream advocates castigated any critical comparison of the Holocaust with other wrenching historical wrongs, colonial or postcolonial, and insisted on the impropriety of any comparison with Israel's contemporary treatment of Palestinians. A year earlier, numerous rabbis teaching at an Israeli pre-military preparation yeshiva (academy) caused an uproar by lauding Hitler to their students. All the "stupid and violent non-Jews," they exhorted, clearly intending Palestinians, "want to be enslaved" by the "genetically superior" Jews. As a "superior race," Jews were obliged to "help those inferior." One of the rabbis explicitly embraced being "racist" and "believing in racism" (Pileggi 2019). The German debate conveniently ignored any condemnation of the Israeli rabbis' casuistry at a state-funded academy, despite swift Israeli criticism of them. Dominant German media were more concerned to reinforce the prevailing vector invoked to discredit German dissidents critical both of Germany's own racisms and Israeli repression today.

*

Modes of racial delineation apply equally to political tensions about immigration and to the technologies of bordering. In Europe, these racial extensions reach across the lines of the historical and contemporary: Muslims, Arabs, Blacks, Jews, Roma, the Indigenous, Asians and South Asians. The line marking insiders as not fully belonging is inscribed in differentiations of "blood," bones, and behavior, culture and character, projected incapacity and presupposed lack of intelligence. The preclusions are enacted in the name of fabricating and maintaining homogeneity, of power in the name of projected purity, in the face of their dreaded undoing. But the maintenance – first of the fantasy of differentiated being and maintenance of purity and capacity, and then of their enactment – is possible only by the compulsions of make-believe. This conservation requires forced constraint of thought and deed, of compelled movement and systematic confining enclosure. (Temporary encampments – over 400 migrant camps today dotted across Europe, for instance – perhaps uneasily collapse the two.) It forecloses possibilities of ways of being, thought, political and cultural expression.

The racially self-empowered and self-entitled – dominantly characterized in terms of whiteness – operate constitutively in terms of offense. They do so in the sense of being offensive, of claiming to be offended ("I am the least racist person in the room"), and being unqualifiedly, limitlessly, on the offense. They do so even if today so often in denial, in claiming or feigning ignorance: "We didn't know," or, increasingly, stressing "unconscious" or "implicit bias." If hidden even from ourselves, then how can we be responsible for the offensive or, worse yet, psychically or physically violent expression. This is the condition of militarizing the racial (Goldberg 2016), of race as weapon: no backing down; taking no prisoners. Race is weaponized while scrubbing the terms of explicitly racial characterization so there is nothing for critics to point to. The smoking gun is always camouflaged in the paper bag of claimed racial ignorance.

This forced preservation of racial entitlement has necessitated technological enablement. The border – once a line in the sand made cartographic, then requiring barbed wire – today resurrects the border wall. As a politics, the wall – the political wall – invariably requires more than cement to maintain its political aims. It always requires, in ever-enlarging ways, supplementation: more wall (higher, longer, wider, deeper); surveillance and policing whether human or technological; oversight and sensor enhancement. A more cemented politics. Political walls are extended, irresolute technologies of civil warring, not their resolution. They are in fact a land grab. A form of imperial state imposition, they colonize not just the land on which they are erected, nor only the land on either side or at either end. They are in effect colonizations of the landscape. They order the contours of the visible, of the lived, of ontic community and the denials marking its way of life. Fortress Europe. Walled America. Moated Australia.

Political walls are racial by conception, design, and implementation. In being about "the lives of others," they are inevitably about ourselves too. The homogenizing intended through political walling is purchased at the cost of lives interrupted and disrupted. Prisons are technologies of walling that embody political practices of disabling, delimiting life's possibilities, and premature death. The racially assigned are those restricted to inescapable racial prospects by those having the power to take themselves to be racially neutral, racially transparent, even a-racial. The explicitly racially assigned are destined on a map of life to existential curtailment in what can be thought, pursued, done, and achieved. It is a map from birth through racial delineation to diseducation, unwork, healthlessness, and the walls of incarceration. Blackness in the reproduced worlds of racist ascription is projected to represent for all the lesson of futureless futures.

Futureless futures are hopeless futures, those slipping from view and not just from grip. The sort of future being left to our children and theirs. The likelihood is approaching of heat domes, uninhabitable areas the soaring temperatures in which will make impossible most life there. Those who can afford it, by contrast, will buy into breathable domes, the next iterations of "biospheres." Given current climatic directions, these biosphere 3.0 or 4.0s will constitute the next generations of hyper-gated communities. These are futures with no common forward-looking capacity because we have thoughtlessly destroyed its conditions of possibility. A future in time with no future in prospect.

As technologies of control, tracking offers longer-term possibilities of virtualizing walls. Techno-tracking enables grid-like criss-crossings of territory. It effectively fashions a different way of thinking about territorial oversight and sensoring. Less the mode of keeping the door locked so much as absolutizing the pervasive monitoring of movement anywhere and everywhere, inside or out, into and out of structures, across landscapes of motion and stasis. Tracking is the drone technology of monitoring made ubiquitous, without the give-away buzz. It is more intrusive but less obvious. Its techno-capillary patterning across the entire map of mobile life provides an info-relay visible only to the monitors. In accepting the cookies in order to nibble at the crumbs the info-collectors throw at us with each incursion into our device-lives, we each reveal our interiorities inductively and probabilistically to those monitoring and their partners, corporate or political. The technologists accordingly brag that they know more about us than we know ourselves. Repressing one's innermost feelings, desires, interests, or concerns no longer suffices to deny one's pending intention, expression, or culpability.

That the operating system of the digital is technologically neutral does not entail that its operating logic or outcomes are too. Indeed, the powerful and monied have their prejudices, leanings, interests, and commitments sewn explicitly or implicitly into the code. In this, digital syntax is no different from natural language. It has its own version of "the Queen's English."

Racial consideration is at work here definitively. Race provides the brush painting the line between the belonging and the unbelonging, the trusted and untrusted. It textures those very characterizations. Racial characterization color-codes the constitutively belonging from the unbelonging. It will translate into the racial coding of info-feeds too, just as voice, gesture, patterns of speech-making, or names and their spelling have tended to. It baptizes the (legitimately) born within from the invaders, the pure from the polluting, the nominally trusted from the projected threat.

For racial states, enemies, like poverty, are always racially defined. Poverty may be as much a profiling of thinking and behavior as of pecuniary wealth. The racial poor are charged as a tax on the better off. They are deemed an eyesore, threatening illness, requiring resources. Enmity is inscribed in – and onto – the racially conceived. The architecture of walling and technology of tracking accordingly are mutually reinforcing, racially composed technologies of circumscription and excision. Those conceived and constituted as racial enemies have always been subjected to surveillance, as Simone Browne (2015) has shown, from slavery to indenture, ghettoization to concentration, incarceration to technologies of identification.

Tracking now offers the possibility of individuating what historically has been group-fashioned, extending the logic of the watch by postracializing – making invisible – the nominally erased terms of racially explicit identification. Racism becomes next to impossible to identify with the erasure of the racial terms of identification. Rightlessness follows from a namelessness enacted in the name of securing rights. A double-edged cut. Life awash with termless racism is a life largely lived in dread on both sides, if differentially, of the conflict shoreline.

*

Civil wars in the end are conflicts over the contours and coloring, the quality and character of civic and social life, and over the levers of state as their embodiment. Like war more generally, civil wars are struggles to the death, or to subjugating surrender for fear of death, whether of life or what one stands for. They are wars over the very fabric of being in the social world. Over the conditions of state control. Over what counts as the civic and civility.

Civility is the inheritance of ways of being and doing in a society, sedimenting into behavior taken as given, as natural. This inheritance of modernizing state-making is racially ordered from top to bottom. Violations or transgressions are taken as attacks on ways of life, on the lifeworld itself. These lifeworlds, I have been insisting, are racially constituted and comprehended. The breached wall is to be plastered up, cemented with the blood and mud of reinvented racialities against invasion and claimed pollution of the invented tradition.

The dread of diversity in Europe is largely if not solely expressed concerning Muslim migrants. In the United States, the object of dread veers between African-Americans, Latinos, Muslims, and, in moments like the pandemic – as earlier in times of wars, political or economic – Asians. It is pushed along by the collapsing universalization of color, culture, and character. Religious identification gels into racial narration, the terms of racial identification largely implicit or dog-whistles carried by more neutral-seeming terms until events prompt eruption into explicit outburst (Valayden 2016).

Racial fabrication never fits the facts on the ground. Like polluting air, religious raciality knows no cartographic borders. Racialities are floating signifiers, so to speak, as much seeping into as swirling about us. They are as much a product of (our) historical seepages as of contemporary geopolitics. The police report for George Floyd's death cited "resisting arrest" despite video evidence to the contrary. The initial autopsy report established cause of death as "chemical intoxication" and "heart disease" rather than what the entire world witnessed: induced asphyxiation from a policeman's knee to the neck for nearly nine long minutes.

As noted above, in the days following Floyd's public police execution, American cities exploded into mass protests against police violence targeting black people. These protests, shaped by organizations like Black Lives Matter, were almost immediately interrupted by violent arson, property damage, and looting. It turns out these flares of destruction were largely initiated by the sort of militiamen who showed up to protest the pandemic lockdowns at the Michigan Capitol and invaded the US Capitol. White neofascist and anarchistic forces descended on protesting cities armed with sledge-hammers, spray-paint cans, and lighters to destroy police cars and businesses, torch buildings and police precincts, and generally escalate violence in the name of sowing chaos and by explicit design to ignite civil war.

Génération Identitaire declared war both on generational political adversaries in France and on declared outsiders within or arriving. It has had institutional partners. French police stop black and Arab men at twenty times the rate of whites. The Boogaloo movement in the United States, by contrast, is a loose-knit network of militia taking the state and police as enemies. "Boogaloo" and its varieties of use like "Big Luau" are slang for a war to protect self-entitling "liberty" from state and police delimitation, the Big Dance with bazookas. Early Boogaloo groups flourished first on the online forum 4chan, recently gravitating to the more open but equally accepting platform of Facebook. As Facebook and Twitter feel compelled to squeeze out their likes, these groups gravitate to a variety of start-up platforms like Dlive. The groups range from hardcore neo-Nazi accelerationists to the more "race-neutral," libertarian, and masculinist Boogaloo Bois. They are identifiable not just by their open inclination to use firearms but also by their protest event uniform of Hawaiian pattern shirts. Boogaloos showed up to support the Michigan Liberty Militia when they marched on the state capitol. But the Bois also traveled to Minneapolis to participate in the protests against George Floyd's murder by police. There they are reported to have led the burning of a police precinct and other buildings as well as incitement to loot local businesses. The Boogaloos bear the torch of an "alt-right" or, more accurately, neofascist remake of America through armed insurrection, egged on with a nudge and a wink by self-serving politicians (Bailey 2020: DeVega 2020).

Taking to the streets to protest racial injustice in a time of pandemic uncertainty speaks to the depth of anguish and anxiety about a world of stolen tomorrows. Lives facing worklessness, unlivable environments, suffocating piles of personal and social debt, viral threats, and intrusive tracking of all aspects of life point to futureless futures. The protests were met initially with escalating law enforcement heavy-handedness. Armed vehicles on the streets, thickening tear gas mixing with fire plumes re-polluting the clearing pandemic skies, rubber bullets not so indiscriminately piercing skin. Intended to re-establish "law and order," to re-settle in a state of mounting uncertainty, the official responses have tended to amplify uncertainty rather than diffuse it. The lax police response to extremist invasion of the US Capitol reinforces the point.

Dread here expresses itself as debilitation, negation, rejection. The unknown as object not of fascination but of aversion, disavowal, abjection, distemper. Slipping social elevation is offset by assertive racially inscribed self-entitlement. Recall the armed white St. Louis couple "defending" their castle built on quicksand. One is not as bad off as feared because better than the racially subordinated. Anything can be declared, done, destroyed in the name of liberty absolutized, without limit. Parading as "freedom," this self-asserted limitlessness – of speech, of practice, of brandishing weapons in liberty's name – is taken as given by those so socially self-empowered. When challenged at its roots, as it is now, the familiar is rendered unrecognizable. The uncertainty experienced by those previously taking the power and right for granted is considered unpleasant, even terrifying. The defamiliarizing of the taken-as-given leaves the structurally empowered at a loss in the face of the self-empowering. The script has been flipped in the face of the uncanniness.

The self-protective shoring up of interacting class and racial advantages has assumed weaponized instrumentalization. Almost everywhere, stay-at-home lockdowns were enforced by armed police and their capacity to exercise significant fines for even minor violators. In China, people were literally locked into their homes. In Italy and Spain, walking just meters beyond designated markers was met with relatively stiff penalties. In the past forty years, the United States has come to devote more than twice as many resources to law enforcement (policing, prisons, the court system) as to cash welfare programs. In 1980, the amounts were roughly equal. As wealth inequality and privatization surged, so too did weaponized policing. Large cities are spending on average 40 percent of their general budgets on policing; in Los Angeles the proportion is 53 percent. Increasingly, police have been retrofitted with military weaponry and trained – in many cases by the Israeli military – to "occupy" and "dominate" their "turf," or "battlespace" (as then Secretary of Defense Mark Esper characterized it during the post-Floyd demonstrations). And they are signing up in droves to be shaped by former military personnel like the leading police trainer Dave Grossman in the mindset of "killology": kill or be killed. (Grossman's clientele are overwhelmingly white male officers.) George Floyd's murder was not a mistake. It was proof of concept.

*

Late modern cycles of warring over contesting conceptions of how to be in the world surfaced as rejection of the 1950s, notching up in the 1980s as the "culture wars." Race and gender were self-evidently the terrain of the battlefield. The ending of formal state apartheid, the fall of the Berlin Wall and the collapse of the Soviet system followed by the growing heterogeneities resulting from economic and technological globalization, intensified the rifts. Tracking started taking hold after 9/11. It was enabled over the ensuing decade by the widespread call to monitor the interactive movements of militants, rapid development of the technology, and elaboration of digitally enhanced network theory.

Airports are ecospheres in which biometric experimentation could be trialed for wider application. As Taiye Selasi (2017) hints at in a searingly rendered essay, airports exemplified between-states in the age of globalization and the financialization of everything. They offered wet labs for developing technologies of tracking. They are controlled byways of mixture, of super-intersectionalities, of mixedupness. Our post-sovereign Tower of Babel. Technically outside of jurisdiction – outside, beyond the law – their indefinability is shored up, cemented, walled into hyper-securitization. International airports exist outside of state sovereignty, as evidenced by the stories with which I started this book. One has passed out of the departed state, not yet entering the desti*nation*. Airports are remade as sites of absolutized authority. Completely walled-in sites, they are the other side of a thin blue line. Here, advanced by computational databases of the algorithmic state, identity is metamorphosed into identification. Biopower is subsumed into biometric power (cf. Ajana 2013).

Airports serve as test-sites for prolific power in the face of its challenge. We, travelers and airport workers alike, were – are? – always just passing through. But the passage is also a freezing in time, into shared states of both suboptimality and hyper-competitiveness: for seats, for space, for resources, for air. We were – are? – here always, hyper-sensitively, at others' behest, ultimately of the petty authoritarians. Racial identification is squeezed between these heightened contestations, pumping up the pulse, covering for the "opacity of selfhood," denuding the "personal." All of us under constant suspicion, but some (a whole lot) more than others. Always on the verge of losing control, of being pulled from the line or one's seat, of facing demands to reveal one's password to the private.

Airports are the only public spaces where being reduced to nakedness can be generally commanded or enforced. Where bearing and baring blackness is once again made into a generalized security project for all, awkwardly, discomfortingly, to witness in the flesh. The results of those experiments are now being applied pervasively. There will come a time when the sort of tracking developed here is technologically advanced not as an externality but by inserting tracking technology into us, ontically programming our techno-being.

The cemented structures of thought, architectures of being, and infrastructures of racism (Sithole 2020) weigh as impingements of both the distant past and more recent (re)turns. Together, they close us off and drag us down. Concentration and refugee camps, prisons, and shanty towns are examples of racial infrastructure, as are policing, courts, even legislatures. Schools, universities, private and public housing can be too. In the past half-century, state authority and securitization have protected prolific profiteering, even pirating enterprise and venture. They have promoted privatization, stripping away more and more of a commons. Tracking is a natural instrument and feature, the next iteration, of this logic of privateering racial capitalism (Robinson 2019).

Tracking also enables racially targeting people with bot-generated political messaging. The algorithmic artificing is impossible to distinguish from human-generated messaging (Schneier 2020). This in turn reinforces racial segregations, in networking, interactions, voting patterns, political outcomes. Tracking as political or policing technology is cemented into infrastructures of racism too.

Dread, as I say, tends to freeze feet in place. It operates as an instrument of incapacitation, a frustrated lashing out, and ultimately violence. But does dread have to foreclose, to drag us down in this way? "Oh, Freedom," the post-Civil War Black freedom chant widely recorded by Odetta, Joan Baez, and others, hauntingly echoes a call to rise up, recommitting to the resistant ring of "Freedom" even – perhaps especially – in the face of civil warring, dread, and possible death:

Before I'd be a slave
I'd be buried in my grave.

The antidote to dread lies in the struggles to retain, sustain, and extend a just, dignified Freedom for all.

8

De-Dreading

For Kierkegaard, dread takes hold with the impossibility of awe, with evaporation of awe's ultimate source. Today, with the conquest of the last frontiers – space, the ocean deep, the highest peaks, the biggest waves – we may find "awesome" this seeming defiance of the laws of physics. But we are generally not *in awe*. To one side of indifference a feeling of being overwhelmed manifests. Here dread tends to reproduce the politics of despair, of compounding violence or political and cultural stand-offs in its wake. In a word, dread contributes to extending apartness, to stressing the logic of segregation. It takes as given the refusals of engagement, the projected torments, despair, and loathing directed at the non-recognizable and presumed non-belonging. It registers that a teleology of progress, that one will leave life's pathway better off than at one's entry point (cf. Feiler 2020), is a dream shattered.

To the other side of indifference, however, dread can also imply that one cares. That care can take hold, even as the abiding sense of dread makes it difficult to get out of bed in the morning, suggests a more complex landscape of concern. What was witnessed in the wake of George Floyd's execution by a policeman on a street in Minneapolis presuming he was just doing his job as the world watched aghast is the Great Refusal (Marcuse

1964). The collective moment of Enough! Floyd's was not the last in a long line of police killing black people in the United States. The public performance of callous police terror and execution to no end other than that it had been done habitually and with impunity in the past, and expressed extended authoritarian power, ignited the bubbling cauldron turning frustration into explosive anger.

For those invested in being white who sense long-sustaining racial power slipping, dread is anxiety about that loss. It signals the erosion of standing, entitlement, privilege, access, and self-assertion. For the racially objectified, dread is continuing to have to live defined by policed authority and violence contouring possibility at every moment. While the details differ within and across states, the logic is broadly generalizable. Dread of losing authority pitted against dread of authority's material and psychic impacts on everyday life.

What followed Floyd's killing reveals the surging commitment by the racially objectified and disinvested to liberatory purpose in the face of pervasive dread, of dreaded processes upon dread-revealing events and closures. The politics of the counter has involved refusals of prevailing politics, reclaiming and remaking the promise of openness. Heterogeneities are messy, uncontainable. It's what makes them so attractive and subject to attack by those threatened by their promiscuity, by the forces of repression. To take to the streets is to insist on turning from the inevitability of futureless futures ensured by things as they are, from the associated despair, to critical and creative rage, to futures filled with aspiration because collectively made.

Street uprisings and protests at their best and biggest indicate both the depth and the breadth of the political concern. There is an immediacy and viscerality to watching in real time the killing by police of defenseless black individuals. This exemplification of the serial viciousness of authority strikes a more resonant chord than the projection of environmental end times thirty years out. The protests remake by repurposing the publicness of the space – street, square – in which the gatherings take place. The heterogeneous public itself is reconstituted as the contesting body politic in the process, in public spaces, in legislatures and institutions, even in the home (Butler 2011).

public [handwritten margin note]

This was borne out in the United States after Floyd's murder, quickly ramping up globally. Coming out of initial pandemic lockdown, cities and towns across America took to the streets following Floyd's execution. Urban centers were closed down, a whole section of Seattle occupied. The American protests were joined by 20,000 in Paris, marking also the fourth anniversary of Adama Traoré's death, long suspected of being asphyxiated by police in a banlieue of the French capital. In the Netherlands, protests insisted on ending enduring racisms, including the blackfacing tradition of *Zwarte Piet* (Black Pete) that Dutch people of color have to endure every December.

Monuments of slave traders, colonizers, and segregationists have been brought to their knees as well by protestors in cities worldwide. The colonial administrator and diamond digger Cecil John Rhodes is being removed from his perch outside Oriel College, Oxford, his alma mater. Even Mahatma Gandhi, the world-historical icon of non-violence, has not fared well, given his repeated, especially early career racist remarks about black people. One statue was removed from the University of Ghana, there is a petition to take down another from Canada's Carleton University, and his sculpted likeness has been defaced in Johannesburg, London, and Amsterdam. Winston Churchill is no longer safe outside Britain's Houses of Parliament. Statues of slave-owning Founding Fathers of the United States George Washington and Thomas Jefferson were pulled to the ground in Portland, Oregon. And in Britain, slave trader Edward Colston's statue was toppled into Bristol harbor. Mirrors are being held up for whites to face directly their violent and exploitative legacy, its representative symbols and their ongoing assertion of distinctly minority global power. Street forces seeking to protect these statues from defacement and destruction have done so under the white-right banner of refusing "replacement."

*

The culture of the street, of the supposedly uncultured, is heard as noise. Noise tends to be thought of as distraction, as inarticulation, even as dread-inducing. It is what one blocks out, attends to only as disturbance. There is a history underlying this too. Noise is heard as the interruption of bourgeois peace and quiet, an annoyance, the intrusion into thinking deep thoughts, enjoying aesthetically pleasing experiences in music, art, or literature, interrupting fine conversation alongside finer wine. It's often the wine that gives the illusion the conversation is so cultured.

This conception misses, or refuses, the sense of noise as the inevitable and inimitable expression of living. Noise is a feature of the everyday life of incessant challenge but also of irritation, even rage. It may be read as an index of sorts, a partially invisible gauge of the unpredictable. In this quasi-historical telling, then, noise runs counter to the imposed dominance of silence, of political shushing. To make noise is to act out, to insist on an even unarticulated or inarticulate concern to receive a hearing. It is to insist on gaining voice in the face of being incessantly silenced.

The sites of the political – from the streets to legislatures to wherever else politics is engaged in and expressed – are noise filled. The resistance to noise, its refusal or shutting or shouting down, is thus political too. This is a constitutive feature of the politics of noise also. Nina Sun Eidsheim (2019) speaks of the heterogeneity of experience, Dylan's/Whitman's multitudes making up all of us, out of which a voice develops and is shaped. One could say the same of the voice on the street. There is no single voice so much as the multivocality of "the people."

The politics of the street, that takes to the street, rather than the everyday that is street politics more generally, can also constrain that heterogeneity. It may produce a streamlined voice leaning to the singular. Monovocality is always a gesture of reduction, tinged with repression. In message, in expression, in volume, in assertiveness, in tone. Hitler infamously reached for the loudspeaker as a technology of conquest, seeking to drown out all others in the public square. Authoritarian regimes insist on dominating the airwaves, and now social media. Any expression not this – any dissidence, even satire, nonconforming comedy – will be read as noise, as static, the left behind. Rather than heard, it operates as distraction, irritation, to be kicked, sometimes literally, aside. When the system breaks down, terror – and, as endgame, The Terror – kicks in. The thud of the boot or truncheon, the hissing of the Molotov cocktail or tear gas, the gushing of water are the noise of the political too, its siren cries. And as with sirens more generally – the sound of twentieth-century modernity, after all – they signal on the flip side the political clamor for another way of being in the world, however muted.

Political voice is expressed and heard to be addressing a political subject or a subject politically. A voice of assertion, contestation, or struggle. The Voice of the leader is a voice recognized by others as a leading voice, not one declaring itself as the voice of authority, imposed. The voice of Authority, His Master's Voice, is decidedly not an authoritative voice. The voice of the people can be understood here as a composite of

voice of the people

the multi-voiced speaking broadly in unison on matters taken to be of general urgency. It is a multi-vocal
amplified voice that the Voice of Authority will insist
on unplugging. It is a sonic boom the Authority fails to
recognize, requiring no authorized electrical source for
its amplification. It generates its own electricity, turns
it up or down but not off, unless the relational source
becomes – is made to be – fractured. It is the voice
drowning out politically induced dread.

Political voice is voice engaging in an exchange. It is
a conversation taken in the broadest sense, even when
shouting at each other, or shouting in a room alone
at political statements fed one through the media, on
matters of political significance. Political voice is constitutively relational, interactive, interactional.

There is always noise, or static, with the political.
Where shouting at each other over politically implicated
conditions reaches the decibel level (the "frothing at
the mouth" stage) where it becomes close to impossible
to make out the points being expressed, noise becomes
akin to television static completely snowing out the picture and sound. Noise is the punctuation in the political
conversation. When excessive, it is less a contouring of
the political than an obstacle to its expression. Noise is
counter to form, to in*form*ation, the disruption of order,
the perturbing intrusion of "world" into structure and
form.

Noise is always already there, accordingly, as constitutive of the political. It signals the limits of order,
the contestation implicitly or consciously enacted, the
incapacity of the political to deliver on its ever-deferred
promissory note, at least in full. Noise does not so much
drown out the political or effective action. Rather, it is
another register in and through which the political is
expressed.

Where noise drowns out all else, the political has
become nothing but civil war, the political by other

means. Civil war, as I argued in the previous chapter, is the more or less irresolvable struggle over ways of living, of being in the world. Perhaps, as Foucault insists, civil war is always at least implicitly being waged, in any political contestation. It is just not how it is ordinarily recognized.

*

Michel Serres characterizes the dominant as sweeping out "the parasite." The parasite stands aside of order, "the white of our dominance," as he puts it. White noise is ambient sound, the unnoticed humming in the background much like the white page behind the print. Inverted, it is the white that dominates, that asserts itself in its normative presence. White noise controls, suppresses counter-noise. "Whoever belongs to the system perceives noises less and seeks to repress them more, the more he is a functioning part of the system" (Serres 2007: 68). Surrendering is waving the white flag, submitting to the dominating – the white – rule of power, of Singularity, of the One. Static, noise, the disruptive have none of the purity historically associated with "white"; they pointedly refuse it. They are constituted by blooming, buzzing flecks of black, grey, and white incessantly, indistinguishably pulsing against and into each other. Refusing imposed form, dominance, domination. Unbounded mixture, the impurities it represents, implies refusal of dreaded racial constitution, of commanded categorization. It violates ordered classification, representing, in short, transgressions of the Law. Mixture is the depurifying noise of the political.

The sites of the parasite, of the incessant asides of power, are the constant making and remaking of the in-common, the uncommon, the counter-normal against control. The parasite constitutes worlds outside time, times against Time, places against Space, atonalities against linearity, open-ended circuitries against repetitiveness, pushing against the enclosed circle, throwing open against battening down (Kowalik et al. 1996). In the face of uniformity, the parasite, the unlocatable, responds not so much with non-conformity as de-conformity, as unmaking the parameters of confinement. The drive is to hold open, to refuse the dominant drives to lock up, lock in, lock down.

The most effective large-scale anti-racist movements – abolition, anticolonial, civil rights, anti-apartheid, in our time #BLM – have been cross-racial, multi-gendered, multi-generational, cross-class, local-global. They are intersectional, interfacing, interactive. Wonderfully and wondrously mixed up. The leadership or, as Black Lives Matter puts it, "leaderful" range across these groups has been made of multitudes, ever mindful of constituencies other than their own. They represent multiplicity, heterogeneity, transitivity. Constituencies that lead have to be coalitions of the open, inviting, exciting, not shutting down by shutting up. But then this has to translate into concrete developments, visible transformations of the commonplace to the greater equality, justice, dignity, respect, and betterment relationally for all.

All lives matter only when every black, brown, and indigenous life, however historically constituted, really does. When no one is picked out as the alien within, targeted, ignored, foreclosed, precluded, "shat out" (in Coetzee's terms), prematurely killed or left to die because ethnoracially serialized. And when everyone is enabled otherwise to get on with their lives with everyone else: when jogging or birdwatching or sitting on a bench in the park; when driving down the highway, swimming at the pool or beach, unlocking their front door, shopping in the store, awaiting a friend at the coffee shop or in a parked car; when protesting on the street. Not when "all lives" signals the violent negation of some for the sake of perpetuating a racially sterile, a *color*-blind, a veil-of-ignorance social *and* economic status quo. Not when it insists on refusing, repressing, erasing, annihilating. The lives of all can matter only when the "all" no longer artificially reduces its universalism to the Chosen of one racio-national deity or another by walling itself within the borders of this or that ethnoracially presupposed turf or territory, enclosed community, neighborhood, or nation (Mbembe 2018).

Only under such conditions can a psychology of weaponizing give way to foreclosing violence. Racial militarization to demilitarizing the social (Goldberg 2016). Tracking and being tracked to forging paths together. Profiling to co-constituting world-making. Humiliation to humility and dignity. The culture of homogeneity to heterogeneities. In short, the political economy of devaluing people for the sake of rampant profiteering and racial power to one of dignified equality. The intensities and suspicions of perpetual civil war only then can open ways to civility, respectful sociality, interactive co-constitution, and politico-economic equality.

Serres insists, playing on Gramsci's wars of position and maneuver, that:

> The producer plays the contents, the parasite the position. The one who plays the position will always beat the one who plays the contents. The latter is simple and naïve; the former is complex and mediated. . . . To play the position or to play the location is to dominate the relation. It is to have a relation only with the relation itself. Never with the stations from which it comes, to which it goes, and by which it passes. Never to the things as such and, undoubtedly, never to subjects as such. (Serres 2007: 38–9)

In positioning, one is concerned with the dance of relationalities and relational moves, with the grids and networkings of the moves being made, not distracted by those making them. One attends to the relations of power exercised by tracking-capitalism and is not seduced or shaped by addictive attention to the manipulating messages social media reinforcingly and reproductively feed us. This, Serres insists, is to stress the "para-" over the "-site." It is to attend to the relation, aside of, next to, between the things or subjects under relation. To the "always mediate," always in relation, in process of inter-action. "Computers never had sex," George Clinton has funkadelically exclaimed, "you have to put the funk in it" (Smithsonian 2019). The "para-" never fixates on the "immediate," the fixed, the given, the one-time action in isolation.

The politics of dread accordingly presupposes a relation to time. It conjures on one side a nostalgia for a lost past, a romantic sense that all was well. Make this or that great *again*. Invariably, this past is reconstructed by repressing its failings, sustained by seeking to suppress its critiques and counters. On the other side, multiple temporalities are in play. With the reconstruction of the past, its repressions and suppressions come to the surface. It is inhabited in all its complexities. The present is produced as a consequence of this more fully articulated, less heroic, past. Hence the contemporary struggles over monumentalizing and its politics of (mis)representation and (mis)recognition.

Future time is under contestation as a consequence also. The overriding struggle in recent years has been to reinstate or extend the conditions of possibility for racial authoritarianisms, to remake states of imposed whiteness in a world not much more than 10 percent white. The more insistent the undertaking, the more its projections resemble the imposed, the fascistic, as Trumpism made clear at the close of Trump's presidency in January 2021. By contrast, the vision for worlds-in-common is for co-habitable futures, as the crises cubed – climatic, pandemic, racial – have rendered abundantly apparent. The anticipated tomorrow is caught between the impossibility of paradise lost for a small global minority and remaking the conditions of possibility for life together for all. What worlds, what futures, what times, we are being asked, are each of us, are we in-common, for?

*

Protest movements have materialized worldwide against militarized policing that racially targets those not white. Social movements are taking on racial policing as the weapon of securing racial domination, social segregation, and pedigreed power otherwise seen to be slipping from grasp. Aspirational calls have been issued to abolish, defund, and redesign the police, to resist refugee restriction and anti-immigrant violence, and more generally to diminish funding streams for repressive state apparatuses (police, military, and law enforcement). These calls underpin the drive to dismantle and redefine the operative power of the social today. They represent a conception of living relationally with others in a sociality of non-violence (Butler 2020).

This has become central to politics in our time. Abolition as a general social counter-principle articulates the horizon of possibilities for refusing institutional racisms and their driving institutionalizations, for undercutting and countering authoritarianisms, dominant and petty. Addressing such questions requires opening up effective spaces for articulating the institutional conditions to enable, sustain, and where necessary redress wrongdoing in dignified ways.

One blowback will likely be the hastened development of tracking-capitalism precisely because it makes much less visible the capacity of the state to track and control the activities, movements, and networks of its citizens. Round-the-clock tracking may render street policing less necessary. But it hardly de-polices society. It simply shifts the mode, making its implications less open to recognition, identification, and contestation. The banality of evil is updating its operating system to anonymize its functionality.

In the morphology of affect underpinning all modes of governing (Stoler 2016), dread often operates as static. Dread concerns the anxiety attending this relational unfixity and unlocatability, of the seen and in a blink the not-seen, the gathered and then gone, of the conventionally ungraspable, the peripheralized at the center. It comes with the fog of indiscernibility in worlds in which authority seizes control. As the hand of command descends, the parasite, the ever aside, evaporates. It dis-appears, only to manifest elsewhere and otherwise, multiplying in and through its unlocatability. The resistant response to the anonymity of evil is to inhabit its operating system, turning it back against its dominant powers. Small examples include the Hong Kong resistance communicating with Telegram, and politically savvy teens effectively using TikTok to undermine a racist Donald Trump rally in Tulsa. The resistance goes virtual and viral.

Dread is awe absent the possibility of identifying the source, rendering reconciliation irrelevant and redress impossible. It is the ceaseless drone soundtracking the everyday. All that is liberated in ever-expanding lockdown, perpetual catastrophe, and endless emergency, generally policed by tracking, is insecurity. Dread expresses the irresolvable tension between the apocalyptic (jihadi, evangelical) promise of afterlife tomorrow and the worldlessness of perpetual flight from global abandonment and ever-present death now. Between the closed, bounded, walled-off states under the web of completely tracked subjects and collectively made and remade freedoms and politically renewed materializations of "the right to have rights" (Arendt 1973). Insistence on the universal right to breathe (Mbembe 2020b) and an emerging anxiety that we all might soon be environmental refugees concretize the conditions relationally tying environmental, viral, racial, technological, and economic conditions interactively together.

*

The counter to dread, then, involves co-developing a collective ecology of caring. Such an ecology is not simply reducible to the one-to-one, the face-to-face. It is not caring as affect, as care-giving. It concerns crafting infrastructures of social care, tools for conviviality (Illich 2001; Klein 2020b). Absent, eroding, and failing social infrastructure tends overwhelmingly to affect communities of color and the poorer more directly and deeply. Flint, Michigan's water crisis is obviously revealing, but so too is the lack of electrification for Bedouin communities in Israel's Negev, or the absence of resources in refugee camps everywhere. Abandoned or undeveloped baseline living conditions – infrastructures of debilitation – are suffered by racially configured populations in informal settlements, indigenous reservations, disinvested neighborhoods and towns. But so too are infrastructures of control, from segregation to policing, and increasingly tracking.

An ecology of caring demands attending to the equality and impacts of enabling social design, resources, and infrastructures of living. It takes as its collective inspiration working together towards equality, respect, and dignity in distinction, without domination (Skaria 2020). And towards putting in place the infrastructural conditions and social practices necessary for all to live dignified lives in the challenged world we co-inhabit. Infrastructures of care are the material conditions for the possibility of dignified living (Held 2007). A recent survey of American youth revealed that, faced with a wide range of listed commitments, "community organizing" was ranked top choice by youth of color and second by whites (white youth chose "voting" as their first, black youth "revolution" – understood as transformative social change – as their second). Community organizing is committed to creating together the social infrastructures of care.

Effective social contestation of street activism and social movement politics translates from the street into institutional shifts, changes, and innovations. It is these developments that will help to produce "institutive" shaping (Esposito 2020). This institutive molding can be sustained over time only by the insistent struggle from the streets. When the adrenalizing energy of street struggles fade, without sustained social organizing, the institutional drive and impact mostly do too. Taking to the streets is the insistent reclamation process of a commons. Commonality

The social goal with current street protests is not for a reinstatement of awe in a deity or fearsome leader. Rather, the strivings in the streets are for an engaged being-, doing-, and achieving-in-common. They are for the making of collective choices in the face of fear and trembling. The practices and struggles of the in-common (Mbembe 2017: 183) are for reimagining and reconstructing a commons, more or less undone over the past half-century. This requires both mobility and mobilization, a re-sourcing, re-pairing, re-making. The pandemic economic impact has somewhat discouraged the taken-for-granted throw-away economy and culture, encouraging the sorts of experimentations in living with finitude much of Africa has long exercised by necessity. The consequent turn is away from radical individuation and possession to lives of relation, co-composition, and repair (Goldberg and Mbembe 2018). The fixes are not simply technical, an immunitarian vaccine for the pandemic which will enable business as before. They are socio-structural and axiological, calling for reparations in value and ways of being, fashioned from living together in the world.

Infrastructure shapes and shifts intent (Bornstein 2017). A defining social infrastructure of a caring commons mobilizes not only for a political economy framed on green principles and technologies but also for a legal framework and culture supporting them. It requires taking as the social ontology not individuated human personhood but ontic porosities and leakages between the conventionally human, technological, and animal. We are already inhabiting interspecies being, "societies of societies," as Kim Stanley Robinson (2020) puts it. This is less conducive to self-interest than to "solidarities" and what Kropotkin (1902/2017) characterized as "mutual aid" (cf. Graeber and Grubačić 2020). Lacking an infrastructure of co-constitution and inter-habitation, one that enables mutual support and enablement, creates the incapacity to address immediate health and survival needs. This becomes ramified in a pandemic outbreak, layered environmental or racial challenges and catastrophes.

The lived condition of our large-scale collective social challenges (the pandemic, racism, the environment) is exhaustion. Individual and social debilitation saps bodies and psyches, social patience and capacity. This, in turn, pressures societies to pursue high-risk undertakings at considerably intensified peril to the wellbeing of all. The undercutting of the social infrastructure of the commons in favor of radically individuated personal responsibility comes with postponed and so significantly enhanced longer-term economic and social costs too. In short, with a political economy of austerity.

The antidote to viral dread, then, is to strive collectively to reimagine and remake the planet in ways more livable for all, as much techno-economically as ecoformationally. It is to imagine the possibility of a sociality without end, a non-teleological ethic, where constantly renewed aspiration refuses the repetitive social conditions of dread-making. Infrastructures of care offer a social ethic without grounds, foundations, or guarantees, with no fixed truths to fall back on. Such an ethic values multiplicities over singularity, pluriversals over universals, co-making through interacting. Imagining new worlds, our worlds anew, entails as their conditions of possibility renewably thinking and living without segregations, social purifications, securitized homogenizations. This Reconstruction 3.0 will necessitate undoing significant inequalities in opportunity, wealth, income, and political power, individually, collectively, globally. It requires undercutting, and waylaying, tracking-capitalism. It demands forgoing ethnoracially and gender-reproduced subjugations, debasements, inequities, and indignities. Enormous individuated wealth comes with inordinate social power undercutting any possibility of equitability.

Equalizing opportunity and resources for dignified living for the least positioned in our worlds will render everyone better off. The less desperation, the less the reach for apparatuses of securitization, the more resources will be available for more meaningful, supportive, and uplifting initiatives. This will help to delimit the heating up climatically and politically, across town and country as much as across wider political and environmental geographies. It has not gone without notice that those states with women leaders have tended to fare considerably better in steering their societies through the pandemic and other catastrophic events (such as the mass shooting in New Zealand) than their male counterparts elsewhere. Men tend to shoot, women to tend. Social movement and care organizations steered by women have exhibited enormous resolve, creativity, and humility in the face of socially daunting and debilitating challenges.

Ecologies of care take their cue, proposal, promotion, and administration from their gender-driven conception and initiation. In its aspirationally idealized conception, mothering undertakes to nurture, taking care of the life-enabling conditions and wellbeing of those for whom responsibility is exercised without smothering them. It involves exemplifying for those in care how to live, to care for others, to enable life. Anyone can exercise this disposition of mothering, and all can fail at it. Othering, by contrast and equally enacted by anyone, alienates those taken not to qualify for conditions of care, to the extreme of directing murderous violence at them. And smothering represses one's own, in the name of caring for them. Ecologies of care, their materializing infrastructures and cultures, are constitutive of living together. They are integrally threaded with ecoformations of equality and dispositions of dignity.

*

Cooling down the temperature socially, environmentally, politically is of a piece with ecoformations of care. This symbolizes also the constitutive dispositions of respect, dignity, and equality on which such ecologies are built and are committed to advancing. In this time out of time, I close with a memorable multidimensional meme, the hashtag for our moment. While not proposed as a governing strategy (Buck 2020), this meme metaphorizes the need to address interactively the dominant challenges of our time, of the time we inhabit with no time left: economically, politically, ethnoracially, pandemically, ecologically. It generalizes for us the contemporary call, the rallying cry, of the street, from the square:

#FLATTENTHECURVE

Flattening the curve across these various domains urgently requires living differently, together, reaching always for the common good.

References

Abbas, Ackbar 1997. *Hong Kong: Culture and the Politics of Disappearance*. University of Minnesota Press.

Abbas, Ackbar 2012. "Adorno and the weather: critical theory in an era of climate change," *Radical Philosophy* 174 (July/August). *https://www.radical philosophy.com/article/adorno-and-the-weather*

Abramovich, Alex 2009. "Phenomenologically fucked," *London Review of Books*, November 19. *https:// www.lrb.co.uk/the-paper/v31/n22/alex-abramovich/ phenomenologically-fucked*

Agamben, Giorgio 1998 *Homo Sacer: Sovereign Life and Bare Life*. Stanford University Press.

Agamben, Giorgio 2020a. "The invention of an epidemic," *European Journal of Psychoanalysis*, February 26. *http://www.journal-psychoanalysis.eu/ coronavirus-and-philosophers/*

Agamben, Giorgio 2020b. "Clarifications," *An und für sich*, March 17. *https://itself.blog/2020/03/17/giorg io-agamben-clarifications/*

Ahuja, Neel 2016. *Bioinsecurities: Disease Interventions, Empire, and the Government of Species*. Duke University Press.

Aiello, Chloe 2018. "Apple has done extraordinary things to protect user privacy, tech investor says," CNBC, October 3. *https://www.cnbc.com/2018/10/ 03/mcnamee-apple-has-done-extraordinary-things- to-protect-user-privacy.html*

Ajana, Btihaj 2013. *Governing Through Biometrics: The Biopolitics of Identity*. Palgrave Macmillan.

Alexander, Michelle 2018. "The newest Jim Crow," *New York Times*, November 8. *https://www.nytimes.com/2018/11/08/opinion/sunday/criminal-justice-reforms-race-technology.html*

Aljazeera 2020. "Coronavirus: travel restrictions, border shutdowns by country," April 1. *https://www.aljazeera.com/news/2020/03/coronavirus-travel-restrictions-border-shutdowns-country-200318091505922.html*

Ambrose, Jillian 2020. "'Hijacked by anxiety': how climate dread is hindering climate action," *The Guardian*, October 8. *https://amp.theguardian.com/environment/2020/oct/08/anxiety-climate-crisis-trauma-paralysing-effect-psychologists?__twitter_impression=true*

Arendt, Hannah 1966–7/2017. "Never-before-published Hannah Arendt on what freedom and revolution really mean," *The New England Review*, June 17. *https://lithub.com/never-before-published-hannah-arendt-on-what-freedom-and-revolution-really-mean/*

Arendt, Hannah 1973. *The Origins of Totalitarianism*. Harcourt Brace Jovanovich.

Armitage, David 2017. *Civil Wars: A History in Ideas*. Yale University Press.

Arnett, Chazz 2019. "From decarceration to e-carceration," *Cardozo Law Review* 41.2. *https://papers.ssrn.com/sol3/papers.cfm?abstract_id=3388009*

Bailey, Holly 2020. "Man linked to far right 'Boogaloo Bois' charged after allegedly shooting at police precinct during Floyd protests," *The Washington Post*, October 23.

Baldwin, Andrew 2017. "Postcolonial futures: climate, race and the yet-to-come," *ISLE: International Studies in Literature and Environment* 24.2 (Spring): 292–305.

Beauchamp, Zack 2017. "This chilling NRA ad calls on its members to save America by fighting liberals," *Vox*, June 29. *https://www.vox.com/world/2017/6/29/15892508/nra-ad-dana-loesch-yikes*

Beck, Ulrich 2011. "System of organized irresponsibility behind the Fukushima crisis," Fukushima News Online, July 6. *https://fukushimanewsresearch.word press.com/2011/07/06/japan-interview-ulrich-beck-system-of-organized-irresponsibility-behind-the-fuku shima-crisis/*

Beckett, Samuel 1958. *Endgame*. Faber and Faber.

Benanav, Aaron 2020. *Automation and the Future of Work*. Verso.

Bendell, Jem 2018. "Deep adaptation: a map for navigating climate tragedy," *IFLAS Occasional Paper 2*, July 27. *https://www.lifeworth.com/deepadaptation.pdf*

Benjamin, Ruha 2019. *Race After Technology*. Polity.

Benkler, Yochai 2002. *The Wealth of Networks*. Harvard University Press.

Benthall, Sebastian and Haynes, Bruce D. 2019. "Racial categories in machine learning," FAT* '19: Conference on Fairness, Accountability, and Transparency (FAT* '19), January 29–31. *https://arxiv.org/pdf/1811.11668.pdf*

Berardi, Franco "Bifo" 2016. "The coming global civil war: is there any way out?" *e-flux* 69 (November). *https://www.e-flux.com/journal/69/60582/the-coming-global-civil-war-is-there-any-way-out/*

Berlant, Lauren 2011. *Cruel Optimism*. Duke University Press.

Bhan, Gautam, Caldeira, Teresa, Gillespie, Kelly, and Simone, Abdoumaliq 2020. "The pandemic, southern urbanisms, and collective life," *Society+Space*, August 3. *https://www.societyandspace.org/articles/the-pan demic-southern-urbanisms-and-collective-life?fbclid= IwAR2emhhdLh0WdJ-GsTG3g2C3C491DdKbOtV zf6jIhP5zzMGYOOEL5TuDoTE*

Blanchot, Maurice 1986. *The Writing of the Disaster*. University of Nebraska Press.

Bornstein, Aaron 2017. "Are algorithms building the new infrastructure of racism?" *Nautilus*, December 21. *http://nautil.us/issue/55/trust/are-algorithms-buil ding-the-new-infrastructure-of-racism*

Breckenridge, Keith 2016. "Biometric capitalism," *Haus*

der Kulturen der Welt, November 16. *https://techno sphere-magazine.hkw.de/p/Biometric-Capitalism-tA QgbSspeqhckkakBq8b5h*

Bridle, James 2018. "Rise of the machines: has technology evolved beyond our control?" *The Guardian*, June 15. *https://www.theguardian.com/books/2018/jun/15/ rise-of-the-machines-has-technology-evolved-beyond-our-control-*

Browne, Simone 2015. *Dark Matters: On the Surveillance of Blackness*. Duke University Press.

Buck, Holly Jean 2020. "The tragic omissions of governance by curve," *Strelka Mag*, May 15. *https://strel kamag.com/en/article/the-tragic-omissions-of-govern ance-by-curve*

Buolomwini, Joy 2018. "We're training machines to be racist. The fight against bias is on," *WiredUK*, April 10. *https://www.youtube.com/watch?v=N-Lxw 5rcfZg*

Butler, Judith 2011. "Bodies in alliance and politics of the police," *transversal texts*. *https://transversal.at/ transversal/1011/butler/en*

Butler, Judith 2020. *The Force of Nonviolence: The Ethical in the Political*. Verso.

Cassidy, John 2014. "Piketty's inequality story in six charts," *New Yorker*, March 26. *https://www.new yorker.com/news/john-cassidy/pikettys-inequality-sto ry-in-six-charts*

Cassidy, John 2020. "Can we have prosperity without growth?" *New Yorker*, February 3. *https://www.new yorker.com/magazine/2020/02/10/can-we-have-pros perity-without-growth*

CBS News 2018. "Big oil asks government to protects its oil facilities from climate change," *Associated Press*, August 22. *https://www.cbsnews.com/news/texas-protect-oil-facilities-from-climate-change-coastal-spine/*

Chakrabarty, Dipesh 2009. "The climate of history: four theses," *Critical Inquiry* 35: 197–222.

Chakrabarty, Dipesh 2015. "The human condition in the Anthropocene," *Tanner Lectures in Human*

Values, Yale University, April 18–19. *https://tanner lectures.utah.edu/Chakrabarty%20manuscript.pdf*

Cheng, Lijing, et al. 2020. "Record-setting ocean warmth continued in 2019," *Advances in Atmospheric Sciences* 37: 137–42. *https://link.springer.com/article/10.1007%2Fs00376-020-9283-7*

Coetzee, J.M. 1986. *Foe*. Penguin.

Coetzee, J.M. 2009. *Summertime*. Viking.

Cohen, Leonard 2016. "Treaty," *You Want It Darker*. Columbia Records. *https://www.youtube.com/watch?v=NU5FPAR7ass*

Comaroff, Jean and Comaroff, John 2001. "Naturing the nation: aliens, apocalypse and the postcolonial state," *Journal of Southern African Studies* 27.3: 627–51.

Cottom, Tressie McMillan 2019. *Thick: And Other Essays*. The New Press.

Critchley, Simon 2020. "To Philosophize Is to Learn How to Die," *The New York Times*, April 11. *https://www.nytimes.com/2020/04/11/opinion/covid-philosophy-anxiety-death.html?smid=fb-share&fbclid=IwAR2LfM9bsE4vJ8tarlvzwLDHwJ7-xwBIfNMMKsurG3-6UW785Fk6GVWHkiA*

Cunningham, Vinson 2020. "The argument of 'Afropessimism'," *New Yorker*, July 13. *https://www.newyorker.com/magazine/2020/07/20/the-argument-of-afropessimism?fbclid=IwAR1fco_WnAwbFNRt7aI8_n2JpkdBJlXx2mzWHrxemK-dEZmpBnsEthR9qnQ*

Daniels, Serena Maria 2018. "When we talk about automation, we also need to talk about race," *Huffington Post*, June 22. *https://www.huffingtonpost.com/entry/automationrace_us_5b20eb7ae4b0adfb826f9f48*

Datson, Lorraine 2020. "Ground-zero empiricism," *Critical Inquiry*, April 10. *https://critinq.wordpress.com/2020/04/10/ground-zero-empiricism/*

dBridge 2016. "Digital dread," algo-music dub, July 6. *https://www.youtube.com/watch?v=9B8ULuIMTJE*

Delsol, Jean-Philippe, Lecaussin, Nicolas, and Martin, Emmanuel (eds.) 2017. *Anti-Piketty: Capital for the 21st Century*. Cato Institute.

220 References

Dempster, Helen and Smith, Rebekkah 2020. "Migrant health workers are on the COVID-19 frontline. We need more of them," Center for Global Development, April 2. *https://www.cgdev.org/blog/migrant-health-workers-are-covid-19-frontline-we-need-more-them*

Deraniyagala, Sonali 2013. *Wave*. Vintage.

Derrida, Jacques 1985. "Racism's last word," *Critical Inquiry* 12.1 (Autumn): 290–9.

DeVega, Chauncey 2020. "Soldiers of the Boogaloo: David Niewert on the far right's plans for a new civil war," *Slate*, May 18. *https://www.salon.com/2020/05/18/soldiers-of-the-boogaloo-david-neiwert-on-the-far-rights-plans-for-a-new-civil-war/?fbclid=Iw AR3zlrwdUKp6BF_ITrhXtFAghLNB_18kExw2FO AkR8k05_4hdWRaAWw0JPk*

Diamond, Jared 2011. *Collapse: How Societies Refuse or Fail to Succeed* (Revised Edition). Penguin.

Doctorow, Cory 2014. "What happens with digital rights management in the real world?" *The Guardian*, February 5. *https://www.theguardian.com/technology/blog/2014/feb/05/digital-rights-management*

Dourish, Paul 2016. "Algorithms and their others: algorithmic culture in context," *Big Data and Society*, July–December, 1–11. *https://www.dourish.com/publications/2017/AlgorithmsOthers-BDS-onlinefirst.pdf*

Edwards, Lin 2010. "Study suggests reliance on GPS may reduce hippocampus as we age," *MedicalXpress*, November 18. *https://medicalxpress.com/news/2010-11-reliance-gps-hippocampus-function-age.html*

Eidsheim, Nina Sun 2019. *The Race of Sound: Listening, Timbre, and Vocality in African American Music*. Duke University Press.

Ellsmoor, James 2019. "United States spends ten times more on fossil fuel subsidies than education," *Forbes*, June 15. *https://www.forbes.com/sites/jamesellsmoor/2019/06/15/united-states-spend-ten-times-more-on-fossil-fuel-subsidies-than-education/?fbclid=IwAR26 mTB--9Jy4_iIzJySBo2LJfnmM6vtRIQXS-VXHoNE sqlzlDfyI0YaZwU#2b3986334473*

Esposito, Roberto 2020. "The biopolitics of immunity in times of COVID-19: an interview with Roberto Esposito," *Antipode*, June 16. *https://antipodeonline. org/2020/06/16/interview-with-roberto-esposito/?fb clid=IwAR2_EmTP_Zjy7JC2fssVd-Bn8zNQnL_I5N 7qmCVirIAWyD8YWKE2OnZan0M*

Evans, Jon 2019. "Facebook isn't free speech, it's algorithmic amplification optimized for outrage," *TechCrunch*, October 20. *https://techcrunch.com/20 19/10/20/facebook-isnt-free-speech-its-algorithmic-amplification-optimized-for-outrage/*

Fahim, Kareem, Kim, Minjoo, and Hendrix, Steve 2020. "Cellphone monitoring is spreading with the coronavirus. So is an uneasy tolerance of surveillance," *The Washington Post*, May 2.

Fawbert, Dave 2019. " 'Eco-anxiety': how to spot it and what to do about it," BBC, March 27. *https://www. bbc.co.uk/bbcthree/article/b2e7ee32-ad28-4ec4-89aa -a8b8c98f95a5*

Feder, J. Lester and Buet, Pierre 2017. "They wanted to be better class of white nationalists. They claimed this man as their father," Buzzfeed News, December 27. *https://www.buzzfeednews.com/article/lesterfeder/the -man-who-gave-white-nationalism-a-new-life*

Feiler, Bruce 2020. *Life is in the Transitions: Mastering Change at Any Age*. Penguin.

Fernandez, Marisa 2019. "The world's 500 richest people saw their net worth increase by 25% in 2019," *Axios*, December 27. *https://www.axios.com/worlds-richest-people-billionaires-net-work-2019-2d41df98-1bad-4779-8844-985be9fd3eec.html*

Finkel, Alan 2019. "The innovation imperative," Australia's Chief Scientist, May 6. *https://www.chief scientist.gov.au/2019/03/speech-the-innovation-im perative*

Fisher, Mark 2017. *The Weird and the Eerie*. Repeater.

Foucault, Michel 1974–5/2003a. *Abnormal: Lectures at the Collège de France*. Picador.

Foucault, Michel 1975–6/2003b. *"Society Must Be Defended": Lectures at the Collège de France*. Picador.

Foucault, Michel 1978–9/2008. *The Birth of Biopolitics: Lectures at the Collège de France*. Picador.

Foucault, Michel 1980–1/2017. *Subjectivity and Truth: Lectures at the Collège de France*. Picador.

Fowler, Geoffrey 2020. "Smartphone data reveal which Americans are social distancing (and not)," *The Washington Post*, March 24.

Freud, Sigmund 1919/1955. "The uncanny," in *The Standard Edition of the Completed Psychological Works*, Vol. XVII. Hogarth Press.

Frey, Carl Benedikt and Osborne, Michael A. 2013. "The future of employment: how susceptible are jobs to computerization," Oxford Martin School, University of Oxford. *https://www.oxfordmartin.ox.ac.uk/downloads/academic/The_Future_of_Employment.pdf*

Frischmann, Brett 2019. "Re-engineeering humanity," *Talking Politics*, September 21. *https://www.talkingpoliticspodcast.com/blog/2019/189-re-engineering-humanity*

Frischmann, Brett and Selinger, Evan 2018. *Re-engineering Humanity*. Cambridge University Press.

Fuller, Matthew and Harwood, Graham 2016. "Abstract urbanism," in Rob Kitchin and Sung-Yueh Perng (eds.), *Code and the City*. Routledge.

Gardiner, Beth 2019. "The plastics pipeline: a surge of new production is on the way," *YaleEnvironment 360*, December 19. *https://e360.yale.edu/features/the-plastics-pipeline-a-surge-of-new-production-is-on-the-way*

Gardiner, Beth 2020. "White supremacy goes green," *New York Times*, February 28. *https://www.nytimes.com/2020/02/28/opinion/far-right-climate-change.html?fbclid=IwAR0mG2EZPnUm6m75QpjkYYF20bI2R8weDfWJ4NAz9hH9FVG-8BTrrdWStSk*

Gattrell, Peter 2019. *The Unsettling of Europe: How Migration Re-shaped a Continent*. Basic Books.

Génération Identitaire 2020. "A declaration of war from the youth of France" (re-upload). *https://www.youtube.com/watch?v=_URBE8PIc3c*

Ghosh, Amitav 2004. *The Hungry Tide*. Mariner Books.

Ghosh, Amitav 2016a. *The Great Derangement: Climate Change and the Unthinkable*. University of Chicago Press.

Ghosh, Amitav 2016b. "Where is the fiction about climate change?" *The Guardian*, October 28. *https:// www.theguardian.com/books/2016/oct/28/amitav- ghosh-where-is-the-fiction-about-climate-change-*

Gibney, Elizabeth 2020. "Coronavirus lockdowns have changed the way the Earth moves," *Nature*, March 31. *https://www.nature.com/articles/d41586- 020-00965-x*

Gilmore, Ruth Wilson 2007. *Golden Gulag: Prisons, Surplus, Crisis and Opposition in Globalizing California*. University of California Press.

Gilroy, Paul 2005. *Postcolonial Melancholia*. Columbia University Press.

Gilroy, Paul 2019. "Never Again: refusing race and salvaging the human," Holberg Prize Lecture, June 4. *https://holbergprisen.no/en/news/holberg-prize/2019- holberg-lecture-laureate-paul-gilroy*

Gilroy, Paul 2020. "Race today: marginality, inequality, creativity and belonging in Britain," Repeater Books, June 25. *https://www.youtube.com/watch?v=xJUvqK QVZG0*

Ginsberg, Allen 1957–9/1984. "Kaddish," in *Collected Poems, 1947–80*. HarperCollins. *https://www.poet ryfoundation.org/poems/49313/kaddish*

Goldberg, David Theo 2009. *The Threat of Race: Reflections on Racial Neoliberalism*. Wiley-Blackwell.

Goldberg, David Theo 2015. *Are We All Postracial Yet?* Polity.

Goldberg, David Theo 2016. "Militarizing race," *Social Text* 129 (December): 19–40.

Goldberg, David Theo 2019. "Coding time," *Critical Times* 2.3: 353–69.

Goldberg, David Theo and Mbembe, Achille 2018. "The reason of unreason: a conversation on *Critique of Black Reason*," *Theory, Culture & Society*, July 3. *https://theoryculturesociety.org/conversation-achille-*

mbembe-and-david-theo-goldberg-on-critique-of-black-reason/

Goold, Imogen 2019. "Digital tracking medication: big promise or Big Brother?" *Law, Innovation and Technology* 11.2: 203–30.

Göpffarth, Julian 2020. "Why did Heidegger emerge as the central philosopher of the far right?" *openDemocracy*, June 23. *https://www.opendemocracy.net/en/countering-radical-right/why-did-heidegger-emerge-central-philosopher-far-right/?fbclid=IwAR11F3n6H ka5a_Ru2QbL8_PZxAnUbud25OMBUMr7zSIPntg 9uoR55vd-0hc*

Graeber, David 2015. *The Utopia of Rules: On Technology, Stupidity and the Secret Joys of Bureaucracy*. Melville House.

Graeber, David and Grubačić, Andrej 2020. "Introduction from the Forthcoming *Mutual Aid: An Illuminated Factor of Evolution*," *truthout*, September 4. *https://truthout.org/articles/david-graeber-left-us-a-parting-gift-his-thoughts-on-kropotkins-mutual-aid/*

Grass, Günter 1965. "Do something." *https://allpoetry.com/poem/12002929-Do-Something-by-G%C3% BCnter-Grass*

Gupta-Nigam, Anirban 2020. "Plastic flowers: overlooking resource scarcity in postwar America," *Theory, Culture & Society* 37.6: 111–33.

Hage, Ghassan 2017. *Is Racism an Environmental Threat?* Polity.

Harari, Yuval Noah 2018. "Why technology favors tyranny," *The Atlantic*, October. *https://www.theat lantic.com/magazine/archive/2018/10/yuval-noah-har ari-technology-tyranny/568330/*

Harari, Yuval Noah 2020. "The world after coronavirus," *Financial Times*, March 19. *https://www.ft.com/ content/19d90308-6858-11ea-a3c9-1fe6fedcca75*

Haraway, Donna 2008. *When Species Meet*. University of Minnesota Press.

Harp, Seth 2019. "I'm a journalist but I didn't fully realize the terrible power of US border officials until they violated my rights and privacy," *The Intercept*, June

22. *https://theintercept.com/2019/06/22/cbp-border-searches-journalists/*

Hartman, Saidiya 2020. "The death toll," in "The quarantine files: thinkers in self-isolation," *Los Angeles Review of Books*, April 14. *https://lareviewofbooks.org/article/quarantine-files-thinkers-self-isolation/#_ftn15*

Harwell, Drew 2019a. "A face-scanning algorithm increasingly decides whether you deserve the job," *The Washington Post*, October 22.

Harwell, Drew 2019b. "Colleges are turning students' phones into surveillance machines, tracking the locations of hundreds of thousands," *The Washington Post*, December 24.

Held, Virginia 2007. *The Ethics of Care: Personal, Political, and Global*. Oxford University Press.

Hofmeyr, Isabel 2019. "Provisional notes on hydrocolonialism," *English Language Notes* 57.1: 11–20.

Holley, Peter 2019. "Wearable technology started by tracking steps. Soon, it may allow your boss to track your performance," *The Washington Post*, June 28.

Holmes, Aaron 2020. "Employees at home are being photographed every 5 minutes by an always on video-service to ensure they are actually working – and the service is seeing a rapid expansion since the coronavirus outbreak," *Business Insider*, March 23. *https://www.businessinsider.com/work-from-home-sneek-webcam-picture-5-minutes-monitor-video-2020-3*

Honig, Bonnie 2021. *A Feminist Theory of Refusal*. Harvard University Press.

hooks, bell 1997. "Representing whiteness in the black imagination," in Ruth Frankenberg (ed.), *Displacing Whiteness: Essays in Social and Cultural Criticism*. Duke University Press.

Hughes, Langston 1967. "The backlash blues," *Broadside Press*, July (Smithsonian).

Illich, Ivan 2001. *Tools for Conviviality*. Marion Boyars.

Ito, Joi 2019. "Forget about artificial intelligence, extended intelligence is the future," *WIRED*, April

24. *https://www.wired.co.uk/article/artificial-intellig ence-extended-intelligence?fbclid=IwAR0dZkNhL9 ErzszcDcatDWl9AJUIcnEAUQVh1n5BZP_BFpdox LkL5jcTuGA*

James, Aaron 2012. *Assholes: A Theory*. Doubleday.

Jaspers, Karl 1933. *Man in the Modern Age*. Henry Holt and Company.

jastej 2019. "An inquiry into dread," *Ideas and Observations*, August 21. *https://idsandobs.substack. com/p/firstly*

Jenkins, Henry 2006. *Convergence Culture*. New York University Press.

Johnson, Akilah and Buford, Talia 2020. "Early evidence shows African Americans have contracted and died of coronavirus at alarming rates," *ProPublica*, April 3. *https://www.propublica.org/article/early-data- shows-african-americans-have-contracted-and-died- of-coronavirus-at-an-alarming-rate?fbclid=IwAR3 bj3d3wFT6G4YOjny_JlFM0caXrzNiFFYQXmg2a OxhbrNQSjCTfPInR50*

Johnson, Carolyn Y. 2019. "Racial bias in a medical algorithm favors white patients over sicker black patients," *The Washington Post*, October 24.

Johnson, Walter 2020. "American bottom," *Boston Review*, January 23. *http://bostonreview.net/class- inequality-race/walter-johnson-american-bottom? fbclid=IwAR0RWOT9AmA0UPUOiJ4IZrGFHV nCjXIWEsVAy2J18_law5ywtkAvm7ZzViI*

Jones, Nicola 2020. "How native tribes are taking the lead in planning for climate change," *YaleEnvironment 360*, February 11. *https://e360.yale.edu/features/ how-native-tribes-are-taking-the-lead-on-planning- for-climate-change*

Kafka, Franz 1920. *The Refusal. https://zork.net/~patty/ oldkafka/krefusal.html*

Kahn, Douglas 2020. "What is an ecopath?" *Sydney Review of Books*, March 3. *https://sydneyreviewof books.com/essay/what-is-an-ecopath/?fbclid=IwAR0 DxRCMtJagsUgbbscXBhXd9lkpTzPNuIjAggnLaq xtBJtu1lgqk6RmUvY*

Kallis, Giorgos 2018. *Degrowth: Vocabulary for a New Era*. Columbia University Press.

Kallis, Giorgos, Paulson, Susan, D'Alisa, Giacomo, and Demaria, Frederico 2020. *The Case for Degrowth*. Polity.

Khalili, Laleh 2020. *Sinews of War and Trade: Shipping and Capitalism in the Arabian Peninsula*. Verso.

Khan, Azeen 2018. "Lacan and race," in Anka Mukerjee (ed.), *After Lacan: Literature, Theory and Psychoanalysis in the Twenty-First Century*. Cambridge University Press.

Khosravi, Shahram 2011. *Illegal Traveler*. Palgrave Macmillan.

Kierkegaard, Søren 1844/1944. *The Concept of Dread*. Princeton University Press.

Klein, Naomi 2011. "Capitalism vs. the climate," *The Nation*, November 9. *https://www.thenation.com/article/archive/capitalism-vs-climate/*

Klein, Naomi 2014. *This Changes Everything: Capitalism vs. the Climate*. Simon & Schuster.

Klein, Naomi 2020a. "How big tech plans to profit from the pandemic," *The Guardian*, May 13. *https://www.theguardian.com/news/2020/may/13/naomi-klein-how-big-tech-plans-to-profit-from-coronavirus-pandemic*

Klein, Naomi 2020b. "A message from the future II: the years of repair," *The Intercept*, October 1. *https://theintercept.com/2020/10/01/naomi-klein-message-from-future-covid/*

Kowalik, Zbigniew, Wróbel, Andrzej, and Rydz, Andrzej 1996. "Why does the human brain need to be a nonlinear system," *Behavioral and Brain Sciences* 19.2: 302–3.

Kreiss, Daniel, Finn, Megan, and Turner, Fred 2011. "The limits of peer product ion: some reminders from Max Weber for the network society," *New Media and Society* 13.2: 243–59.

Kropotkin, Peter 1902/2017. *Mutual Aid: A Factor of Evolution*. CreateSpace Independent Publishing Platform.

Lakhani, Nina 2020. " 'Heat islands': racist housing policies in US linked to deadly heatwave exposure," *The Guardian*, January 13. *https://www.theguardian. com/society/2020/jan/13/racist-housing-policies-us-deadly-heatwaves-exposure-study*

Landau, Noa 2020. "In dead of night, Israel approves harsher coronavirus tracking methods than gov't stated," *Haaretz*, March 17. *https://www.haaretz. com/israel-news/.premium-cellphone-tracking-author ized-by-israel-to-be-used-for-enforcing-quarantine-or ders-1.8681979?fbclid=IwAR0phGi_LMEgxrJIw4sv 3TIoCF-5vbEIgHTnyx-vfeNdVSC3t6tzOICzaM4*

Lardieri, Alexa 2019. "Robots will replace 20 million jobs by 2030, Oxford report finds," *US News and World Report*, June 26. *https://www.usnews.com/ news/economy/articles/2019-06-26/report-robots-will-replace-20-million-manufacturing-jobs-by-2030*

Latour, Bruno 2018. *Down to Earth: Politics in the New Climatic Regime*. Polity.

Lévy, Bernard-Henri 2020. *The Virus in the Age of Madness*. Yale University Press.

Lewis, Michel 2018. *The Coming Storm*. Audible.

Ligaya, Armina 2014. "You're being followed: new digital tracking technologies keep tabs on your every move," *Financial Post*, May. *https://business.financial post.com/financial-post-magazine/digital-tracking-privacy*

Lusher, Adam 2017. "Fake news website created to test Donald Trump supporters' gullibility – Reveals they will believe anything," *The Independent*, March 10. *https://www.independent.co.uk/news/world/ameri cas/us-politics/fake-news-donald-trump-supporters-gullible-believe-anything-barack-obama-paedophile-hillary-clinton-a7623441.html?fbclid=IwAR0Hxo 3G28h0GqSlnQ1e-lAqNvhpnU5gZywezFVzIOyZ zdBWWv4XVXskc5o*

Lynch, Wayne 2020. "Wayne Lynch on the Black Summer: something has changed, something has shifted," *Surfing World*, November 6. *https://surf*

*ingworld.com.au/wayne-lynch-on-the-black-sum
mer/?fbclid=IwAR0b68bc_pU8_82nL-ZZ5vCpr
LK7CJJKeR80cfE9EkA_gqNKdtSUi6rJ6Ao*

Marcuse, Herbert 1964. *One-Dimensional Man: Studies in the Ideology of Advanced Industrial Society*. Beacon Press.

Marks, Oliver 2018. " 'Digital' confusion, disasters . . . and opportunities beyond the hype," ZDNet, March 19. *https://www.zdnet.com/article/digital-confusion-disasters-and-opportunities-beyond-the-hype/*

Matache, Margareta and Bhabha, Jacqueline 2020. "Anti-Roma racism is spiraling during COVID-19 pandemic," *Health and Human Rights Journal*, April 7. *https://www.hhrjournal.org/2020/04/anti-roma-ra cism-is-spiraling-during-covid-19-pandemic/*

Mazza, Ed 2019. "The real Americans in Trump's new ads are foreign stock models," *Huffington Post*, April 7. *https://www.huffpost.com/entry/trump-facebook-ad-stock-models_n_5d1d7f12e4b0f312567eb8ae?utm_medium=facebook&utm_campaign=hp_fb_pages&utm_source=main_fb&ncid=fcbklnkushpmg000000 63&fbclid=IwAR2RlHttXdfG4gy2vCx7HK5tAO MZI9bheMHkt2s3iTe9dSkvLszKm25jca8*

Mbembe, Achille 2016. "The society of enmity," *Radical Philosophy* 200.1, *https://www.radicalphilosophy. com/article/the-society-of-enmity*

Mbembe, Achille 2017. *Critique of Black Reason*. Duke University Press.

Mbembe, Achille 2018. "The idea of a borderless world," Lecture, University of Augsburg, May 9. *https://www.youtube.com/watch?v=2oYCXNgwPqw*

Mbembe, Achille 2019. "Life futures and the future of reason," European Graduate School, October 26. *https://www.youtube.com/watch?v=uv11y10XaLY*

Mbembe, Achille 2020a. "The paranoia of the Western mind," School of Resistance, October 17. *https:// howlround.com/happenings/school-resistance-epi sode-eight-paranoia-western-mind?fbclid=IwAR2k5 uaIlHdvNC7P6cD7dHAWW-AdakLHs2uSdIWppo 3Hcyw_gILTWUe2YEE*

Mbembe, Achille 2020b. "The universal right to breathe," *Critical Inquiry*, April 13. *https://critinq.word press.com/2020/04/13/the-universal-right-to-breathe/*

McEwan, Ian 2019. *Machines Like Me*. Penguin.

McKinsey Global Institute 2017. *Jobs Lost, Jobs Gained: Workforce Transitions in a Time of Automation*. December. *https://www.mckinsey.com/ featured-insights/future-of-work/jobs-lost-jobs-gain ed-what-the-future-of-work-will-mean-for-jobs-skills-and-wages*

McLane, Hannah 2020. "A disturbing medical consensus is growing. Here's what it could mean for Black patients with coronavirus," WHYY: PBS, April 10. *https://whyy.org/articles/a-disturbing-medical-con sensus-is-growing-heres-what-it-could-mean-for-black-patients-with-coronavirus/?fbclid=IwAR0EXXmJu LwGI9SnsZCJxRO-KZmN2wFdUcNgyhPpnXGYE cBaQo0kJm5DEc4*

McNamee, Roger 2019. *Zucked: Waking Up to the Facebook Catastrophe*. Penguin Press.

Meleagrou-Hitchens, Alexander and Brun, Hans 2013. "A neo-nationalist network: the English Defence League and Europe's counter-jihad movement," ICSR. *https://icsr.info/wp-content/uploads/2013/03/ ICSR-Report-A-Neo-Nationalist-Network-The-Eng lish-Defence-League-and-Europe%E2%80%99s-Counter-Jihad-Movement.pdf*

Mendes, Margarida 2018. "Molecular colonialism," *Matter Fictions: Inhabitants-TV*, 125–40. *http://in habitants-tv.org/oct2018_colonialismomolecular/Ma rgaridaMendes_MatterFictions_EN_126-141.pdf*

Milanovic, Branko 2019. *Capitalism, Alone: The Future of the System That Rules the World*. Harvard University Press.

Miller, Ryan 2019. "46% of whites worry becoming a majority-minority nation will 'weaken American culture,' survey says," *USA Today*, March 21. *https:// www.usatoday.com/story/news/nation/2019/03/21/ pew-survey-whites-fearful-minority-country-will-weaken-american-culture/3217218002/*

Mitchell, Timothy 2011. *Carbon Democracy: Political Power in the Age of Oil.* Verso.

Mittelman, Elisheva 2020. "Air pollution from fossil fuels costs $8 billion per day, new research finds," *YaleEnvironment 360*, February 12. *https://e360. yale.edu/digest/air-pollution-from-fossil-fuels-costs-8-billion-per-day-new-research-finds*

Moir, Nick, et al. 2020. "Behind the lens: on the front-lines of the bushfire crisis," *Sydney Morning Herald*, January 20. *https://www.smh.com.au/interactive/ 2020/behind-the-lens/live/?fbclid=IwAR3UL4-xoKs6 Tl8I7AlIuLAKFNUoZxE5FW2cBAqDvBncHPHK 1SqELGAaxKs*

Molla, Rani 2019. "The robot revolution will be worse for men," *Vox Recode*, December 12. *https://www. vox.com/2019/1/28/18185061/robot-automation-jobs-employment-revolution-worse-men-brook ings*

Monella, Lillo Montalto and Palfi, Rita 2020. "Orbán uses coronavirus as excuse to suspend asylum rights in Hungary," *euronews*, March 3. *https://www.euro news.com/2020/03/03/orban-uses-coronavirus-as-ex cuse-to-suspend-asylum-rights-in-hungary*

Moore, Michael 2020. "Planet of the humans." Rumble Media. *https://vimeo.com/ondemand/planetofthehum ans/433436007*

Morton, Timothy 2013. *Hyperobjects: Philosophy and Ecology After the End of the World.* University of Minnesota Press.

Naughton, John 2019, "'The goal is to automate us': welcome to the age of surveillance capitalism," *The Guardian*, January 20. *https://www.theguardian. com/technology/2019/jan/20/shoshana-zuboff-age-of-surveillance-capitalism-google-facebook*

Navarro, Peter 2006. *The Coming China Wars: Where They Will be Fought, and How They Can be Won.* FT Press.

New England Center for Investigative Reporting 2014. "New analysis shows problematic boom in higher ed administration," *Huffington Post*, February 6. *https://*

www.huffpost.com/entry/higher-ed-administrators-growth_n_4738584

Norquist, Grover 2001. "Morning Edition interview," National Public Radio, May 25. *https://www.npr.org/templates/story/story.php?storyId=1123439*

Obermeyer, Ziad, Powers, Brian, Vogeli, Christine, and Mullainathan, Sendhil 2019. "Dissecting racial bias in an algorithm used to manage the health of populations," *Science* 366.6464: 447–53. *https://science.sciencemag.org/content/366/6464/447*

O'Connor, M.R. 2018. "Ditch the GPS. It's ruining your brain," *The Washington Post*, June 5.

Offill, Jenny 2020. *Weather.* Knopf.

Olsen, Hallgeir 2016. "Great song: Nina Simone – Backlash Blues," *Born to Listen*, January 16. *https://borntolisten.com/2016/01/21/great-song-nina-simone-backlash-blues/*

Oxford Economics 2019. *How Robots Change the World: What Automation Really Means for Jobs and Opportunity.* June. *https://www.oxfordeconomics.com/recent-releases/how-robots-change-the-world*

Pasquinelli, Matteo 2014. "The eye of the algorithm: cognitive Anthropocene and the making of the world brain," November 5. *http://matteopasquinelli.com/eye-of-the-algorithm/*

Pearce, Fred 2020a. "Long shaped by fire, Australia enters a perilous new era," *YaleEnvironment 360*, January 16. *https://e360.yale.edu/features/long-shaped-by-fire-australia-enters-a-perilous-new-era*

Pearce, Fred 2020b. "Why clouds are the key to new troubling projections on climate change," *Yale Environment 360*, February 5. *https://e360.yale.edu/features/why-clouds-are-the-key-to-new-troubling-projections-on-warming*

Piketty, Thomas 2014. *Capital in the Twenty-First Century.* Belknap Press.

Piketty, Thomas and Saez, Emmanuel 2003. "Income inequality in the United States, 1913–1988," *Quarterly Journal of Economics* CXVIII.1: 1–39. *https://eml.berkeley.edu/~saez/pikettyqje.pdf*

Piketty, Thomas, Saez, Emmanuel, and Zucman, Gabriel 2019. "Simplified distributional national accounts," *AEA Papers and Proceedings* 109: 289–95. *http:// gabriel-zucman.eu/files/PSZ2019.pdf*

Pileggi, Tamar 2019. "Embracing racism, rabbis at pre-army yeshiva laud Hitler, urge enslaving Arabs," *The Times of Israel*, April 30. *https://www.timesofisrael. com/embracing-racism-rabbis-at-pre-army-yeshiva-laud-hitler-urge-enslaving-arabs/*

Preciado, Paul B. 2020. "Learning from the Virus," *Art forum*, May–June. *https://www.artforum.com/print/ 202005/paul-b-preciado-82823*

Ray, Sarah Jaquette 2020. *Climate Anxiety: How to Keep Your Cool on a Warming Planet*. University of California Press.

Rini, Regina 2019. "Deepfakes are coming. We can no longer believe what we see," *New York Times*, June 10. *https://www.nytimes.com/2019/06/10/opin ion/deepfake-pelosi-video.html?fbclid=IwAR3hL3 1vTood_s_R6SSslcAJHMSRU4sB3I-UmNzeX7Gv6r af6msiL1Qk9TU*

Robbins, Jim 2020. "Salvation or pipe dream?" A program grows to protect up to half the planet," *Yale Environment 360*, February 13. *https://e360.yale.edu/ features/salvation-or-pipe-dream-a-movement-grows-to-protect-up-to-half-the-planet*

Robinson, Cedric 2019. *On racial capitalism, black internationalism, and cultures of resistance*. Pluto Press.

Robinson, Kim Stanley 2020. "The coronavirus is rewriting our imaginations," *New Yorker*, May 1. *https:// www.newyorker.com/culture/annals-of-inquiry/the-coronavirus-and-our-future*

Rorlich, Justin 2019. "Homeland Security will soon have biometric data on nearly 260 million people," *Quartz*, November 7. *https://qz.com/1744400/dhs-ex pected-to-have-biometrics-on-260-million-people-by-2022/*

Ross, Martha and Bateman, Nicole 2019. "Meet the low-wage workforce," *Brookings Institute Reports*, November 7.

Roulet, Thomas and Bothello, Joel 2020. "Why 'de-growth' shouldn't scare businesses," *Harvard Business Review*, February 14. *https://hbr.org/2020/02/why-de-growth-shouldnt-scare-businesses*

Sassen, Saskia 2014. *Expulsions: Brutality and Complexity in the Global Economy*. Harvard University Press.

Satter, Raphael 2020. "Deepfake used to attack activist couple shows new disinformation frontier," *Technology News*, July 15. *https://www.reuters.com/article/us-cyber-deepfake-activist/deepfake-used-to-attack-activist-couple-shows-new-disinformation-frontier-idUSKCN24G15E*

Schechtman, Joel, Bing, Christopher and Stubbs, Jack 2020. "Cyber-intel firms pitch governments on spy tools to trace coronavirus," *Reuters Technology News*, April 28. *https://www.reuters.com/article/us-health-coronavirus-spy-specialreport/special-report-cyber-intel-firms-pitch-governments-on-spy-tools-to-trace-coronavirus-idUSKCN22A2G1*

Schneider, Dan 2015. "1-800 Dial-a-Crowd," *The Atlantic*, July 22. *https://www.theatlantic.com/business/archive/2015/07/crowd-hiring-politics-campaign-2016/399002/?fbclid=IwAR1q6vPpd-us9G09Vl_gzAzxHWSJd6_JLHg9FTYrTm_RawGYa5yNGdNIHeA*

Schneier, Bruce 2020. "Bots are destroying politics as we know it," *The Atlantic*, January 7. *https://www.theatlantic.com/technology/archive/2020/01/future-politics-bots-drowning-out-humans/604489/*

Schradie, Jen 2019. *The Revolution That Wasn't: How Digital Activism Favors Conservatives*. Harvard University Press.

Scott, James 2017. *Against the Grain: A Deep History of the Earliest States*. Yale University Press.

Seghers, Anna 1944/2013. *Transit*. New York Review Books.

Selasi, Taiye 2017. "Airport," *Dictionary of Now: Violence*, Haus der Kulturen der Welt, May 11. *https://www.hkw.de/en/app/mediathek/video/56533*

Serres, Michel 2007. *The Parasite*. University of Minnesota Press.

Servigne, Pablo and Stevens, Raphael 2020. *How Everything Can Collapse*. Polity.

Shaw, Matt 2020. "Eyal Weizman barred from US ahead of Forensic Architecture retrospective," *The Architect's Newspaper*, February 19. *https://archpa per.com/2020/02/eyal-weizman-barred-from-us/?fbc lid=IwAR1k05FJLkVrRXVk4-ZicAF0WKP7fwZw NEhCggrowfx4PnGUyANhkTX44T4*

Shrivastava, Kumar Sambhav 2020. "Documents show Modi Govt building 360 degree data base to track every Indian," *Huffington Post*, March 17. *https:// in.finance.yahoo.com/news/aadhaar-national-social-registry-database-modi-015438503.html?guccount er=1*

Shute, Nevil 1957. *On the Beach*. Heinemann.

Siegel, Eric 2018. "What if the data tells you to be racist? When algorithms explicitly penalize." KDNuggets, Sept. *https://www.kdnuggets.com/2018/09/siegel-when-algorithms-explicitly-penalize.html*

Simon, Ed 2020. "On pandemic and literature," *The Millions*, March 12. *https://nltimes.nl/2020/03/14/ dutch-researchers-first-find-covid-19-antibodies-rep ort*

Simone, AbdouMaliq 2020. "Detection," Foundry (UCHRI), April. *https://uchri.org/foundry/detection/*

Sithole, Tendayi 2020. *The Black Register*. Polity.

Skaria, Ajay 2020. "Thinking with Gandhi on racism and violence: a letter to a friend," ABC Religion and Ethics, July 6. *https://www.abc.net.au/religion/thinking-with-gandhi-on-racism-and-violence/12424422?fbclid=Iw AR3RPeLJapZGCXPM1rboztjf_ZHIClygYZNpCry EMqfjGendAAFbS24xJE0*

Skow, Bradford 2015. *Objective Becoming*. Oxford University Press.

Sloterdijk, Peter and Stiegler, Bernard 2016. "Welcome to the Anthropocene: a debate with philosophers," Radbout University, June 27. *https://www.youtube. com/watch?v=ETHOqqKluC4*

Smithsonian 2019. "Sonic futures: the music of Afrofuturism," Smithsonian Museum, December 15. *https://www.youtube.com/watch?v=mWnFnzuUIjk &fbclid=IwAR34kGomcaKnuHU10VYh8H3tdnml BdGf0E0u-kq8XxjvG18F56XMgbe6bMc*

Spillers, Hortense 2017. In George Yancy (ed.), *On Race: 34 Conversations*. Oxford University Press.

Srinivasan, Ramesh 2019. "How bias in technology drives inequality, interview with Ana Kasparian," #*NoFilter*, YouTube TV, April 15. *https://www.youtube.com/ watch?v=_meJ0j2Eels&t=412s&fbclid=IwAR 0P2TwTf8fyfpY6QzLUMYn5sKZ6AGc9Vk_1b15e 8xEM79kAMV4-qCnDRvk*

Srnicek, Nick 2016. *Platform Capitalism*. Wiley.

Stiegler, Bernard 2018. *The Neganthropocene*. Open Humanities Press.

Stiegler, Bernard 2019. *The Age of Disruption*. Polity.

Stoler, Ann Laura 2016. *Duress: Imperial Durabilities in Our Time*. Duke University Press.

Tanous, Osama 2020. "A new episode of erasure in the settler colony," *Critical Times*, April 9. *https:// ctjournal.org/2020/04/09/a-new-episode-of-erasure- in-the-settler-colony/*

Thacker, Eugene 2012. "Cosmic pessimism," *Continent* 2.2: 66–75.

Thacker, Eugene 2015. *Cosmic Pessimism*. Univocal Publishing.

Thaler, Richard and Sunstein, Cass 2008. *Nudge: Improving Decisions About Health, Wealth, and Happiness*. Penguin Books.

Topol, Eric 2019. *Deep Medicine: How Artificial Intelligence Can Make Medicine Human Again*. Basic Books.

Tsjeng, Zing 2019. "The climate change paper so depress- ing it's sending people to therapy," *Motherboard: Tech by Vice*, February 27. *https://www.vice.com/en_ us/article/vbwpdb/the-climate-change-paper-so-dep ressing-its-sending-people-to-therapy*

Uricchio, William 2012. "The algorithmic turn: photo- synth, augmented reality and the changing implications of the image," in Goran Bolin (ed.), *Cultural Technologies: The Shaping of Culture in Media and Society*. Routledge.

Valayden, Diren 2016. "Racial feralization: targeting race in the age of 'planetary urbanism'," *Theory, Culture & Society* 33.7–8: 159–82.

Victor, David 2020. "Deep decarbonization: a realistic way forward on climate change," *YaleEnvironment 360*, January 28. *https://e360.yale.edu/features/deep-decarbonization-a-realistic-way-forward-on-climate-change*

Virilio, Paul 1983/2008. *Pure War*. Semiotext(e).

Virilio, Paul 2012. *The Administration of Fear*. Semiotext(e).

Viveiros de Castro, Eduardo 2019. "Indigenous populations are better prepared than us for future catastrophes," *Investigate Europe*, July 25. *https://www.investigate-europe.eu/publications/indigenous-populations-are-better-prepared/?fbclid=IwAR2dt0z-kaiXXsFwn3n70iN0mKX1bdUNV0wHpsU9iERItPqhQfkvMlVu_vU*

Voorhees, Jessica van 2020. "Ramping up," *New Yorker*, April 13. *https://www.newyorker.com/magazine/2020/04/13/inside-a-new-york-er*

Wallace, Rob, Liebman, Alex, Chaves, Luis Fernando, and Wallace, Rodrick 2020. "COVID-19 and Circuits of Capital," *Monthly Review*, March 27. *https://monthlyreview.org/2020/03/27/covid-19-and-circuits-of-capital/?mc_cid=a45d929946&mc_eid=3acbcadec3&fbclid=IwAR0ilZnkJFJ_JbfmOM4TxQfnJeTze7AfIbCD3Ev75J2LK6BvgxRlcFSqtVw*

Wark, McKenzie 2020. "The schadenfreude of history," *Commune*, January 16. *https://communemag.com/the-schadenfreude-of-history/?fbclid=IwAR323nv6Qis5mHCuxwQ36gzg7v3gTnczaJBaa9rv8i4mXb_MwA4k5Thdf5o*

Waters, Muddy (McKinley Morganfield) 1964. "You can't lose what you ain't never had," Chess Records. *https://www.youtube.com/watch?v=VcjowO17SyA*

Weber, Max 1921/2015. "Bureaucracy," in *Rationalism and Modern Society*. Palgrave-Macmillan.

Weinstein, Adam 2020. "The coronavirus coups are upon us," *The New Republic*, April 3. *https://newrepublic. com/article/157170/coronavirus-coups-hungary-ser bia-pandemic-authoritarianism?utm_content=buffer cb3cc&utm_medium=social&utm_source=facebook. com&utm_campaign=buffer&fbclid=IwAR0azV1Rg Lb1l5sS6KJdf5C7QYAEn0e1465dzP-op4Q4Ge4 RHehGwMb4dJI*

Weizman, Eyal and Sheikh, Fazal 2015. *The Conflict Shoreline: Colonialism as Climate Change in the Negev Desert*. Seidl.

Whitehead, Mark 2020. "Neuroliberalism: welcome to government in the 21st century," *openDemocracy*, March 15. *https://www.opendemocracy.net/en/trans formation/neuroliberalism-welcome-government-21st-century/*

Wilderson, Frank B. III 2020. *Afropessimism*. Liveright.

Wile, Rob 2014. "A venture capital firm just named an algorithm to its board of directors – here's what it actually does," *Business Insider*, May 13. *https://www. businessinsider.com/vital-named-to-board-2014-5*

Williams, David R., Lawrence, Jourdyn A., and Davis, Brigette A. 2019. "Racism and health: evidence and needed research," *Annual Review of Public Health* 40: 105–25.

World Inequality Lab 2018. *World Inequality Report.* *https://wir2018.wid.world/*

Wright, Jennifer 2018. "Why stripping US citizens of their passports is a precursor to genocide," *Harper's Bazaar*, September 7. *https://www.harpersbazaar. com/culture/politics/a23010174/stripping-american-citizens-passports-genocide/?fbclid=IwAR1qmz4TzA xE9yRLbKNkc3ivLXeymEDPusrBEvC6SmBBq7U 7mwS2zQVViS4*

Xu, Chi, Kohler, Timothy A., Lenton, Timothy M., Svenning, Jens-Christian, and Scheffer, Marten 2020. "Future of the human climate niche," *PNAS: Proceedings of the National Academy of Sciences*, May 4. *https://www.pnas.org/content/early/2020/04/ 28/1910114117*

Zittrain, Jonathan 2019. "The hidden costs of automated thinking," *New Yorker*, July 23. *https://www.newyorker.com/tech/annals-of-technology/the-hidden-costs-of-automated-thinking*

Žižek, Slavoj 2020. *Pan(dem)ic! COVID-19 Shakes the World*. Polity.

Zuboff, Shoshana 2019. *The Age of Surveillance Capitalism: The Fight for a Human Future at the Frontier of Power*. Public Affairs Books.

Index